זכור ימות עולם

Shiras Ha'azinu

SWEET HARMONIES OF JEWISH DESTINY

זכור ימות עולם

Shiras Haazinu

SWEET HARMONIES OF JEWISH DESTINY

MOSHE M. EISEMANN

COVER ILLUSTRATION:
Haggadah Shel Pesach, Mantua, 1560.

Rabbi Moshe M. Eisemann
403 Yeshiva Lane, Apt. 1B
Baltimore, MD 21208
(410) 484-7396

www.kishinievyeshiva.org

Designed by Misha Beletsky

Edited by Adina Gewirtz

This book was set in
Adobe Brioso Pro and Narkiss Classic MFO

ISBN 978-0-9817642-1-4

10   9   8   7   6   5   4   3   2   1

Printed in the USA

CONTENTS

RABBI AHARON FELDMAN

ROSH HAYESHIVA
NER ISRAEL RABBINICAL COLLEGE
STUDY: 400 MT. WILSON LANE (410) 484-7200
RESIDENCE: 409 YESHIVA LANE (410) 653-9433
FAX (410) 484-3060
BALTIMORE, MARYLAND 21208

פורים דמוקפין תשס"ט

Rabbi Eisemann has deeply influenced the students at Ner Yisroel with his classes for over thirty years. It is therefore a matter of great joy for me to learn that he is now disseminating his teachings in book form where they will be available to the general public.

From the essays I have seen it is clear that they are inspiring and incisive in their analysis of their respective topics, as well as beautifully presented through elegant and masterful writing.

It is my hope that this book will be well received by all lovers of Torah learning and that it will be given all the recognition which it truly deserves.

With respects,

Aharon Feldman

Aharon Feldman
Rosh Yeshivas Ner Yisroel
Baltimore, MD

PROLOGUE

THE WORD *PROLOGUE* IS DERIVED
FROM THE GREEK
PROLOGOS
TRANSLATED LOOSELY AS
"BEFORE" (*PRO*) "THE DISCOURSE" (*LOGOS*).

THIS BOOK REALLY BEGINS
WITH THE CHAPTER THAT I CALLED
"INTRODUCTION."

THE MATERIAL
THAT PRECEDES THAT CHAPTER
IS QUITE LITERALLY THE
PRO LOGOS.

IT NEEDS TO BE SAID
BEFORE THE DISCOURSE BEGINS.

A PREVIEW OF WHAT WE CAN EXPECT
TO LEARN ABOUT HA'AZINU

Why a prologue? Why not plunge straight into the book?

Here is why. Most of us know almost nothing about Ha'azinu, and if you are going to read a book, you must, at the very least, have some idea of where you might be heading. Without at least the beginnings of a solid appreciation for the precious gift we are about to unwrap, this book is going to bore you to tears. We have reams of questions that we are going to ask. Why should you care? We have some really exciting answers that we will offer. Why would they concern you?

There is a mystery about Ha'azinu. It is a gift that the Ribono shel Olam gave us, one we are meant to use. So He told us in VaYeilech (Devarim 31:21): והיה כי תמצאן אתו רעות רבות וצרות ועונתה השירה הזאת לפניו לעד..., *It shall be when they are beset by many constricting evils, this song will testify to them....* However, for practical purposes it seems to have been shunted aside. I have been associated with various wonderful *yeshivos* for over sixty years, years that saw a great deal of history, much of it dreadful beyond description, pass over us. Not once do I recall that we were advised to turn to Ha'azinu for guidance or comfort. A major piece of *Yiddishkeit* seems to have slipped away from us. We are missing things that live at the very center of informed Judaism.*

So now we know why we need a prologue.

Come, we have important work ahead of us.

WHAT DOES THE RIBONO SHEL OLAM
SAY ABOUT HA'AZINU?

Here is a *Midrash* that we are going to use as a springboard for our discussion. It comes from Midrash Zutah, Shir HaShirim 1.

---

* It took me all the way to chapter 20, the final chapter of this book, to be able to suggest an answer. I do not think it is a particularly good one. It seems weak to me. Still, it is the best that I was able to do. Why not try your own hand at coming up with an answer?

עשר שירות הן: שירת אדם שירת אברהם שירת הים שירת הבאר **שירת**
משה שירת יהושע שירת דבורה שירת דוד שירת שלמה ושיר לעולם הבא.
There are ten *shiros:* . . . *Shiras HaYam* . . . *Shiras Moshe* . . .

The context makes clear that שירת משה describes Ha'azinu.
In what way is it Moshe's *shirah?* He did not author it; it
was handed to him from heaven (Ramban 31:19). Certainly
we would suppose that it is less "his" shirah than is אז ישיר,
which he composed. Still, the Midrash calls that one simply
שירת הים. This is a very strong question. Anything less than a
very strong answer will not do.

Ha'azinu is introduced to Moshe Rabbeinu for the first time
in VaYeilech. It is there that we first learn that the Ribono shel
Olam has a poem that is destined to play a very large role in
our history. We will not understand much about Ha'azinu if
we do not first learn VaYeilech.

Here is the background. We are at the very end of Chumash,
the day upon which Moshe Rabbeinu is going to die. The
Ribono shel Olam has just informed him that not long after his death, the people, seemingly forgetful of all that they
have experienced, will lose their religious bearings and stam-
pede straight into the prevailing culture of committed idol
worship.

Moshe Rabbeinu must have wondered why the Ribono
shel Olam was telling him all this. He knew well that such a
defection from their covenantal obligations would lead to
God's wrath and retribution. But what was he to do about it?
What, in the last few hours remaining to him, could he do that
he had not done in forty years of conscientious stewardship?

The Ribono shel Olam has an answer. There is a great deal
that he can do. Moshe Rabbeinu's last few hours will be busy
ones. God is about to hand him the text of a poem. He is to
write it down, teach it to the people, and make sure that they
learn it by heart. It is very, very precious. In some way, not at
this point fully specified, it will see them through the difficult
periods that lie in wait for them.

To us it sounds almost bizarre. What is a poem going to do
to alleviate stark tragedy? But you know, dear Reader, you and

I live in times in which we ought to be as leery of glib questions as we surely are of glib answers. We have lived through times and places in which there was little more than a stubborn clinging to a half-remembered Torah to see us through. Words pack power. Moshe Rabbeinu was not shocked by what the Ribono shel Olam told him; neither should we be.*

TRACING HA'AZINU THROUGH VAYEILECH

There is mystery in how VaYeilech introduces us to Ha'azinu. Both that which is said and that which is left unsaid convey the sense that there is more here than a superficial reading would yield. It is quite clear that the Ribono shel Olam wants our full attention.

Let us spend a few minutes looking around VaYeilech. Let us trace what the Ribono shel Olam told Moshe Rabbeinu about Ha'azinu, and what He did not tell him. Ha'azinu is introduced in verse 19. There, after having described the suffering that would follow our anticipated perfidy, the Ribono shel Olam informs Moshe Rabbeinu that there is an antidote. There is a song. He is to write it down, teach it to the people, and "place it in their mouths." Nothing is said about the message, only about the form. It is to be a poem. Apparently the Ribono shel Olam expects the words of that poem to speak for themselves.

In verse 22 we are told that Moshe Rabbeinu did what he had been told to do. He wrote the shirah and taught it to the

---

* I still remember when, after the war, the first poor remnants from the concentration camps came straggling to England. My friends and I were children. We probably felt superior to them. But soon enough they taught us things that we had never known before. They knew songs that we had never heard. One was לולי תורתך שעשועי אז אבדתי בעניי, *Had Your Torah not been my delight, I would have perished in my afflictions* (Tehilim 119:92). Another was Tehilim 119:49–51, זכר דבר לעבדך על אשר יחלתני, זאת נחמתי בעניי כי אמרתך חיתני. זדים הליצוני עד מאד, מתורתך לא נטיתי, *Remember Your word to Your servant through which You have given me hope. This is my comfort in my affliction that Your promise has preserved me. Though the arrogant have cruelly mocked me, I have not swerved from Your teaching.* Those songs went straight to our hearts. I guess that we grew up some through that experience.

people. The *pesukim* then turn to other interests. We would have expected the matter to end there. However, the story of the shirah is picked up once more in verse 28. There we are told that Moshe Rabbeinu sent messengers to gather the entire people. He is about to invite heaven and earth to become witnesses to the shirah's contents* and wants the people to be present. Verse 30 leads straight into *parshas* Ha'azinu where, indeed, he recites Ha'azinu beginning with his invitation to heaven and earth.

Here is a problem. Moshe Rabbeinu had already done all that the Ribono shel Olam told him to do. He had written down Ha'azinu and taught it to the people. Nowhere had the Ribono shel Olam told him to recite it in the presence of the people. Moshe Rabbeinu had only a few more hours to live. Could he not have left the technicality of summoning heaven and earth as witnesses to Yehoshua?[1]

Apparently he could not. Why? Why is Ha'azinu *Shiras Moshe*? Wherein lies the affinity of Moshe Rabbeinu *as* Moshe Rabbeinu to this particular poem? We are back at the question that started us out on this track. Why is Ha'azinu שירת משה?

HEAVEN AND EARTH ARE TO BE THE WITNESSES

Moshe Rabbeinu's insistence that he personally summon heaven and earth as witnesses places this invitation at the very center of the drama. Still, to our modern sensibilities it sounds strange, does it not? In what sense can inanimate objects be called as witnesses? What does it all mean?

Rashi steps in (32:1). ולמה העיד בהם שמים וארץ? אמר משה, אני בשר ודם למחר אני מת . . . לפיכך העיד בהם שמים וארץ, *Why did Moshe Rabbeinu choose the cosmos as witness? He thought, "I am mortal. Who will replace me after my death?" It was for this reason that he chose heaven and earth to be the witnesses.* Rashi's statement opens the door a crack. Heaven and earth are to replace Moshe Rabbeinu after his death. What does that mean? In

* ואעידה בם את השמים ואת הארץ.

6

which of his capacities does he need to be replaced? How can "heaven and earth" replace him? Again: what does it all mean?

You, dear Reader, have probably understood by now that all these questions are designed to edge us closer to our main problem. There seems to be a mysterious bond between Moshe Rabbeinu *as* Moshe Rabbeinu and *Shiras Ha'azinu*.

What is it?

We will approach the issue obliquely.

WHAT ILLS IS HA'AZINU DESIGNED TO HEAL?

After Yehoshua's death we were caught up in a religious downward spiral, in a frenzied pursuit of *avodah zarah*. Ramban to verse 16 states categorically that this transgression and *no* other occupies Ha'azinu.[2]

Do we know something about Moshe Rabbeinu that would help us understand why he, and only he, would be the one to pass Ha'azinu, the Torah's main thesis about the evils of avodah zarah, on to the people?

Well, yes! At the very least we can affirm a connection, if only in a negative sense. Moshe Rabbeinu's presence among the people seems to have doused any inclination to follow the lures of the idol worship that had been their all-encompassing expression of worship throughout the long dark years of the Egyptian exile.* Before the day upon which Moshe Rabbeinu failed to return as anticipated, there is no whisper on the part of the people that it would be nice to have some tangible image to which they would be able to pay obeisance.** Nevertheless,

---

* Please do yourself a favor and at least read through Yechezkel chapter 20, where our apparently natural affinity to idol worship is spelled out in detail. Here are just a few pesukim referring to what went on during the Egyptian exile: ו. ביום ההוא נשאתי ידי להם להוציאם מארץ מצרים . . . ז. ואמר אליהם איש שקוצי עיניו השליכו ובגלולי מצרים אל תטמאו . . . ח. וימרו בי ולא אבו לשמע אלי איש שקוצי עיניהם לא השליכו . . . ואמר לשפך חמתי עליהם . . . .

** You may want to see *Kuzari, ma'amar* 1:97, in his discussion of the *Eigel*. He argues that in those times the need for something tangible upon which to focus one's prayers was universal. Even while Moshe Rabbeinu was with them, the Jews looked upon the ענני כבוד to fill that role.

7

on the very first day after his nonappearance, we have three thousand benighted souls cavorting around a golden calf.

Everything points to the idea that it was the presence of Moshe Rabbeinu that obviated the need for some physical presence among them. Remember, it took less than a day after his unexplained disappearance to have service of the *Eigel* in full swing.[3]

I think that the explanation is simple enough. From what we have written in endnote 2, we have seen that avodah zarah is the natural form of worship for people whose reality is grounded in the physical world (אשר חלק ה' אלהיך אתם). But Moshe Rabbeinu had taught us by means of ten fearsome plagues and a split sea that our Jewish world was not circumscribed by any laws of nature. He had made a shambles of every physical assumption; water simply *does not* turn into blood. He was a true son of Avraham Avinu and, so to speak, dwelt with his forefather *above* the stars. How, in his presence, could עכו"ם (עובדי כוכבים ומזלות) be considered even a distant option?

All this would hold true as long as Moshe Rabbeinu lived. In the event, it held true even after Moshe Rabbeinu had died, as long as Yehoshua was still alive. Moshe would be living on in his beloved *talmid* (Rashi, VaYeilech, Devarim 31:29). However, that does nothing for the much more difficult question. What would protect us during the endless centuries that we would have to traverse on our trek toward Moshiach, centuries during which Moshe Rabbeinu would no longer be with us?

Enter heaven and earth as his surrogates.

How will they set about doing their job?

Before we continue, let us take an inventory so that we will not forget where we are heading. We have discovered a new threesome. It consists of Ha'azinu, Moshe Rabbeinu, and שמים וארץ. Here is how it works. Ha'azinu spells out certain truths; Moshe Rabbeinu embodies those truths and therefore authenticates their message. It follows that Ha'azinu's ability to do its job is dependent upon Moshe Rabbeinu. But Moshe Rabbeinu is mortal. *Shamayim* and *Eretz* will be able to take his place.

To do our job we will need to define all three elements: Ha'azinu, Moshe Rabbeinu, and שמים וארץ.

Ha'azinu: This book has no purpose other than finding out how we are to understand Ha'azinu's message. A prologue is not the place to quote an entire book. Here is my suggestion. Take a little time off and glance at the Introduction and, if you have the time, at chapter 7A. These two essays will get you where you need to get just now. Briefly, their thesis concerning Ha'azinu's message is this: We must never permit the stern features of the judge to obscure the loving face of the father. All that happens, even heavy sorrow and suffering, has its ultimate source in God's mercy. If we are so inclined we could word this as follows: Ha'azinu's theology projects the truth of אחרית הימים, when, as Pesachim 50a teaches, the blessing of דיין אמת will fall into disuse. Even when terrible things happen we will say הטוב והמטיב.

We are left with Moshe Rabbeinu and the cosmos.

MOSHE RABBEINU'S LAST MOMENTS ON HAR NEVO

Verse 34:1 in VeZos HaBerachah tells how, after he had given his final blessings to the twelve tribes, Moshe Rabbeinu ascended Har Nevo. From the vantage point of the mountaintop, the Ribono shel Olam allowed Moshe Rabbeinu to see various parts of Eretz Yisrael. Rashi attempts to explain what was special about the particular places comprised by that list.[4] For our purposes, the individual places are less important than the general thrust of the passage.

Here are the comments that Rashi makes on these two verses.

א. **את כל הארץ** הראהו את כל א"י בשלותה והמציקין העתידין להיות מציקין לה. **עד דן** הראהו בני דן עובדים עבודת כוכבים שנאמר ויקימו להם בני דן את הפסל והראהו שמשון שעתיד לצאת ממנו למושיע. ב. **ואת כל נפתלי** הראהו ארצו בשלותה וחורבנה והראהו דבורה וברק מקדש נפתלי נלחמים עם סיסרא וחייליותיו. **ואת ארץ אפרים ומנשה** הראהו ארצם בשלותה ובחורבנה והראהו יהושע נלחם עם מלכי כנען שבא מאפרים. וגדעון שבא ממנשה נלחם עם מדין ועמלק. **ואת כל**

ארץ יהודה בשלותה ובחורבנה והראהו מלכות בית דוד ונצחונם. **עד הים**
האחרון ארץ המערב בשלותה ובחורבנה. ד"א אל תקרי הים האחרון אלא
היום האחרון הראהו הקב"ה כל המאורעות שעתידין ליארע לישראל עד
שיחיו המתים.

Rashi is offering a potpourri made up of happy circumstances and tragic disappointments. First there is the ubiquitous "שלותה וחורבנה," *the times of serene tranquillity contrasted to
the ruins that would be left after these had been laid waste,* that
occurs no less than five times in the commentary to the two
verses. What could have been the point of allowing Moshe
Rabbeinu to see all this horror? Then there is the matter of
heroes and villains to whom this panoramic view of the
land would introduce him. Let us take *shevet* Dan as a random example. Among its sons, Moshe Rabbeinu's prophetic
eye picked out Shimshon, perhaps the holiest man who ever
lived,* while at the same time apprehending that the tribe as a
whole was steeped in avodah zarah. And so it goes on and on.

What can all this mean?

This is what I think.

I think that, in making Ha'azinu his own, Moshe Rabbeinu
had earned the right to have the details of the puzzle filled in
for him.

Let me explain what I mean by that last phrase. I will use
the metaphor of the tapestry with which, I am sure, we are all
familiar. The obverse side is beautiful; the reverse side is ugly.
The beauty of the obverse side is created by the tangled mass
of the reverse. Ugliness can and does yield beauty. Perspective
matters. All depends upon the side that you see.

On the towering heights of Har Nevo, Moshe Rabbeinu
had finally severed the last ties that bound him to anybody at

---

* If you are shocked by that description, you owe it to yourself to learn the
few pages in *Yisrael Kedoshim* in which R. Tzadok HaKohen of Lublin discusses Shimshon. As just a tiny sample we might take his interpretation of the
Gemara's statement (Sotah 10a) that Shimshon was lame in both his feet: חיגר
בשתי רגליו (Sotah 10a). R. Tzadok explains that, although all of us are planted
firmly in this physical world through our feet, Shimshon was "lame." He lived
completely in the land of the spirit.

all besides the Ribono shel Olam. In that world, he was ready for the true truth. He was ready to see the real tapestry.

This requires a little more explanation.

At a level that can be at least a little meaningful to us, we should try to understand something about the Ribono shel Olam's כבוד. What do the *mal'achim* mean when they say מלא כל הארץ כבודו, *His* כבוד *fills the whole earth* (Yeshayahu 6:3) and why do they feel the need to proclaim this?

Here is what I think. If we know what constitutes a חלול ה', we should be able to work out what would generate כבוד שמים. Yechezkel 36:20 speaks of the חלול ה' that comes about when we are driven into exile. Our captors would say, עם ה' אלו ומארצו יצאו, *these Jews are said to be His very special people and yet He was not able to prevent us from dragging them into exile.* It does not take much to extend this same idea to any apparent miscarriage of justice at the hand of the Ribono shel Olam. If a righteous person suffers, it seems as though the Ribono shel Olam is unable to stand by His obligations. If the wicked prosper, they seem to find it easy to circumvent the Torah's threats.

We can understand the need for the mal'achim's proclamation. It is certainly not obvious that the כבוד of the Ribono shel Olam, as we have now defined it, fills the earth. In what sense, then, is their proclamation true?

In terms of the parable that we suggested earlier, we might say that the reverse side of the tapestry represents *chilul HaShem*, the obverse side כבוד שמים. As we said earlier, perspective matters. The mal'achim see the obverse side of the tapestry and know the truth of what they proclaim.

Here, as I understand it, is what happened on Har Nevo. At Shemos 13:18 Moshe Rabbeinu had begged the Ribono shel Olam הראני נא את כבודך, *Could You please allow me to perceive Your* כבוד. In terms of our present discussion we might say that he was begging to be shown the truth beneath the truth: "Allow me to see You and experience You as the mal'achim do. Free me from my entanglement in the myriad questions that, since I am human, dog me as they dog every other human. At this moment of triumph, when through my prayers I achieved everything for which I asked, can You, in Your bountiful love, not grant me this too?" The Ribono shel Olam had refused him, כי לא יראני האדם וחי, *for a human being, still living in this world, and therefore still tied to this world, such a perception lies out of bounds.* Is it not possible that now, on Har Nevo, as Moshe Rabbeinu was about to depart this world, as he had already severed all ties to the living, it was given to him to understand God's כבוד in real terms? The כבוד of the Ribono shel Olam lives on the obverse side of the tapestry.

In these last few moments of his life, Moshe Rabbeinu was finally permitted the perspective for which he had pleaded so many years ago.[5] He was shown the ups and downs of Jewish history and the key to understanding the *yichud* of the Ribono shel Olam, the essential unity that underlies it all. We are beginning to understand why Ha'azinu, the poem that, as we saw above, propounds this truth, could be called *Shiras Moshe.*

SINCE THE DEATH OF MOSHE RABBEINU HEAVEN AND EARTH HAVE BEEN "ON DUTY," STANDING IN FOR HIM

Is there anything about this that we can grasp? Can heaven and earth as "witnesses" mean anything to us at all? It seems to me that there are various levels at which this might be understood. Each of these levels could stand alone; in aggregate they make an imposing team.

At its most simple, I could suggest that we take Noach's rainbow as paradigm. I have the Ramban's suggestion (Bereishis 9:12) in mind. Ramban believes that the rainbow's efficacy as אות ברית was based on a combination of two elements. The first is the fact that *any object at all* can be designated by contracting parties as a memorandum to their agreement.* ** God chose to make the rainbow the earnest of his undertaking and that solves the problem. Ramban could have rested his case with this observation, but adds a little polish. Since the bow of

---

* כי כל הדבר הנראה שיושם לפני שנים להזכירם ענין נדור ביניהם יקרא אות.

** As one example among many, we need only think of the pile of stones that Yaakov and Lavan designated as witness to the covenant that they had just concluded.

the rainbow is inverted, with the feet downward, indicating that all intentions are absolutely peaceful, it is a particularly suitable symbol to select.

We can use the same principles in understanding the selection of heaven and earth as witnesses. Moshe Rabbeinu's choice might have been arbitrary without trading in any of its power. In fact, though, since by either granting or withholding fertility heaven and earth are the tools for implementing the rewards or punishments envisioned in the covenant, they are more appropriate than other symbols that might have been chosen.

At a slightly deeper level it could be argued that the absolute predictability* that governs the orbits of the denizens of the heavens, to which earth also belongs, is a potent argument against the caprice that is the hallmark of the pantheon. If Ha'azinu's aim is to discredit idolatry, heaven and earth are worthy allies in the battle.

I believe that we can dig more deeply and perhaps come closer to the truth. From earlier in this essay we recall that Ha'azinu can be viewed as a defense of the כבוד of the Ribono shel Olam. The כבוד of the Ribono shel Olam is undermined when we are surrounded by apparently unanswerable questions in the areas of צדיק ורע לו and רשע וטוב לו. When such situations occur, it appears that the Ribono shel Olam is not capable of keeping His promises. Ha'azinu's argument is that perceived evil as much as perceived good is the handiwork of the Ribono shel Olam. Both contribute to, and ultimately lead to, the desired end.

It occurred to me that Ha'azinu may have inspired Dovid HaMelech when he wrote in Tehilim 19:1 that: השמים מספרים כבוד אל. It could be that the following is far-fetched, but then again it may not be. The heavens (and perhaps also the earth) proclaim the כבוד of the Ribono shel Olam by providing all manner of examples from nature in which seeming disasters are, in fact, the means to promoting a significant overarching good.

---

* That stands in contrast to the anticipated entropy.

Here is an example:* From superficial reading I have picked up that some (perhaps all) environmentalists believe that forest fires that start naturally** ought not to be extinguished artificially. The idea is to let nature take its course. These periodic "disasters" are not disasters at all but constitute nature's way of removing impediments to the forest's healthy development. They get rid of superfluous undergrowth and dead trees, while making room for new trees to let down roots and so on and on. I may not have understood it all correctly, but, to the extent that I am right, it serves beautifully as a metaphor. Not all serious dislocations are tragic. They may be stepping-stones on the way to great and wonderful developments.[6]

IT IS TIME TO MOVE ON
TO THE BOOK.
I HOPE THAT THIS PROLOGUE
HAS WHETTED SOME APPETITES,
STIMULATED SOME THINKING.
WITH R. NECHUNIAH BEN HAKANAH
LET US PRAY THAT ישמחו בנו חברינו.
WE ARE SETTING OUT
ON A LONG AND DIFFICULT JOURNEY.
LET US PRAY
THAT WE DO NOT LOSE OUR WAY.

---

* I am not taking sides in a major מחלוקת between environmentalists and logging interests. In the first place I have no natural leaning toward either side, but, even more important, I know practically nothing about the entire issue. I just believe that, if my information is correct, it is a good *mashal* to the point that I am trying to make.
** Fires caused by lightning rather than as a result of careless stewardship over campfires.

L et me tell you how I came to write this Introduction. I was about halfway through the book and had been going through a mild to moderate case of writer's block.* Although writing up until then had been an exhilarating experience— hardly a day passed without some new discovery—I felt that the early chapters were simply not sufficiently focused. Ha'azinu turned out to be so multifaceted, touching upon such a variety of profoundly significant themes, that I found myself veering off in all kinds of directions. It was not so much that there was no logical core where all the topics could meet and cohere; it was that that core was deeply lodged in my own mind and I lacked the writing skills to make sense of it all to my readers. I realized that I would have to do a lot of rewriting and felt that it was all beyond me.

Then one night there was a change for the better. Since the time that I decided to learn Ha'azinu seriously, I had fallen into the habit of checking it out whenever I happen upon a *sefer* on Chumash. On that particular night, I picked up the fifth volume of the late great Rav Elie Munk's *The Call of the Torah* and, to a not inconsiderable extent, my life changed. Right at the beginning of his Ha'azinu commentary he points his readers to Rosh HaShanah 31a where, I believe, an important key to the mysteries of Ha'azinu is hidden. This source had escaped me and I will be eternally grateful to him for making me aware of it.

Let us take it slowly and carefully. This whole book will begin to sparkle once we open our hearts to what we are about to learn.

We all know that at the end of each day's *Shacharis* we recite the שיר של יום, the chapter from Tehilim that the *Levi'im*

---

* I Googled "Writer's Block" and found that there are 3.6 million references. It seems that I am not alone.

sang in the Beis HaMikdash while the daily *tamid** was being brought. Each day has a different chapter and the Gemara provides reasons for the choices. It was very important for Chazal to understand why a particular chapter was chosen for that particular day. The Gemara then asks what text was sung to accompany the Musaf sacrifice that was brought on *Shabbos*.[1] The Gemara answers, הזי״ו ל״ך.

What can this possibly mean?

For our purpose in this essay, we should notice one important detail even before we get to the answer to this question. That is that the Gemara does not ask what it means. It appears that the expression הזי״ו ל״ך was commonly used and whoever volunteered that answer felt confident that he would be understood. That is very, very significant.

So let us analyze what we have here. I have inserted an apostrophe in both words to indicate that rather than two words that demand to be treated as words, these two units are a listing of letters כ, ל, ו, י, ז, ה. The meaning is as follows. The Gemara had asked what scriptural passage was used for the shirah with which the Levi'im accompanied the Musaf sacrifice on Shabbos. The answer is that they sang passages from Ha'azinu. The system was as follows: The shirah was to be divided into six segments, each beginning with the initial letter indicated by the הזי״ו ל״ך code.** Each Shabbos only one of these segments was sung so that in the course of six weeks the entire shirah was recited. After that they went back to the beginning.[2]

Now, it is very clear from the Gemara that, although הזי״ו ל״ך is primarily a mnemonic code to help us remember the points at which the breaks were to be made, it was also understood as two words, הזיו לך, *the light [that permeates all] is to be traced to You*. Were this not the case, the Gemara would have been meaningless. The question had been, "What was sung?" An

---

* There were two *temidim* (sing. תמיד) that were brought every day (hence תמיד, *that which is constant*). The morning tamid was brought as the first sacrifice of the day; the evening tamid brought the daily sacrificial service to a close.

** Here is Rashi's system. Other Rishonim set the system up differently: "ה" האזינו "ז" זכור ימות עולם, "י" ירכבהו על במתי ארץ, "ה" וירא ה' וינאץ, "ל" לולי כעס אויב, "כ" כי ידין ה' עמו.

16

answer that asserts "Here is a code to tell you where to make the necessary breaks" will obviously not serve. If the question would have been posed to us today, we would have answered, "They sang the shirah part of 'Ha'azinu'; they divided it into the following segments." Where we would have identified the passage that was used as we do the other *sidros* in the Torah, by the initial word האזינו, they had a different name for this *parshah*. They called it by a highly suggestive, descriptive name, *"The light[3] [that permeates all] is to be traced to You!"*[4]

Do you realize what a treasure we have uncovered? We now have an explicit source that tells us how Chazal looked upon this shirah that is so chock-full of the horrifying experiences that would dog us throughout our history. They looked upon it as exuding an insistent luminosity that would never permit itself to be dimmed by even the cruelest suffering.

What a find![5] Let us use our heads and take this information to wherever it might lead us. Now is not the time to sit back and think happy thoughts. Let us remember that Ha'azinu was given to us so that it might help us in times of trouble. Let us make sure to read the owner's manual. What buttons must we push to make the system work?

I will make you a promise right now. The passage that I will soon quote from the writings of the late, great R. Gedalia Schorr will shake you deep down where it counts. Listen carefully; it will pay.

While writing the early chapters of this book, I had been disturbed by the fact that Ha'azinu delivers its message in the form of a song.[6] Why music when, until the very end, the shirah is one long litany of obdurate sinning leading to more obdurate sinning, crushing sorrows following upon crushing sorrows, dismal failures begetting ever new disasters? In our analysis of the relevant texts we will discover plausible explanations that will open our eyes to profoundly significant truths.

However, for this introductory chapter I want to take a different road. I want to find the source of the luminosity of which "הזיו לך" speaks. Just for the rest of this chapter let us learn from the holy שפת אמת as his teachings are conveyed to us by R. Gedalia Schorr in his *Ohr Gedalyahu* to BeShalach.* Here is a paraphrase:

> The fact that Ha'azinu is considered to be a shirah in spite of all the suffering that it describes comports with Tehilim 101:1, חסד ומשפט אשירה, *God's judgment, not less than his kindness, moves me to song.*

Devarim 31:17–19 tells how one day, crushed by all manner of suffering, we would claim that our suffering could only have happened to us because the Ribono shel Olam had forsaken us; left us in the lurch.** God considers such a thought sinful. He would never leave us. He tells us, "It is 'I' who am hiding My face from you."*** It is true that My face is hidden, but it is 'I', present among you as always, Who is doing the hiding."

That, R. Bunim from Peshischa preached, is the message that Ha'azinu teaches us. We sing even when we are the victims of God's anger, because as long as He is with us, we feel safe and cared for in His arms.

In verse 39, Ha'azinu calls out to us, ראו עתה כי אני אני הוא, *See now that it is I, even I Who am He.* "I" is first person; it implies a presence, we use "he" when we talk about a third person who is not in front of us. "Please understand," God is calling out to us, "that even when you experience Me as 'He' it is really 'I' Who am there at your side."

There is much to sing about even when we suffer.

Isn't this something? Even we who are very, very far from being initiates into the world of *sisrei Torah* can see something of the glow that shimmers through the darkness of Ha'azinu's sorrowful depiction of huge swaths of Jewish history. It seems to me a great pity that the music of Ha'azinu has somehow,

---

* In the text I will offer the piece in translation. I will provide the Hebrew to salient phrases in these footnotes.

** על כי אין אל-הי בקרבי מצאוני הרעות האלה.

*** ....ו."אנכי" הסתר אסתיר פני

over the centuries, become stilled, that we have somehow fallen out of the habit of referring to Ha'azinu as הזיו לך.

I do not know whether I have convinced you, but after this introductory essay I have surely convinced myself that I made a good choice when I decided to devote this book to a contemplation of Ha'azinu.

Let us go on together to put some body to the glorious ideas that we have garnered here. We now know where we have to end up. We can expect to have to cross some hilly country. These steep inclines will not deter us. Yeshayahu (40:4) has taught us that, with redemption in sight, *valleys will be raised, hills and mountains made low, rugged ground become level and ridges changed to plains.**

We could stop right here and the Introduction would, so to speak, have earned its keep. But, if we were not to ask the following question, we would be guilty of sloppy learning. Here is the question: We started this essay by noting that the first half of Rosh HaShanah 31a identifies the specific psalms that the Levi'im sang on each day and offers explanations why this psalm and this day belong together. It is what we would have expected. The appropriation of a given psalm by a given day would certainly not have been haphazard.

Why, then, is no explanation offered for the twinning of Ha'azinu with the Musaf on Shabbos? The appropriation is stated but we are not told why. Well, why? It appears that the connection is so obvious that it does not have to be spelled out.

I must admit that it was not obvious to me but, after some heavy thinking, I feel that I may have the answer. Ha'azinu is a *Shabbos-dikke* song. If Musaf on Shabbos needs a shirah, Ha'azinu is the ideal choice.

Here is why.

The shirah associated with Shabbos morning is, of course,

___

* כל גיא ינשא וכל הר וגבעה ישפלו והיה העקב למישור והרכסים לבקעה. I have borrowed the translation from the Jewish Publication Society's offering.

Tehilim 92, which, alone among the other psalms associated with particular days, actually identifies itself as מזמור שיר ליום השבת.... Certainly we would have expected that a psalm thus identified would live up to its billing and tell us things about Shabbos. All of us who have been reciting this *mizmor* every Shabbos, all our lives, know that this is not at all the case. If we were challenged to define its central message, we would probably say that it contrasts the transience of the successes enjoyed by the wicked* with the permanence of the bliss that lies in store for the righteous.** Now why would this be a מזמור שיר ליום השבת?

Here is a short quote from Rav Hutner:

שורש הענין של עונג שבת נעוץ הוא בתורה בפרשה של גמר מעשה בראשית, שהרי כן כתוב בתורה: וירא אלהים את כל אשר עשה והנה טוב מאד, ויכולו וגומר, וישבת וגומר, ויקדש וגומר. הנה נתפרש לנו בכאן כי השביתה והקידוש של שבת באים הם מתוך ראיה של "טוב מאד" בכל הבריאה כולה. . . העונג שבת שלנו הוא דוגמת ראיה של "טוב מאד" אשר בה הסתכל הקב"ה בעולמו בגמר מעשה בראשית. וחכמים פירשו כי ויכולו היינו "כלילא דבתי." משל למלך שבנה פלטין וגמרו ראה אותו וערבה לו. אמר הלואי שיהא הפלטין מעלה חן בעיני כל שעה כשם שהעלה חן לפני בשעה זו. העלאת חן של העולם היא פנימיותה של תיבת "ויכולו" המשמשת פתיחה לפרשה של קדושת שבת. עד כמה שהאדם איננו נקי מהרגשה של תרעומות כלפי סדר הנהגות העולמות, בה במדה נעדרת היא ממנו הרגשת קדושת שבת .

The *mitzvah* that commands us to enjoy Shabbos (*oneg Shabbos*) is rooted in the Torah passage that describes the final stages of Creation. There it is written, *And Elohim saw all that He had wrought* AND, BEHOLD, IT WAS VERY GOOD. . . . This passage is then followed by ויכולו, which in turn is followed by וישבת, which is followed by ויקדש. Clearly the fact that the Ribono shel Olam "rested" on Shabbos and then "sanctified" it derives from the fact

---

* בפרח רשעים כמו עשב ... להשמדם עדי עד, [We know that] though the wicked sprout like grass ... it is only that they may be destroyed forever.

** צדיק כתמר יפרח ..., The righteous bloom like a date palm ...

that He had looked out upon all that He had wrought and found that it was VERY GOOD.

Our enjoyment of Shabbos (oneg Shabbos) is rooted in the fact that, at the end of Creation, the Ribono shel Olam had determined that all was *very good*. Our Sages have taught us that the word ויכולו (from כלה, *to bring to an end*) hints at the celebration that we make when we have built a house and are ready to move in.* They say that [God's celebration of the world that He had now created] can be compared to a king who had built a palace and was pleased with what he had wrought. He prayed that his pleasure should never become attenuated. That whenever in the future he would look at this building, he might feel the same pleasurable thrill.

It transpires that the satisfaction with His world that gave pleasure to the Ribono shel Olam lies at the root of the word ויכולו, which, in turn, opens the parshah that deals with the sanctity of Shabbos. It becomes clear that anybody who has complaints about the running of the world (the wicked prosper, the righteous suffer, and so on) will never really know the joy of Shabbos.

We had been surprised that a psalm that introduces itself as Shabbos's song should not say anything at all about Shabbos. Its theme, that the successes of the wicked are transient as also are the pains that Tzadikim sometimes have to bear, seemed unconnected to Shabbos. We now, of course, understand that on the contrary, that theme spells out precisely what Shabbos is all about. Shabbos is the day upon which the טוב מאד of Creation comes into its own for us. It is, after all, a מעין עולם הבא, a piece of the future that finds its way into our present. Pesachim 50a teaches that the hallmark of עולם הבא is that the division of events into categories of good and bad, where on the first we recite the *berachah* הטוב והמטיב and on the second, דין האמת, will fall away. Everything, even events that,

---

* כלילא דבתי.

21

in our present state of little understanding, would warrant a berachah of דין האמת will merit the berachah of הטוב והמטיב.

The message of Tehilim 92 is that what appears to be bad is really good. In the first part of this essay we have learned that this is also the theme of Ha'azinu = הזיו לך. The choice of Ha'azinu as the shirah for the Musaf of Shabbos indeed requires no explanation. Its message is identical with that of מזמור שיר ליום השבת.

There is one last postscript that belongs in this Introduction. It is the kind of thing that ought to engage our attention. Let us think about the issues and then we will be done. Here is the language of the Rambam in Hilchos Tefilah 13:5.

כל העולה לקרות בתורה פותח בדבר טוב ומסיים בדבר טוב אבל פרשת האזינו קורא הראשון עד זכור ימות עולם והשני מתחיל מזכור ימות עולם עד ירכיבהו והשלישי מירכיבהו עד וירא ה' וינאץ והרביעי מן וירא ה' וינאץ עד לו חכמו והחמישי מן לו חכמו עד כי אשא אל שמים ידי והששי מכי אשא אל שמים ידי עד סוף השירה ולמה פוסקין בה בעניינות אלו מפני שהן תוכחה כדי שיחזרו העם בתשובה.

When people are called up to read from the Torah (*aliyah*), the breaks should be made such that both the opening and the closing of that segment deal with happy matters. This applies to the whole Torah with the sole exception of Ha'azinu. There, some of the breaks occur at places that deal with sinning and suffering....

Why was an exception made for Ha'azinu? It is because Ha'azinu is exhortative and it is to be hoped that when people hear of these sorrowful events, they will repent.

Rambam's explanation for the fact that Ha'azinu is an exception is his own.* I suspect that Sefas Emes and his school might have worded the answer a little differently. If we take

---

* There is no source for it in Chazal. See *Kesef Mishneh*.

together all that we have learned in this Introduction, we might have said the following: Ha'azinu is different because in its context the bad things are also "good."

"A gutten Shabbos!"

Some First Very Tentative
Steps Toward Understanding Ha'azinu[1]

*J*ust about a year ago, on a particularly blustery winter day, it happened that parshas Ha'azinu was very much on my mind. It kept crowding into my thoughts, played havoc with my equanimity because everything seemed so threatening. The times just seemed to demand special attention. It was only natural to turn to the one parshah that holds the keys to the mysterious progression of events we know as Jewish history.[2]

So I searched for, and found, Ha'azinu. I knew that VaYeilech (Devarim 31:21) tells us that, *When they will have been beset by many constricting* troubles, this* SHIRAH *will bear witness to them. . . .* I felt that I was doing the right thing, for, even if at this point I had no clear picture of what Ha'azinu's message might be, it was clearly something that was intended to help us through brutal times. Consulting Ha'azinu seemed to be the Jewish thing to do; it seemed a way of doing what God would have us do.

But, having turned there, I began to wonder. What relevance did these forty-three verses have to the Bush, Olmert, Abbas** triumvirate that was posing such danger to Eretz Yisrael? What exactly *is* Ha'azinu? Is it speaking to me and, if it is, what is it saying? How is it supposed to help me? How important is it in our lives? I found myself wondering what, from a purely practical standpoint, would happen if Ha'azinu were suddenly to disappear? Would we feel ourselves substantively impoverished? If yes, why? I began to feel like someone who had bought a newfangled and complicated machine, only to discover that no owner's manual was enclosed. Which of the many buttons was I supposed to press?

Then I faced a whole slew of other questions that we really

---

* The Hebrew reads רעות רבות וצרות. Both R. Samson Rafael Hirsch and R. Dovid Tzvi Hoffman prefer to translate וצרות as an adjective rather than taking it as a noun.

** By the time you read this, these names may be meaningless to you. Unfortunately, as I write, they are very real. They all deserve to be forgotten.

ought to be asking. For me, and I suspect for you, too, Ha'azinu is simply a parshah in the Torah, as are Bereishis, Noach, and Lech Lecha. I do not know it by heart[3] and I most certainly do not know any tune associated with it. For me, and I suspect for you, too, Ha'azinu lives in the *Aron HaKodesh,* is taken out once a year, and then, once *kri'as HaTorah* is over, is lovingly returned there. Is there something wrong with our Judaism? Have we been ignoring the Ribono shel Olam's wishes by allowing *Shiras Ha'azinu* to slip away from us? The Ribono shel Olam seems to have cared so much that Ha'azinu should accompany us through life.[4] It seems a small enough thing to ask of us. Did we go wrong?

If so, when?

If so, how?

If so, why?

These are reasonable questions and deserve careful thought. However, before plunging into textual analysis for some answers, we have one more task that demands our attention. We need a working definition of what it is that we are planning to analyze. What does Ha'azinu purport to be? We must know this before we have a feel for what questions to ask. We must certainly know it before we can develop an instinct for the kinds of answers that can make the cut. Let us responsibly approach the task that we have set ourselves. Berachos 28b recommends that upon entering a Beis HaMidrash we ask that לא אכשל בדבר הלכה, *the Ribono shel Olam protect us from egregious errors.* As we set out to understand a little more about Ha'azinu, we ought earnestly to make that same entreaty.

So what is Ha'azinu all about?

Let Ramban in his concluding remarks to Ha'azinu, speak.

וכך הזכירו בספרי (האזינו מג), גדולה שירה זו שיש בה עכשיו ויש בה לשעבר ויש בה לעתיד לבוא ויש בה בעולם הזה ויש בה לעולם הבא ולזה רמז הכתוב שאמר (פסוק מד) ויבא משה וידבר את כל דברי השירה הזאת באזני העם, הזכיר "כל" להגיד שהיא כוללת כל העתידות למו, ואם היא

קטנה בדבור, כי ביאר להם עניניה הרבים:* ואלו היתה השירה הזאת מכתב
אחד מן החוזים בכוכבים שהגיד מראשית אחרית כן היה ראוי להאמין בה
מפני שנתקיימו כל דבריה עד הנה לא נפל דבר אחד, ואף כי אנחנו נאמין
ונצפה בכל לב לדברי האלהים מפי נביאו הנאמן בכל ביתו, אשר לא היה
לפניו ואחריו כמוהו, עליו השלום.

And it is in these terms that Sifrei describes Ha'azinu.
"This song is great indeed for in it you may find guidance
regarding the present, the past and the future. It teaches
lessons regarding this world and the next. . . . It does all
this although it is really a short composition. In spite of
its terseness it covers many different areas. Now even if
this shirah had been composed by one of the star gaz-
ers who somehow managed to scan world history, logic
would have demanded that we believe him because, at
least up to the present, all that he predicted has come
true. Accordingly it stands to reason that we are bound
to believe God's words as they were conveyed to us by
the mouth of His most trusted servant, he whose greatness was not equaled by anyone who preceded him or
followed him."

Very clearly, this shirah is a national treasure with which we
all ought to be familiar. We were meant to treasure it, sing it,
and remember it. We had been taught its meaning by Moshe
Rabbeinu himself** and understood it sufficiently well to be
inspired by it and pass it on down the generations. Used as
it was meant to be used, there was every expectation that it
would never be forgotten as long as it was needed.*** If nothing
else, the knowledge that disloyalty to the Ribono shel Olam
would bring severe punishments in its wake would surely help

---

* This is a daring statement. Ramban seems to be saying that Moshe Rabbeinu,
on that occasion, not only told the people the text of Ha'azinu, but also spelled
out all the implications that lie beneath the text. Ramban's language makes
clear that none of this is expressed in the Torah's words. He adduces that (without assigning a source) to the extra "כל."

** See the previous footnote. See also Devarim 31:19, ולמדה את בני ישראל שימה בפיהם,
and Ramban there.

*** Verse 21, כי לא תשכח מפי זרעו.

us withstand the siren-song of assimilation. At the same time, the knowledge that even the most painful troubles would ultimately yield to the warmth of reconciliation with the Ribono shel Olam would arm us with an intuitive optimism about the purpose of Jewish life and the luster that is indigenous to Jewish living.

I said *if nothing else*. The truth must of course be that there is a great deal more besides the two points mentioned in the previous paragraph. We can claim this with confidence, since those two truisms are attested in numerous places in the Torah and, as they stand, seem to add nothing substantive to what we already know.* Once more, it becomes obvious that we have a difficult job ahead. Let us pray to the Ribono shel Olam for help and, figuratively, roll up our sleeves. תחזקנה ידינו!

---

* The first truism, that derelictions would be punished, can be found in many places of which the second parshah of kri'as Shema and the *tochochos* in both BeChukosai and Ki Savo are examples. An eloquent presentation of the second truism, the promise of ultimate redemption, can be found in Nitzavim (Devarim 30:1 and onward).

Text Analysis Begins

*W*hy, of all things, a shirah, a song?* If you glanced at endnote 6 in the Introduction and endnote 4 in the previous chapter, you will recall that Ramban takes this description very seriously. *Ha'azinu is called a* SONG *because as a song it is meant to accompany* KLAL YISRAEL *through the generations.* Just look at some of the verses and judge whether you feel like putting them to music. Here is an arbitrary selection: *My anger has kindled a fire, burning to the lowest depths. It shall consume the land and its crops, setting fire to the foundations of the mountains. I will heap evil upon them, striking them with My arrows* . . . (verses 22 and 23) and so on. Can you think of an appropriate tune? Shlomo HaMelech wrote in Mishlei 25:20, *He who sings songs to one whose heart is heavy is like one who wears a flimsy coat on a freezing day.* . . . Artificial happiness is an insult and displays insensitivity; it simply does no good. With Shlomo HaMelech in Koheles 2:2 we can say, *I said of . . . joy, "What does it accomplish?"*

Of course the fact is that Ha'azinu has a happy ending. The last few verses speak of a time when God's retribution will have run its course, when mercy will have taken over, and when, finally, history will move toward a glorious finale. But does that make the "in-between" centuries of suffering the stuff of musical celebration? We will have to dig a little deeper.

The time has come to turn to another of Ha'azinu's puzzles. Twice in VaYeilech (Devarim 31:19** and 21***) the Torah refers to Ha'azinu as testimony.[18] It is designed to bear witness for the Ribono shel Olam.**** Let us scan some of the *meforshim* to see what they make of this.

---

* See endnote 1 to the previous chapter.
** ‏למען תהיה לי השירה הזאת **לעד** בבני ישראל . . .‏
*** ‏והיה כי תמצאן אתו רעות רבות וצרות וענתה השירה הזאת לפניו **לעד** כי לא תשכח מפי זרעו כי ידעתי את יצרו אשר הוא עושה היום בטרם אביאנו אל הארץ אשר נשבעתי.‏
**** I base this assertion on the word ‏**לי**‏ in verse 19.

RASHI (to verse 21)

ועדה השירה הזאת לפניו לעד שהתריתי בו בתוכה על כל המוצאות אותו.
THE SHIRAH WILL BEAR WITNESS: *that I warned them about all the experiences that will pass over them.*

RAMBAN (also to verse 21)

Ramban's comment is directed at the latter part of the verse that reads, כי ידעתי את יצרו הוא עושה היום, *for I know firsthand how their inclination toward evil is expressing itself right now.* Ramban explains that had the Ribono shel Olam not had firsthand knowledge of our sorry record, it would have been inappropriate to spell out in detail all the terrible transgressions that lay in store for us. Here is his language: ואם לא חטאו ישראל במדבר ולא נודע יצרו בפועל
לא היה הגון **שיעיד** בהם שירה לאמור גלוי לפניו שתחטאו **ואעידה** בכם
שתמצאנה אתכם רעות רבות וצרות כזה וכזה .... *Had the Ribono shel Olam not had firsthand experience of what their inclination toward evil could do to them, it would not have been fitting that He have this* SHIRAH *bear witness that He knew quite well that they would sin and that He would proclaim testimony that these and those terrible troubles would overtake them.*

R. Dovid Tzvi Hoffman also focuses upon verse 21, but takes a very different approach to the issue. Here is the verse as he understands it: והיה כי תמצאן אתו רעות רבות וצרות
וענתה השירה הזאת לפניו לעד (כי לא תשכח מפי זרעו) כי ידעתי את יצרו אשר
הוא עושה היום בטרם אביאנו אל הארץ אשר נשבעתי. I have placed the phrase כי לא תשכח מפי זרעו in parentheses because R. Hoffman claims that it is parenthetical to what is being said.* If so, it follows that the phrase after the parentheses is the direct object of what preceded it. In this case, the meaning shifts, and the shirah bears witness that the Ribono shel Olam knew that the people were prone to sinning even before He brought

---

* The phrase is meant to answer the question: What guarantees that the shirah will still be known centuries later when it might be needed? God promises that it will never be forgotten.

them into Eretz Yisrael. In this case, the message is one of great comfort. If the Ribono shel Olam knew about the people's propensity to sin, and knew absolutely that, after their entry into the land, they would in fact become disloyal with acts of the basest treachery, why did He bother to bring them to Eretz Yisrael? Clearly He must also have known that there is an indestructible core of goodness that makes everything worthwhile, and that even the most dreadful exile will, in the end, lead to triumph.

At this point it would be a good idea to glance back at the Introduction to review the ideas of the Sefas Emes and R. Gedalia Schorr. There I paraphrased R. Schorr's ideas; here I offer a short quote. The Rebbe, R. Bunim from Peshischa, taught that "we are called upon to believe that the Ribono shel Olam is with us in even our darkest moments. It is in order to teach us this truth that we were given the shirah. That is the meaning of the words, וענתה השירה הזאת לעד. The purpose of its testimony is to make clear this very point that even in our suffering the Ribono shel Olam is always with us."

The chapter that we are now about to bring to an end has dealt with two issues: the question of why a composition so full of suffering and sorrow should have been expressed as a song and the exploration of what might be the testimony that is contained in the shirah. Are they related? It is too early to tell. I have the feeling that, as we progress in the book, we will be forming some opinions concerning this issue. The essays that follow will continue to explore both these subjects and should lead us to a more solid understanding of Ha'azinu, at least in general terms.

Come with me. We have much to do.

THREE

Rashi on "Eidus"

*H*ere, once more, is Rashi's language in his commentary to verse 21:

וענתה השירה הזאת לפניו לעד שהתריתי בו בתוכה על כל המוצאות אותם. This SHIRAH will bear witness: *that, through what it has to say, I warned them of all the experiences that would pass over them.*

Rashi's comment is terse. He trusts us to read carefully and thoughtfully. Come! We should not let him down.

Context matters and, if we are to understand verse 21 correctly, we will have to read it together with verses 19 and 20.

יט. ועתה כתבו לכם את השירה הזאת ולמדה את בני ישראל שימה בפיהם למען תהיה לי השירה הזאת לעד בבני ישראל.

כ. כי אביאנו אל האדמה אשר נשבעתי לאבתיו זבת חלב ודבש ואכל ושבע ודשן ופנה אל אלהים אחרים ועבדום ונאצוני והפר את בריתי.

כא. והיה כי תמצאן אתו רעות רבות וצרות וענתה השירה הזאת לפניו לעד כי לא תשכח מפי זרעו כי ידעתי את יצרו אשר הוא עשה ...

19. Now commit this shirah to writing and teach it to the Israelites. Make them memorize it. Do this so that this song might serve Me לעד* against** the Israelites.

20. For, when I bring them into the land flowing with milk and honey that I promised their ancestors, they will eat and be satisfied and live in luxury. They will then turn to foreign gods and worship them despising Me and violating My covenant.

21. When they are then beset by many constricting troubles this song will testify before them since it will not be

---

* I left לעד untranslated because, for the moment, I want to leave the possibilities open.
** Thus, R. S. R. Hirsch.

forgotten by their descendants. For I know their inclination...*

Rashi makes his comment on the word לעד that appears in verse 21. Now the same word also occurs in verse 19. Why did Rashi not comment on that "לעד"? The question seems simple enough and seems to call for some explanation. I am puzzled by the fact that none of the Rashi commentators that are available to me offer any thoughts. I suspect that the answer that I am about to suggest was obvious to them.

The wording of the two verses is sufficiently dissimilar to allow for some interpretive conjecture. Here are the two phrases next to each other:

VERSE 19

למען תהיה לי השירה הזאת לעד בבני ישראל

So that this shirah might serve Me לעד**

VERSE 21

וענתה השירה הזאת לפניו לעד

This shirah will testify before [the people]***

Here is my analysis.

It seems to me that "היה לעד" (verse 19)**** does not describe the act of testifying in a court. Rather it identifies someone or something as a *reminder*, who or that would jog memories (*"testify"*) when needed.[1] If this is correct, then verse 19 is saying that Ha'azinu is to be "on call" throughout our history to bring to mind, when required, any of the many, many truths that it contains. The role that Ha'azinu is to play in our trek through history is in no sense limited to the particular piece of information that the Ribono shel Olam had warned us of

---

* I have borrowed some of this translation from R. Aryeh Kaplan's *The Living Torah*.

** The shirah does not testify; rather it "serves" the Ribono shel Olam, is useful to Him.

*** Here Ha'azinu *does* testify in a formal sense.

**** The object of the verb, היה, is introduced with the prefix ל.

the punishments that would lie in store for us if we allowed ourselves to embrace idol worship.* That narrow meaning would be entirely inappropriate in verse 19.

The prefix ב, used in verse 19, usually indicates that the testimony in question is given *against* a person.** You may recall from endnote 2 in the previous chapter that ע ו ד is not limited to formal testimony in court. It can be used for any speech that is intended by the speaker to be taken with absolute seriousness.***

The meaning of verse 19 is clear. Ha'azinu is a treasure that Klal Yisrael is to guard closely over the centuries. On the long, long road to אחרית הימים many difficult situations will arise. This shirah is a resource for finding complex answers to complex questions. The Ribono shel Olam was telling Moshe Rabbeinu that his parting gift to Klal Yisrael is a very precious one.

Verse 21 is a different story altogether. Here we are dealing with an eventuality that verse 19 had predicted. This verse foresees a time when we will have strayed after idol worship and, as predicted countless times in the Torah, this treason will have brought great suffering in its wake. The verse anticipates that when these troubles overtake us we will question the fairness of this retribution. How could we possibly have anticipated that we would be hit so severely? Had we been warned, we would certainly not have succumbed to the enticements offered by the surrounding culture. Ha'azinu, the verse tells us, will do exactly what it was designed to do. It will, as it were, pull the evidence out of its files. There had been ample warning.

We sum up what we have now learned, as follows: Rashi believes that Ha'azinu was intended to be the repository of the many truths that each in its own way, in its own time, could and—if we but cared enough to look—would guide us along the path leading to Messianic redemption. The testimony

---

* This is Rashi's interpretation in verse 21. That same word in verse 19 has a much, much broader range of meanings.

** לא תענה ברעך עד שקר.

*** העד העד בנו האיש לאמור לא תראו פני בלתי אחיכם אתכם.

mentioned in verse 21 is only one single example of what it would be able to do.

We have taken the first necessary step; we have worked out what precisely Rashi is saying. We are now ready to tackle the "why." Specifically, why was it necessary to provide Ha'azinu as a warning of what would happen if the people veered "off the *derech*" and adopted idolatrous cults? The Torah itself is full of such warnings. We need only think of the second parshah of *kri'as Shema* or the *tochachos* of BeChukosai and Ki Savo. What does Ha'azinu say about the consequences of idol worship that has not been said many times before?

Three possible answers occurred to me and I will share them with you in a moment. First, a short preamble is in place. We are discussing the question to what extent the Israelites had been forewarned (וענתה השירה הזאת . . . שהתרתי בו בתוכה [רש"י]). The term התראה is familiar to us from our Gemara learning. We know that no corporal punishment* is normally administered unless the accused had been warned (התראה) about the consequences of his deed. In our discussion we will be drawing upon some of the laws governing that legally required act of warning. It must be stressed that the התראה of which the Gemara speaks and that which Rashi addresses here are in no way legally the same. If I assume that the one can throw light upon the other, that is only in the most general terms. No halachic comparison is intended.

Now to the three possibilities:

1. The laws governing the legal התראה allow for even the smallest possibility that the subject may have forgotten knowledge that we are sure he once had. Accordingly, in order for the התראה to fulfill the legal requirement, the subject must perform the action against which he had been warned *immediately* after the warning had been

---

* This incorporates death or flogging.

given. If there was a break of even a few seconds,* we deem the subject not to have been warned. In this event, the התראה must be repeated.** For this reason Rambam (Sanhedrin 12:2) rules that even a *talmid chacham* cannot be subjected to corporal punishment if he has not been warned. We give him the tiny benefit of doubt that he might have forgotten even that which we are absolutely certain he once knew. It seems possible that it is for that reason that the Torah's many warnings that sin would be followed by retribution do not qualify as adequate התראה. They may all have been forgotten. Ha'azinu is different. It is to be a popular song, designed to be a constant companion to the people.*** It is precisely in order to assure that it would *always* be fresh in their minds that the Ribono shel Olam insisted that it should have the character of a shirah.

2. Rambam (Sanhedrin 12:2) gives the wording of the legally required התראה as follows: "פרוש או אל תעשה שזו עבירה היא וחייב אתה עליה מיתת בית דין או מלקות" "Desist or do not do [what you are planning to do] for it is sinful and would result in your incurring the death penalty or a flogging." From this language it appears that it is not sufficient to give the warning in general terms. It is to be addressed to the subject personally.**** Perhaps, then, this could explain the difference between the other *parshios* and Ha'azinu. The latter is a prophecy addressed by Moshe Rabbeinu to the totality of Klal Yisrael—"You *will* do this, you *will* be punished in this or that manner." It has the character of a direct address, something in which the other parshios fall short.

---

* תוך כדי דבור.

** Rambam, Sanhedrin 12:2. See also *Ketzos HaChoshen* on Choshen Mishpat 28:8.

*** See endnotes 3 and 4 to chapter 1. See also Ibn Ezra to verse 21, where he explains the word לפניו in the phrase וענתה השירה הזאת לפניו with the words כמו נגדו, והטעם, שלא יזה העד ממנו רק עמו יהיה תמיד.

**** "This action is forbidden. One who transgresses the prohibition is subject to death or flogging."

3. Something tells me that this, the third option, is somehow more correct than the other two. I cannot offer any proof, but it feels right to me. I believe that the warning expressed in Ha'azinu projects a gravitas that the warnings contained in the other parshios lack. It is all a matter of context—and context matters. In Ha'azinu, the description of the sins that the people were going to commit as they waxed fat and began kicking, the dreadful suffering to which they would then be exposed, is consciously, and of course purposefully, displayed against the background of Jewish history. We come upon these heart-wrenching sorrows while the imagery of the mighty eagle, curbing his fierce aggressiveness as he gently flutters above his young, is still warming our hearts. A glance down the page transports us to a future of vindication and reconciliation. And there in the middle am I, ugly and stupid, small and bad and pathetic. Above all, wrong, foolishly and inexcusably wrong. Unaware of who I might be, who I might yet become, blithely trading gold for tinsel, eternal bliss for temporal intoxication. It is a sad, sad picture. A sad picture and therefore a peerless warning.

This has been one of those "one-word" Rashis that puts us all endlessly in his debt. Look back and think back to the time we have now had with him in this chapter. Can you think of a better way to spend a couple of hours?

Come now. We have more fields to plow, more harvests to gather in. Let us move on to the Ramban.

Ramban on "Eidus"

*Y*ou may recall Ramban's ideas from chapter 2. In contrast to Rashi, who has the *eidus* in verse 21 function as no more than a warning of the suffering that lay in store for us, Ramban, while agreeing to that, has it testify also to the fact that we would one day succumb to the blandishments of the idolatrous cults that would surround us in Eretz Yisrael.*

Let us see where this approach will take us.**

To get where we need to go, we will first have to take a detour. Specifically, we will need to spend some thought on the passage in VaYeilech that runs from verse 16 till verse 23. Here is the passage:

טו. ויאמר יהוה אל משה הנך שכב עם אבתיך וקם העם הזה וזנה אחרי אלהי נכר הארץ אשר הוא בא שמה בקרבו ועזבני והפר את בריתי אשר כרתי אתו. טז. וחרה אפי בו ביום ההוא ועזבתים והסתרתי פני מהם והיה לאכל ומצאהו רעות רבות וצרות ואמר ביום ההוא הלא על כי אין אלהי בקרבי מצאוני הרעות האלה. יח. ואנכי הסתר אסתיר פני ביום ההוא על כל הרעה אשר עשה כי פנה אל אלהים אחרים. יט. ועתה כתבו לכם את השירה הזאת ולמדה את בני ישראל שימה בפיהם למען תהיה לי השירה הזאת לעד בבני ישראל. כ. כי אביאנו אל האדמה אשר נשבעתי לאבתיו זבת חלב ודבש ואכל ושבע ודשן ופנה אל אלהים אחרים ועבדום ונאצוני והפר את בריתי. כא. והיה כי תמצאן אתו רעות רבות וצרות וענתה השירה הזאת לפניו לעד כי לא תשכח מפי זרעו כי ידעתי את יצרו אשר הוא עשה היום בטרם אביאנו אל הארץ אשר נשבעתי.

16. HaShem said to Moshe, "You are about to die. [Some time after your death,][1] this nation will rise up and stray

---

* שיעיד בהם שירה לאמור גלוי לפניו לפני שתחטאו ואעידה בכם שתמצאנה אתכם רעות רבות וצרות כזה וכזה. I do not want to make a big issue of the differences between Rashi and Ramban that I have now noted. Particularly after seeing in the previous essay how widely Rashi can be expanded once we consider what has and has not been said in verse 19, it is perfectly possible that, in the end, Rashi and Ramban are in full agreement with each other. Certainly the thoughts that will occupy us in the present essay can be true for Rashi as much as I believe them to be true for Ramban.

** As a matter of fact it will take us very far. However, we will return to the Ramban at the very end of this long and complicated chapter.

after the alien gods of the land into which they are coming. They will abandon Me and violate the covenant that I had made with them. 17. On that day, My anger will boil against them and I will abandon them and hide My Presence from them, so that they fall prey [to their enemies]. When they will have been beset by many constricting troubles, they will say on that day, 'It is because my God is no longer with me that these evils have befallen us.'² 18. On that day I will utterly hide My Face because of all the evil that they have done in turning to alien gods. 19. So now, write down this shirah and teach it to the Israelites so that they will know it fluently in order that this shirah will serve Me as testimony in the matter of the Israelites. 20. When I bring them to the land flowing with milk and honey that I promised their ancestors, they will eat, be satisfied and live in luxury. They will then turn to foreign gods and worship them, despising Me and violating My covenant. 21. When they are then beset by many evils and troubles, this song shall testify for them like a witness, since it will not be forgotten by their descendants. I know their inclinations through what they are doing right now even before I have brought them to the Promised Land."

Over the years this passage has always caused me anguish. I could never understand why the Ribono shel Olam chose to break Moshe Rabbeinu's heart just hours before he was to leave this world.* Could anything that he might hear during those last awesome hours** have been more devastating? In

---

* Sanhedrin 101a provides us with a lesson on what to say to a dying man. R. Tarfon, R. Yehoshua, and R. Elazar ben Azariah vied with one another for the best way to shower the dying R. Eliezer with praises. Even R. Akiva, who chose a different route, did so only because R. Eliezer would still be able to use the lesson that R. Akiva thought ought to be taught at such a moment.
** See Yalkut Shimoni, VaYeilech 31, for a detailed description of Moshe Rabbeinu's final hours.

a couple of short verses much of his life seems to have been laid bare as a failure. Nothing much seems to have changed. The people, his people, seemed to have remained as vulnerable to the blandishments of idolatry as they had been back in Egypt. Forty years in his "Yeshiva" seem not to have made much difference.

And furthermore, for whose teachings would they be willing to trade in what they had learned at Moshe Rabbeinu's feet? Their neighbors in Eretz Yisrael, churning around in the filth of their ugly superstitions,* sorcerers and pillagers, true heirs to Canaan and Cham, would be their teachers. His students, in whom he had invested so much belief and trust and, yes, so much love,** would jettison him and what he had taught them like so much flotsam. And for what? For what? For what?

What pain. What indescribable pain!

Over the years this has truly puzzled me.

But I was wrong to be puzzled. I had misread the thrust of the entire passage. The weight of God's communication lay not in the announcement of the impending sickness but in the anticipation of the miraculous cure. The Ribono shel Olam was giving the dying Moshe Rabbeinu the most precious farewell gift that could be imagined. He was giving him the gift of Ha'azinu.

Come with me. We are about to begin some wonderful and profoundly moving learning. It will concern the greatest *shiduch* of all times. Moshe Rabbeinu and Ha'azinu belonged together. It was to be a marriage of like to like. It, more than any other, was a marriage made in heaven. It simply had to come about.

Here is the history of my discovery. I began to wonder whether perhaps there was a closer tie between Moshe

---

* See Sanhedrin 64a for a description of the Pe'or service. In all honesty I cannot say with any certainty that this particular idol was served in Eretz Kenaan. Nevertheless, we can get an idea of the morality and aesthetics of these cults.

** ‏כי תאמר אלי שאהו בחיקך כאשר ישא האומן את היונק‏... (BeMidbar 11:12).

Rabbeinu and Ha'azinu than I had suspected.* On the slightest of slight hunches I went to my search program looking for the expression שירת משה. Maybe something would turn up. Wonder of wonders; it actually occurs in Midrash Zutah to Shir HaShirim 1. Here is the quote:

עשר שירות הן: שירת אדם שירת אברהם שירת הים שירת הבאר **שירת**
משה שירת יהושע שירת דבורה שירת דוד שירת שלמה ושירת לעולם הבא
[שנאמר] שירו לה' שיר חדש.

My suspicion was confirmed. Ha'azinu is not just an anonymous shirah; it is *Shiras Moshe*. I do not yet know in what way it is his shirah, nor do I know how the relationship came about.** However, the fact itself was a mighty revelation. I just had to make up my mind where to take it.

I would like to spend some time with the Gemara in Nedarim 38a.

אמר רבי יוסי ברבי חנינא לא ניתנה תורה אלא למשה שנאמר ולזרעו כתב
לך פסל לך מה פסולתן שלך אף כתבן שלך משה נהג בה טובת עין ונתנה
לישראל ועליו הכתוב אומר טוב עין הוא יבורך וגו' מתיב רב חסדא ואותי
צוה ה' בעת ההיא ללמד אתכם ואותי צוה ואני לכם ראה למדתי אתכם
חוקים ומשפטים כאשר צוני ה' אלהי אותי צוה ואני לכם ועתה כתבו לכם
את השירה הזאת השירה לחודה למען תהיה לי השירה הזאת לעד לבני
ישראל אלא פילפולא בעלמא.

R. Yose bar Chaninah taught that when the Ribono shel Olam gave Moshe Rabbeinu the Torah, He intended that it belong only to him and his descendants [not to the Jewish people as a whole]. Moshe, in his generosity, shared it with everybody. The Gemara cites proof texts to prove that this cannot be true. It is clear that all along the Torah was intended for everybody. The Gemara

---

* If you are suddenly being hit by a feeling of *déjà vu*, you are not mistaken. We have already discussed the concept of *Shiras Moshe* at length in the Prologue. Please glance at chapter 1, endnote 1. What I wrote in the Prologue was based on the research I did for the current chapter. Please do not let this confuse you.
** In the meantime I have written the Prologue and much has changed for me. In that essay I discuss these issues at length.

concludes that R. Yose was referring only to פלפולא בעלמא, *making use of Talmudic dialectic to reach Talmudically correct conclusions.* This power was originally intended for only Moshe Rabbeinu and his descendants. His kindness persuaded him to share it with the rest of Klal Yisrael.

Why was it originally intended that only Moshe Rabbeinu should be entrusted with this potent tool? And, if he alone was imbued with particular intelligence and could therefore be trusted more than anybody else, by what right did he feel himself empowered to share this gift with others? Would not those other, unendowed people inevitably draw incorrect conclusions?

Maharal in his *Chidushei Aggadah* to Nedarim explains that Moshe Rabbeinu's particular affinity to *pilpul* lay in the fact that he was gifted with something that Maharal calls שכל עליון. I do not know what precisely this might mean. I do not think that it has anything to do with a particularly high IQ. Rather it must be describing a mind that was totally in tune with the sacred world of Torah thought. Moshe Rabbeinu understood, and felt at home with, the axioms and values that lie at the root of the Torah's prescriptions. If, for example, he concluded that from the Torah's *x* and *y* it should follow that *z* should be treated or understood in such and such a manner, then that conclusion was correct in as much as it was reached by a mind that worked in absolute tandem with Torah ideas. His thinking could never be deflected by preconceptions and value systems that were foreigners in that holy land, for the very good reason that such intruders were never permitted entry into the קדש קדשים that was his field of battle in his מלחמתה של תורה.

So now we are back with a really major problem. If such a level of self-abnegation is really required if pilpul can hope to have legitimacy, then how could Moshe Rabbeinu, even granting his עין טוב, have handed it over to everybody else? Would that not be an open invitation for the construction of reams and reams of פלפולא של הבל?

Here is what I believe to be the answer.

I believe that Moshe Rabbeinu's faculty for perceiving the

Divine will lay in his self-definition as ונחנו מה (Shemos 16:7 and 8). That "מה" is a very potent word. Of course, as with every rhetorical question, the phrase is not interrogative but assertive. It is saying that, were you to ask anybody "What (מה) is inside this person's mind of his own personality or thoughts?" there would be no answer because, in truth, there is nothing at all of any of that. People who find it important to answer this query as it regards Moshe Rabbeinu are condemned to live out their lives under the shadow of a lifelong question mark. There was nothing at all in Moshe Rabbeinu's mind besides receptivity to the Ribono shel Olam's wishes.[3]

Pilpul ought to be reserved for people in the "מה" category. Anything less than that, any situation in which the "מה" could hope for even the tiniest answer, would have to be excluded. Any אמת that a person not in the "מה" category might produce must emerge tainted by their confused and garbled preconceptions and prejudices.

How then could Moshe Rabbeinu have passed pilpul on to the masses?

In my opinion there can be only one answer to that question. Once Moshe Rabbeinu decided that he wanted to share his prowess in pilpul with the people, he would necessarily have to pass on to them the wherewithal that could make it happen. At least in their learning, they, too, would be able to live under the protection of the "מה." At least in their learning they would be able to rid themselves of their pettiness; to clear their minds and make themselves accessible to the absolute truth.*

Now let us move from pilpul to Ha'azinu.

Even at this early stage of the book you have certainly picked up that, taken as a whole, this is a happy song. Somehow the knowledge that ultimate triumph awaits us makes the trip a little easier. With the introductory chapter in mind, we could say that the זיו of הזי"ו ל"ך is sometimes hard to discern, but,

---

* I cannot pretend to have any idea of how this transfer took place. We are standing on holy ground. We would be well advised to take off our shoes of self-assertion and realize that there are limits to what we can expect of ourselves.

for all that, it is always present. There is a luminosity, sometimes brilliant, at other times dim, that lights up our difficult history in all its stages. What casts that light? Ha'azinu. Who put it into Ha'azinu? With a certain amount of diffidence I am willing to hazard an answer. Moshe Rabbeinu put it there with his pilpul faculty. Pilpul, as we have defined it, partakes of an intuitive understanding of the Ribono shel Olam's ideas. The Ribono shel Olam's *hashgachah* that, from behind the curtains, pulls the strings that produce the performance described in Ha'azinu are, to Moshe Rabbeinu, an open book. It is Moshe Rabbeinu's song because he, among all mankind, was best able to sing it.[4]

Way back in this chapter I asked why the Ribono shel Olam chose to break Moshe Rabbeinu's heart so shortly before he had to die. What point was there in telling him that soon after his and Yehoshua's death the people would betray all that they had covenanted to the Ribono shel Olam and all that Moshe Rabbeinu had taught them? I reasoned from the fact that Moshe Rabbeinu did nothing to attempt to forestall these tragedies that it is evident there was in fact nothing he could do. So why torture him?

I mentioned that this question had been based on a terrible misconception under which I had labored. Now I think I have discovered the truth. The shirah that Moshe Rabbeinu was to teach the people with so much care and with an insistence that they keep it always at their side and in their mind was not something that had an objective existence independent of Moshe Rabbeinu. It was *his* SHIRAH. When the Ribono shel Olam broke the dreadful news to Moshe Rabbeinu that in the not-too-distant future his people would turn to idol worship, that was only half the story. The point of telling this to Moshe Rabbeinu was to let him know that even though he was about to die, even though the road that his people would have to travel through history would be rocky and dangerous, he would not leave them unprotected. He would be their constant protector and guide, their רעיא מהימנא, *their conscientious shepherd. His* Ha'azinu would never leave them.

We began this essay with an attempt to discover to what

facts Ha'azinu is meant to testify. We saw that Rashi limits the testimony to the fact that we had been warned. One day severe punishment would overtake us for our sins. There is to be no appeal to ignorance of the results of our actions. We had been warned. Ramban, as we saw above, takes it further.

Why is Ramban interested in expanding Rashi's ideas? Why should our transgression be included in Ha'azinu's testimony?

If I am right in the analysis that I have offered in this chapter, the following explanation becomes possible. It is all part of the "pilpul" by which *Shiras Moshe* is energized. We suggested earlier that the luminosity that lights up even the tragic periods of our history is generated by a mind-set that is completely congruent with the thinking of the Ribono shel Olam. →The historiography that is yielded by such thinking is all-encompassing. Once we will have been granted a peek at the obverse side of the tapestry,* we will understand why *every* detail of our experiences, the awful as well as the stellar, will have played a role in the final *dénouement* toward which Ha'azinu leads us. One day we will understand.

---

* See the Prologue for details.

R. Dovid Tzvi Hoffman on "Eidus" I

*H*ere, once more, is how we presented R. Dovid Tzvi Hoffman's reading of the VaYeilech passage:

R. Dovid Tzvi Hoffman also centers his remarks upon verse 21, but takes a very different approach to the issue. Here is the verse as he understands it: והיה כי תמצאן אתו רעות רבות וצרות וענתה השירה הזאת לפניו לעד (כי לא תשכח מפי זרעו) כי ידעתי את יצרו אשר הוא עשה היום בטרם אביאנו אל הארץ אשר נשבעתי. I have placed the phrase כי לא תשכח מפי זרעו in parentheses because R. Hoffman claims that it is parenthetical to what is being said.* Given this, it follows that the phrase after the parentheses is the direct object of what preceded it. The meaning is: The shirah is to bear witness that the Ribono shel Olam knew that they were prone to sinning even before He brought them into Eretz Yisrael. The message is one of great comfort. It is this: If the Ribono shel Olam knew about the people's propensity to sin, and knew absolutely that, after the entry into the land, they would in fact prove to become disloyal to their beginnings in acts of the basest treachery, why did He bother to bring them to Eretz Yisrael? Clearly He must also have known that there is an indestructible core of goodness that makes everything worthwhile, and that even the most dreadful exile will, in the end, lead to triumph.

Our task is clear. We must find out the nature of this "indestructible core of goodness." We will devote this chapter to discovering what exactly it is that we are talking about.

What is the secret? What are the links in the invisible chain that hold us safe even at the point at which we are wavering

---

* It answers the question: What guarantees that the shirah will still be known centuries later when it might be needed? God promises that it will never be forgotten.

at the very edge of the unforgiving chasm? The logic of totally
unfettered freedom of choice* ought really to demand that if
we choose to take that final leap to total eclipse, we should be
free to do so. Ha'azinu seems to be taking us into very choppy
waters. We have to find some help.

There is no way out of our conundrum without readjusting
our definitions. In asking our question we assumed that freedom of choice (*bechirah*) is absolute. There simply are no limits to what each of us can decide to do. It turns out this is not
true; there is, in fact, one reservation. The ultimate triumph
of good over evil, the final vindication of Klal Yisrael and,
through Klal Yisrael, of the Ribono shel Olam, is not given us
to alter. We can approach the very brink, but the Ribono shel
Olam will not allow us to take the leap.

To grasp the enormity of what we have just said, let us
ponder a small excerpt from one of the late Rav Hutner's
ma'amarim (*Pachad Yitzchak* to Yom Kippur 6:7):

> ... That promise constitutes a limitation on the other-
> wise guaranteed freedom of choice. Were that freedom
> absolute, then the balance between "good" and "evil"
> should have been exactly equal. But that is not the case.
> This promise implies that although "evil" is empowered
> to oppose the "good," to make war against it and to put
> obstacles in its path ... it is not empowered to destroy
> the "good" totally. It is simply a given that in the end "all"
> will find its place with the sacred.[1]

That is the message that Ha'azinu sends. It is the one message that should be able to get through to even the benighted
dropouts to whom the shirah is addressed. It extends hope to
the hopeless, discovers the lovable in even such unfortunates
as have spent a lifetime in covering their spark of sanctity under layers of the blackest evil.

How does this principle work in real life? Earlier we spoke

---

* בחירה חפשית.

of an invisible chain that pulls us back from the brink. What links make up this chain?

We will find the answer in Ramban's commentary to verses 26 and 27 of the shirah.

Here is the background.

Immediately before these two verses the Ribono shel Olam had deplored our execrable lack of gratitude for all the kindness and generosity with which He had always showered us. There simply was no excuse. In verse 26 the Ribono shel Olam reveals that He had seriously considered breaking off His relationship with us. He would leave us to wither on the vine; would sunder His relationship with us and permit us to be swallowed up by our exile.*

Here is verse 26:

אמרתי אפאיהם אשביתה מאנוש זכרם.

I had considered destroying them utterly, causing them to be erased from human memory.[2]

Verse 27 immediately makes clear that what was contemplated in verse 26 would not, under any circumstances, occur. It provides the reason:

לולי כעס אויב אגור פן ינכרו צרימו פן יאמרו ידנו רמה ולא יהוה פעל כל זאת.

Were it not that the anger of the enemy was pent up, lest their tormentor misinterpret, lest they say, "Our hand was raised in triumph and it was not HaShem Who accomplished all this."

Let us put the information contained in these two verses together and see what it sounds like. *If the Ribono shel Olam were able to do so, His preference would be to simply erase us from human memory. Unfortunately, from His point of view, He is unable to do so because the* umos ha'olam, *drunk on their own arrogance,*

---

* This rendering is based on our discussion of the Ramban's ideas, in chapter 12.

would ascribe our disappearance to their own might and would deal the Ribono shel Olam out of the equation. What a shame for Him! Against His will He will have to continue dealing with us!

That sounds awful, does it not? None of us want to feel that the Ribono shel Olam has absolutely no interest in us, would in fact be glad to consign us to oblivion, but is "unable" to do so because of the pesky umos ha'olam who would misread the signs. What does that do to the הבוחר בעמו ישראל באהבה that we recite so proudly every morning?*

Ramban picks up this really disturbing problem and cites a number of other verses in TaNaCh that convey similar ideas.[3] Quite apart from the fact that this does not do much for our self-respect, the whole thesis is of course absolutely impossible. It militates against everything we hold dear, everything that we know beyond doubt or cavil.

Let us learn and try to understand Ramban's ideas on this subject.

> והטעם בטענה הזאת, איננו כרוצה להראות כחו בין שונאיו, כי כל הגוים כאין נגדו מאפס ותוהו נחשבו לו אבל השם ברא את האדם בתחתונים שיכיר את בוראו ויודה לשמו, ושם הרשות בידו להרע או להטיב, וכאשר חטאו ברצונם וכפרו בו כולם לא נשאר רק העם הזה לשמו, ופרסם בהם באותות ובמופתים כי הוא אלהי האלהים ואדוני האדונים ונודע בזה לכל העמים והנה אם ישוב ויאבד זכרם, ישכחו העמים את אותותיו ואת מעשיו ולא יסופר עוד בהם, ואם אדם יזכיר כן, יחשבו כי היה כח מכחות המזלות והכוכבים וחלף ועבר והנה תהיה כוונת הבריאה באדם בטלה לגמרי, שלא ישאר בהם יודע את בוראו רק מכעיס לפניו, ועל כן ראוי מדין הרצון שהיה בבריאת העולם, שיהיה רצון מלפניו להקים לו לעם כל הימים, כי הם הקרובים אליו והיודעים אותו מכל העמים:
>
> וזה טעם כי ידין ה' עמו ועל עבדיו יתנחם (פסוק לו), שיזכור ה' ברחמים כי הם עמו מאז, ויזכור כי הם עבדיו שעמדו לו בגלותם כעבדים לסבול הצרות והשעבוד, וכענין שנאמר (ישעיה סג ח) ויאמר אך עמי המה בנים לא ישקרו וכבר רמזתי בבריאת האדם סוד נשגב ונעלם צריך ממנו שנהיה לו לעם והוא יהיה לנו לאלהים, כענין שנאמר (ישעיה מג ז) כל הנקרא בשמי ולכבודי בראתיו וגו'.

The logic of God's reasoning in these verses is not

---

prompted by a desire to impress His enemies with His strength, for All the nations are as nothing before Him; He looks upon them as carrying neither weight nor value. [Rather, He was motivated by the following consideration.] The Ribono shel Olam created mankind with the purpose that they would acknowledge their Creator and be thankful to Him. And [in order that this might reasonably be accomplished] He empowered humans [with free choice], enabling them to do good or evil. [As history developed] all of mankind chose to follow the path of sin and to deny the Ribono shel Olam. Only this one nation (Israel) remained true to Him and it was through their history that He made His omnipotence known to all.

If God were ever to destroy His people, their history, and therefore the evidence of His omnipotence, would be irretrievably lost. Nobody would even remember all the wondrous miracles that He had wrought for them, and even if this or that one were remembered, people would ascribe what happened to natural or occult agencies. Thus the purpose of creating man would be totally frustrated for nobody would acknowledge the Ribono shel Olam anymore. Only people who provoke Him would be left.

→It follows that the very fact that the Ribono shel Olam willed the world into existence must guarantee that He will want the *benei Yisrael* to remain *His* people to all eternity. Only they will be able to carry the truth to the nations, since they alone are close to Him and know Him intimately.

→This is the meaning of the verse (in Ha'azinu 32:36, the verse that leads into the final comforting section of God's speech, the section that culminates with a glance at the Messianic future) *When, after the Ribono shel Olam will have judged His people [and exposed them to great suffering] and will have then decided that the time has come to deal mercifully with His servants . . .* then God in His mercy will remember that they have always been His people, and will further remember that they are His servants who throughout their exile remained true to Him, willingly bearing suffering and servitude. As it is written in Yeshayahu 63:8, *Surely they are My people, children that will not deal falsely* . . .

Please do read this passage very, very carefully. I have a confession to make. I have learned this Ramban many, many times in the course of many, many years; I have taught it in countless classes, I have written about it as the need arose, and, if truth be told, I practically know it by heart. Even so, I cannot say with any degree of certainty that I really know *peshat* in what Ramban is saying. Even as I am writing these words, I have the Ramban open in front of me and am trying to read it with new eyes and a new heart (בכל יום יהיו בעיניך כחדשים) to see what he is really saying. It is clear to me that the answer is hidden somewhere in the paragraphs that I marked with those important-looking arrows, but, even today, it is not totally clear to me what he means.

I have written this little introduction in order to put you on notice that your guess is as good as mine. I am about to tell you what now appears to me to be the correct interpretation. Please feel free to substitute your own understanding if you feel that it fits Ramban's language more smoothly.

Here is my suggestion. The Ramban introduces his solution with the information that it is based on verse 36.* Here is the verse together with its translation.

כי ידין ה' עמו ועל עבדיו יתנחם . . .

When, after the Ribono shel Olam will have judged His people [and exposed them to great suffering]** and will have then decided that the time has come to deal mercifully with His servants . . .***

---

* . . . וזה טעם, כי ידין ה' עמו

** Based on Rashi to verse 36, כשישפוט אותן ביסורין.

*** Based on Rashi to verse 36, . . . ויתנחם הקב"ה על עבדיו לשוב ולרחם עליהם.

→ Apparently, things are going to get better when the Ribono shel Olam decides to move from the mode of "דין" *pure justice,** to the mode of "רחמים" *mercy.***

Now in order for us to understand this change from "justice" to "mercy," we must spend a few moments clarifying for ourselves what the role of mercy might be for the Ribono shel Olam, Who is the שופט כל הארץ, *the God of justice.*

As some of you may recall, this question is raised by R. Moshe Chaim Luzzatto, the RaMChaL, in his *Mesilas Yesharim*, chapter 4. He wonders how God's attribute of Mercy can interact with His attribute of Justice without compromising its integrity. He explains that, indeed, if mercy were to demand the complete cancellation of the appropriate punishment, that would be incompatible with pure justice. However, if the punishment will be administered but mercy succeeds in somehow mitigating the degree to which it is executed, that would be an application of mercy that leaves justice intact.[4] One of the three means of mitigation that RaMChaL proposes is that mercy might argue in favor of softening the intensity of the punishment that is to be meted out.

This insight will enable us to understand verse 36 as follows. כי ידין ה' עמו, *when HaShem will have punished His people [to the extent that the suffering that they have experienced up to this point may, once the attribute of Mercy takes over, be considered sufficient]* ועל עבדיו יתנחם *and He therefore turns to mercy in dealing with His servants.*

Now *halachah* recognizes another great principle that we may now muster to our cause (see Mishnah, Maccos 23a, codified by Rambam, Sanhedrin 17:7 and 8[5]). It states that, once the sinner has been punished to the degree required by the

---

* When, in his commentary to verse 26, Ramban explains his ideas about the meaning of אפאיהם (see next chapter), he begins with the words יאמר כי היה ... **במדת הדין** להיותנו כן בגלות לעולם ...

** I have marked this paragraph with an arrow because this insight is fundamental to our understanding of the structure of Ha'azinu and, by way of that, the structure of Jewish history. The final גאולה will come when the Ribono shel Olam's הנהגה will change from דין to רחמים.

halachah, he is reinstated as a person in good standing and no more stigma is attached to him.

We may now state Ramban's answer to the depressing problem that we raised earlier in this essay, as follows. Klal Yisrael's performance during the dark years of our exile, taken as a whole, will have been less than stellar. If truth be told, we had, quite simply, failed our test. Strict justice would demand that we remain in *galus* permanently until, in the natural flow of history, we would ultimately sink into oblivion. We would be neither the first nor the last experiment that, having failed, would be condemned to such a fate. However, the Ribono shel Olam cannot allow that to happen. We recall the quote from the Ramban above, that *it follows that the very fact that the Ribono shel Olam willed the world into existence must guarantee that He will want the benei Yisrael to remain His people for all eternity.* So, what is to be done? The attribute of Mercy provides an answer. It is more than simply a technical adjustment, determining that such and such an amount of suffering may be sufficient to satisfy justice's demands. It is much more than that. It can and does change the mood from a grudging bowing to circumstances, to a feast of love and reconciliation.

Here is how. The attribute of Mercy will be pressed into service so that less than the entire stretch of exile will be deemed sufficient.[6] That period of intense suffering (see endnote 7) would be the time subsumed under, כי ידין ה' עמו. The attribute of Mercy is waiting in the wings to make sure that at the first possible moment the path to rehabilitation can be undertaken. That would be the point described as ועל עבדיו יתנחם. Once that happens,* the Ribono shel Olam, now unencumbered by any remaining stigma from the early disappointments, will be able to concentrate on Ramban's promise that *then God in His mercy will remember that they have always been His people, and will further remember that they are His servants who throughout their exile remained true to Him, willingly bearing suffering and servitude.*[7]

---

* At this point I must ask you to have a little patience. The exact nature of "Once that happens . . ." will become clear in the following chapter.

It follows that all the verses that Ramban quoted to show that God's help is to be extended to us not because of His love for us but only in order to avoid a chilul HaShem can now be reinterpreted. That is not at all what is meant by any of these verses. The need to preserve Klal Yisrael in order that the nations not forget that there is a Ribono shel Olam is no more than an explanation of why He will resort to the quality of mercy. Once He will have done so, the entire picture changes. With the period of punishment foreshortened, with all stigmas of the past eliminated, God can concentrate on the heroism and loyalty that we, as a people, showed throughout the dark exile years. Every morning we can say הבוחר בעמו ישראל באהבה with a clear conscience and a singing heart.

R. Dovid Tzvi Hoffman on "Eidus" II:
Further Thoughts on Justice Giving Way to Mercy

*P*lease take the time to glance back at endnote 5 to the previous chapter. At this point I am officially backing down from what it says there. I know that all I had to do was simply to erase it and be done with it. I decided against that because I want to share with you what I thought then and what I think now. As I was struggling with the issues with which I grappled in the previous chapter, I had the feeling that enough is enough. We are, after all, learning Ha'azinu, not *Mesilas Yesharim*. I needed to make use of an insight that RaMChaL noted in the fourth chapter of his magnum opus, and that I did. I did not feel responsible for defending that particular *chidush* against all objections that might be raised. That is what I said in that endnote.

Since then I have had the time to think long and hard about Ha'azinu and it struck me that the Ribono shel Olam's change of heart כביכול (verse 36), the moment in which He decided that His people had suffered enough and that it was time to invoke the quality of mercy, is probably the very fulcrum that supports the message that makes Ha'azinu what it is: the key to unblighted optimism concerning the future of Klal Yisrael that made us so happy when we first began to understand it in chapter 4.

So let us back down gracefully from the earlier footnote and learn a little *Mesilas Yesharim*.

The following quote is taken from the fourth chapter, How to Acquire Vigilance.* Immediately before this passage RaMChaL makes the point that in as much as the Ribono shel Olam is the God of truth, He must treasure justice—the practical application of truth as the judge sees it. From this it would follow that transgressions must be punished according to the strict letter of the law. RaMChaL then wonders how it would be possible for mercy to be injected into the process.

---

* I have taken the English rendering from Ofek's *The Complete Mesillat Yesharim*. My translations will also draw upon that excellent rendition.

Here are his thoughts:

ואם תאמר, אם כן, מדת הרחמים למה היא עומדת, כיון שעל כל פנים
צריך לדקדק בדין על כל דבר? התשובה, ודאי, מדת הרחמים היא קיומו של
עולם, שלא היה עומד זולתו כלל וכלל. ואף על פי כן אין מדת הדין לוקה,
וזה, כי לפי שורת הדין ממש, היה ראוי שהחוטא יענש מיד תיכף לחטאו
בלי המתנה כלל, וגם שהעונש עצמו יהיה בחרון אף, כראוי למי שממרה
פי הבורא יתברך שמו, ושלא יהיה תיקון לחטא כלל, כי הנה באמת, איך
יתקן האדם את אשר עיות והחטא כבר נעשה? הרי שרצח האדם את חברו,
הרי שנאף, איך יוכל לתקן הדבר הזה? היוכל להסיר המעשה העשוי מן
המציאות.

You might ask: What then is the attribute of Mercy for, if
justice must be exacted for everything with precision no
matter what? The answer is that the attribute of Mercy
is certainly what preserves the world; for by no means
could it endure without it. Still, the attribute of Justice
is not compromised. For according to the strict application of the law, a sinner should be immediately punished,
as soon as he sins, without any delay whatever and also
with the wrath that befits one who rebels against the
word of the Creator. Moreover the sins should be utterly
irreparable: for in truth how can a person rectify what
he has made crooked once the sin has already been committed? Suppose someone murders his fellow or committed adultery, how can he possibly rectify this? Can he
undo a deed once done?

RaMChaL has made the point that we can isolate three areas in which mercy would be able to mitigate the demands
of a merciless justice without offending against its essential
demands. Absolute justice would demand that punishment
be administered immediately, that it be applied with the full
fury of which an offended deity would be capable, and that
there be no way to rectify the sinner's transgression.

The paragraph immediately following the section that we
have quoted then explains that in each of these areas mercy
could be applied without compromising the demands of justice. It could argue that the sinner be given some time before

he will be punished, that something less than the full fury that he deserves might be accepted as adequate, and that there should be a possibility of doing *teshuvah*.

This is as far as we took the RaMChaL in the previous chapter. The obvious problem stares us in the face. How can RaMChaL argue that these leniencies do not compromise the demands of justice? Why is it not a compromise when justice demands absolute consistency and mercy offers even minor adjustments? Do compromises not compromise?

RaMChaL was a prolific writer and enriched Klal Yisrael with many different *sefarim*. Whenever things look a little murky in one of his books, there is always a reasonable chance that there may be a passage somewhere else that can throw light on the matter. In this situation, that is indeed the case. In *Derech HaShem*, RaMChaL discusses the interplay between the Ribono shel Olam's love for His people, a love that would surely incline toward the quality of mercy, and the need for the quality of *Mishpat*, one that may well stand in contradiction to the dictates of *Rachamim*.

Here is a little of what he writes in his *Derech HaShem* (part 2, chapter 8):

ממה שיבחן מאד בהשגחתו ית', הוא היות יסוד כל סדרי ההשגחה ודרכיה – יושר המשפט וקו הדין, וכענין שנאמר, שבט מישור שבט מלכותך, וכתוב, מלך במשפט יעמיד ארץ. ואמנם ידענו באמת, שאין חפצו של הקב"ה אלא להטיב, והנה הוא אוהב את ברואיו כאב האוהב את בנו, אלא שמטעם האהבה עצמה ראוי שייסר האב את בנו להטיבו באחריתו, וכענין שנאמר, כי כאשר ייסר איש את בנו ה' אלקיך מיסרך. ונמצא, שהמשפט והדין עצמו ממקור האהבה הוא נובע, ואין מוסרו של הקב"ה מכת אויב ומתנקם, אלא מוסר אב הרוצה בטובת בנו וכמ"ש. ואולם משרש זה נולדים שני ענינים, האחד – שהמוסר עצמו יהיה ממותק ולא קשה ואכזרי, כי האהבה עצמה תמזוג את הדין ברחמים.

It must be very clear to us that the underlying principle by which the Ribono shel Olam dispenses His providence is the need to deal according to the demands of justice along the path defined by law. . . . However we know with absolute certainty that God wishes only to be kind and that He loves His creatures as a father loves his child. [Is there not a contradiction between a stance guided by justice and law, and the expression of parental love? The answer is that] it is love itself that demands adherence to justice and that he chastise his child [when necessary] in order to guarantee that his end will be happy.... We can now see that an adherence to law and justice becomes necessary as an expression of love. The punishments that the Ribono shel Olam metes out do not derive from hatred or vengeance but, on the contrary, they must be understood as the discipline that a loving father would impose upon his son.

Once this is understood we can see that there are two results that grow out of this premise: The first is that the chastisement itself will somehow be softened (lit. sweetened) and not applied harshly or with cruelty, for love (the source of the need to chastise) will dilute justice with mercy...

The application of this passage to the *Mesilas Yesharim* that we were unable to understand earlier is, of course, perfectly clear. *Absolute justice is not an absolute good.* Justice and law are invoked only to the extent that mercy itself requires consistency and discipline. *Mesilas Yesharim* is simply saying that a softening in the three areas that he suggests will not impair either of these.

It seems to me that what we have now learned from RaMCHaL is really no more than a reflection of what Chazal point out to us right at the beginning of the Torah.

We recall that in the first chapter of Bereishis in which the process of the actual Creation is described, the Ribono shel Olam is always called Elohim. In the second chapter, in which more details are filled in, the Ribono shel Olam becomes HaShem Elohim, a combination of two names. Rashi to Bereishis 1:1, where the name Elohim occurs for the first time, comments as follows:

ברא אלהים ולא אמר ברא ה' שבתחלה עלה במחשבה לבראותו במדת
הדין וראה שאין העולם מתקיים והקדים מדת רחמים ושתפה למדת הדין.
והיינו דכתיב ביום עשות ה' אלהים ארץ ושמים.

ELOHIM CREATED: [The name used is] Elohim, not
HaShem. [HaShem is not used here because] originally
it was God's intention to create a world that would [be
governed] by the standards of the attribute of Justice.*
Upon seeing that a world [that was subject to such high
standards] would be unable to exist, He placed the Shem
Havayah before Elohim and thus placed [the attribute of
Mercy]** into partnership with the attribute of Justice.

Normally, I would shy away from analyzing a Rashi like
this, coming close, as it does, to sisrei Torah where I have no
business to be. However, I have the feeling that it is possible to
come just a little closer while still maintaining an appropriate
distance.

It appears to me that the word Rashi uses, הקדים, *He placed
before,* is boundlessly significant. I do not recall ever thinking
particularly deeply about this Rashi, but if somebody would
have asked me what I remember of what Rashi says, I probably would have answered that the Ribono shel Olam decided
to give the attribute of Justice a junior partner whose task it
would be to sand away the rough edges and still make it possible for the new system to, at the very least, hew closely to the
original plan.

The use of הקדים does not allow for this facile philosophiz-
ing. The new Name placed before the old one seems to imply a
total change of perspective. In the new world, nothing at all is
as it would have been.[1]

Now if we take a look at this new partnership (HaShem

---

* The name Elohim is associated with the attribute of Justice. There is a hint to
this in that the numerical value of 86 (אלהים) equals the numerical value of הוא
דיין (Gur Aryeh).

** The שם הויה, written י and then ה and then ו and then ה, can also, in the alpha-
betical system known as את בש גר, be expressed as מ and then צ and then פ and
then ץ, which has the numerical value of 300, which equals the numerical value
of ברחמים (Gur Aryeh).

Elohim), we will see that it is by no means an equal one. It is not only that the new partner (HaShem) is placed before the old one, but also that the four-lettered name of the Ribono shel Olam is what is known as the שם העצם, God's actual name, the one that, to the extent that it is possible, describes Him, while Elohim describes not what He is* but what He does. See Rashi to Bereishis 2:5, ה' הוא שמו, אלהים שהוא שליט ושופט על כל, "HaShem" is His name; "Elohim" [conveys the idea that] He rules over and judges everything.

We do not have to go further in order to make the point that is important to us. By now it should be clear that the solution that we found in the *Derech HaShem* is actually expressed in the composite name, HaShem Elohim. HaShem *is* the God Who dispenses nothing but goodness (הטוב הגמור, see the first footnote below). However the Ribono shel Olam also *administers* justice, presumably as RaMChaL explains, because without it there would not—really, could not—be the absolute good that the Ribono shel Olam desires.

We have not heard the last about the interplay between דין and רחמים. Later on in this book** when we contemplate the meaning of *pasuk 4,* הצור תמים פעלו כי כל דרכיו משפט, there will be other highways and byways to explore. For our immediate purposes, as we are still thinking about the general purpose of Ha'azinu, this chapter taken together with the previous one will do.

Let us now move on to the Rebbe, R. Bunim from Peshischa, as his ideas have been passed down to us through the Sefas Emes and R. Gedalia Schorr.

---

* Gur Aryeh writes as follows: ועוד, ששם בן ד' הוא שם העצם המורה על אמתתו, ואמתתו היא הטוב הגמור המשפיע לכל הנמצאים.

** Chapter 15.

The Sefas Emes on "Eidus" I

*O*nce again, I would like to return to the idea mentioned in both the Introduction and chapter 2: The Rebbe, R. Bunim from Peshischa, taught . . . that we are called upon to believe that the Ribono shel Olam is with us in even our darkest moments. It is in order to teach us this truth that we were given the shirah. That is the meaning of the words וענתה השירה הזאת לעד. The purpose of its testimony is to make clear this very point: Even in our suffering the Ribono shel Olam is always with us.

Ever since I wrote the introductory chapter and became acquainted with the ideas of the Rebbe, R. Bunim, as developed by the Sefas Emes and put into final form by R. Gedalia Schorr, these ideas have defined Ha'azinu for me. Even as I was trying my best to understand Rashi's and the Ramban's approaches, even as I delighted in the simple and, because of that, highly persuasive reading of R. Dovid Tzvi Hoffman, I sensed that this fourth attempt to identify the eidus function of Ha'azinu speaks to my heart more personally than do the others. I am sitting in front of my computer ready and excited to begin an analysis. I think that we are about to find one of the very important keys to understanding Ha'azinu.

But first we have to ask a very basic question. Where, in the text of Ha'azinu, are we taught the idea that the Ribono shel Olam is with us in even our darkest moments?* I have read and reread the shirah many times and, try as I may, I cannot find that this idea is stated there in so many words.

---

* In the long piece from the *Ohr Gedalyahu* that I quote in the Introduction, R. Schorr demonstrates that the idea can be read into verse 39, ראו עתה כי אני אני הוא. Do please look back there and delight yourself by this deep, deep understanding of that verse. However, while I firmly believe in the validity of that brilliant פרשנות, it certainly is not meant, nor does it claim to be meant, at the פשט level. The statement that Ha'azinu testifies to this truth can certainly not rest on that reading of verse 39. Testimony by its very nature requires that its assertions hold true at the level of peshat. R. Schorr's brilliant insight certainly makes no claim that that reading is the simple meaning of the text.

I think that I know the answer, but feel diffident about sharing it with you. It does not seem to have the satisfying heft of a *lomdishe* insight. Still, for what it is worth, here it is. I think that the answer is the very question that we asked in chapter 2 and that has been lurking beneath the surface ever since we left that chapter. Only the assumption that the Ribono shel Olam is *always* there with us can give this record of pain and gore and blood the character of a song. Only the knowledge that, even as we suffer, He is there watching and weighing, taking care that nothing that should not happen happens, can make music of Jewish history. The notes to which Ha'azinu was sung are the sweet harbingers of our אחרית הימים. They speak to us of a time when every ברוך דיין אמת will turn into a ברוך הטוב והמטיב (see Pesachim 50a).

If, then, the theme of Ha'azinu is the celebration of the Ribono shel Olam's loyalty to us even under circumstances in which we commit the most egregious sins, then we are able to attach a name to this message that lifts this shirah to the very center of Jewish being. We can state without equivocation that Ha'azinu is a commentary on the *segulah* status to which we rose as we stood at Sinai (Shemos 19:5).

Let us spend a couple of paragraphs jogging our memories of the Sinaitic experience and then we can return to our Ha'azinu musings.

We recall the famous four expressions of redemption from the beginning of VaEira: והוצאתי, והצלתי, וגאלתי, ולקחתי. Ramban at Shemos 6:6 has this to say regarding the fourth expression, ולקחתי אתכם לי לעם, בבואכם אל הר סיני ותקבלו התורה, כי **ולקחתי** שם נאמר והייתם לי סגולה, *the fourth term,* ולקחתי, *was not fulfilled while they were still in Mitzrayim [as were the other three]. It became a reality later, when they arrived at Sinai and accepted the Torah. On that occasion the Ribono shel Olam said to them, "You shall be My* סגולה." Ramban is defining God's "nation" as His "segulah."

At Shemos 19:5 Ramban defines segulah as, דבר נחמד, לא ימסרנה המלך ביד אחר, *a precious possession, something that the king would never entrust to another.*

At Sinai the Ribono shel Olam promised us that He would

never leave our fate in any hands but His own. Even in our darkest moments we are cradled in His arms.[1]

I really think that we have finally reached a point at which we can say with reasonable certainty what it is that we are celebrating when we live our lives to the beat of Ha'azinu's music. We glory in the knowledge of who we are, and what our role is and ought to be in the scheme that the Ribono shel Olam has mapped out for our world. We know from where we come and to where we are heading. With that understanding in hand, we will be able to summon the fortitude to negotiate the treacherous, obstacle-laden chunks of history that we have had, and will have, to negotiate on the passage from here to there.

Background to Ha'azinu's Historiography

*H*a'azinu is a poem, a shirah. That is how it is written and that is how we are expected to open our hearts to its song. So let us think about poetry. What, above all, distinguishes it from prose?

Here is a thoroughly inadequate formulation, which will offend all kinds of writers but which contains enough truth to serve our purposes in this essay. Prose sets out to inform; poetry to move. Fifty people who read a passage written in prose will walk away with recognizably similar ideas; the same fifty people who read a poem will probably have been touched in fifty very different ways.*[1]

Here is how I was touched when I read the opening verses of *Shiras Ha'azinu*.**

Poetic language tends to be allusive. A well-crafted line can replace reams of descriptive and factual material. All the poet asks of us is that we open our hearts to his promptings. The first few lines of a poem are the most unforgiving of carelessness. Make a mistake there and all is lost. How can we make sure that we truly plumb the poet's dreams?

So, let us open our hearts to Ha'azinu. VaYeilech tells us that it aims to bring comfort to a broken people. Who are these people? Why are they broken? Luckily, we have all this data readily available.

It is all spelled out in VaYeilech (Devarim 31:16–21).

ויאמר יהוה אל משה הנך שכב עם אבתיך וקם העם הזה וזנה אחרי אלהי
נכר הארץ אשר הוא בא שמה בקרבו ועזבני והפר את בריתי אשר כרתי
אתו. וחרה אפי בו ביום ההוא ועזבתים והסתרתי פני מהם והיה לאכל
ומצאהו רעות רבות וצרות ואמר ביום ההוא הלא על כי אין אלהי בקרבי
מצאוני הרעות האלה. ואנכי הסתר אסתיר פני ביום ההוא על כל הרעה

---

* You may want to spend some time with Maharal, *Nesivos Olam, Nesiv HaAvodah*, chapter 12.

** Please note that in chapter 14 I demonstrate that the shirah proper begins with verse 7. The first six verses must be viewed as an introduction to the main body.

אשר עשה כי פנה אל אלהים אחרים. ועתה כתבו לכם את השירה הזאת
ולמדה את בני ישראל שימה בפיהם למען תהיה לי השירה הזאת לעד בבני
ישראל. בעתי לאבתיו זבת חלב ודבש ואכל ושבע ודשן ופנה אל אלהים
אחרים ועבדום ונאצוני והפר את בריתי. והיה כי תמצאן אתו רעות רבות
וצרות וענתה השירה הזאת לפניו לעד כי לא תשכח מפי זרעו כי ידעתי את
יצרו אשר הוא עשה היום בטרם אביאנו אל הארץ אשר נשבעתי.

HaShem spoke to Moshe, "You are about to die. [Know
then that in the future] this people will strike out on a
new path straying after the strange idols [that prolifer-
ate in the] land to which it had come, thereby forsaking Me and transgressing the covenant that I had forged
with them. "My anger will be kindled against them and
will bring all manner of punishments upon them. . . . It
will come about when they will be subjected to all these
painful experiences that this shirah will testify as witness before them . . ."

It could not be clearer. This shirah is designed to bear witness to people who have lost their bearings. Not so long ago, a
loving and fertile land had welcomed them and made them
feel at home. They lacked nothing and, as we all tend to do
when things go well, they stopped thinking. They had looked
around at their neighbors and found them all worshipping
their local deities to whom, apparently quite naturally, these
ascribed their own well-being. That seemed to make a lot of
sense.[2] It appeared to be a prudent course to follow. The invisible, intangible God of their fathers seemed too far away to really matter. Thoughtful and responsible husbandry appeared
to demand that they deal with the local, eminently approach-
able gods who, so they thought, clearly influenced their daily
lives and whose approbation mattered in very practical ways.

It all seemed very logical and they felt that they had every
right to expect further help and lots of smooth sailing into the
future. But, horror of horrors, things did not work out that
way at all. Dreadful plagues scythed through their communities causing death and havoc; natural disasters, locusts, blight,
and marauding wild animals took their cruel toll; military de-
feats on all fronts brought home to them how awfully vulner-

able they really were. None of these had been in the script that they had so lovingly written for themselves.

We can feel for them. Can this history-wracked nation be helped?

The Ribono shel Olam says, "Yes! Tell them this. I knew all along that this would happen. I prepared an elixir that will help them out of their doldrums. It will not cure them. For that they will have to do teshuvah and the energy for that must grow within their own souls. But it will help them understand; it will bring them to their senses by reminding them who they are and what destiny awaits them. It is a shirah that does not flinch from describing the rocky, torturous paths that they will have to negotiate on their way to Messianic redemption, but it does guarantee that redemption will come."

Jewish history has been, and still is, a harrowing trip. It seems unending, does it not? And yet, and yet, it can be encapsulated in forty-three short verses! Ha'azinu knows the secret of inspired teaching. Its message is sharp, focused, and clear. And, wonder of wonders, it turns out to be quite simple.

What will this shirah tell the bewildered and sorely crushed masses? The background that we have now provided will help us to decipher the message. Come now and let us begin. Our analysis deserves a chapter of its own.

Ha'azinu's Historiography

$\mathcal{W}$e ended the previous chapter by asking what Ha'azinu will tell the bewildered and sorely crushed masses. What, in broad terms, is Ha'azinu's message?

We can feel very confident in asserting that Ha'azinu is a tract that, in one way or another,* is teaching us history. There appears to be the assumption that knowledge of who we are, where we come from, and where we are heading can help to salve the inevitable pain that we will meet along the way. And that makes sense. There is much evidence that in the dark, mid-century years, those who were imbued with a self-confident sense of their Jewishness were better able to cope with unimaginable horrors than those who were not.

That, however, does not mean that our problem is solved. "History," standing on its own, does not tell us much. What history? Is it world history?** Is it Jewish history? Is it neither or both? How do we find out?[1]

I suppose that one way would be to consult the Rishonim and learn from them how they read the material. Here, for example is Rabbeinu Bachya: ודע כי כלל הפרשה הזאת שהיה משה מתוכח לישראל ומגיד להם מראשית אחרית ואת כל הקורות אותם לעתיד והתחיל מבריאת העולם וסיים בענין ימות המשיח ..., *You must realize what this tract is all about. It is an account of Moshe Rabbeinu instructing the people, taking them from their very beginnings all the way to the end. He told them everything that would ever happen to them in the future, beginning with Creation and taking them all the way to the Messianic era.* That is as clear a statement as we are likely to get.

Ramban, too, seems to subscribe to this same notion. In his concluding remarks to Ha'azinu he writes: השירה הזאת הבטחה מבוארת בגאולה העתידה על כרחן של מינין וכך הזכירו בספרי (האזינו מג), גדולה שירה זו שיש בה עכשיו ויש בה לשעבר ויש בה לעתיד לבוא ויש בה בעולם הזה

---

* With this phrase I am hinting at our discussion, in the previous chapter, of the various properties of poetry and prose.

** See Ramban to Bereishis 5:1.

ויש בה לעולם הבא ולזה רמז הכתוב שאמר (פסוק מד) ויבא משה וידבר את כל דברי השירה הזאת באזני העם, הזכיר "כל" להגיד שהיא כוללת כל העתידות למו, עניניה הרבים להם ביאר כי בדבור, קטנה היא ואם. This shirah *anticipates future redemption, the infidels notwithstanding. Sifrei makes this very clear. "This song is of the utmost importance for it speaks of the present, the past and the future, this world and the World to Come…"*

In spite of these seemingly clear statements, I will argue that none of this is yielded by the simple text. By this I mean that it is simply not true that the text, at the peshat level, tells us *everything that would ever happen to them in the future.* It is manifestly obvious that, if indeed Ha'azinu is as wide-ranging as these Rishonim claim it to be, it must be by means of invoking *remez, derush,* and *sod* to augment the peshat.

What, then, is Ha'azinu telling us at the peshat level?

My search for a coherent peshat understanding began with the final verse of the shirah, ostensibly a peek into the Messianic future. הרנינו גוים עמו כי דם עבדיו יקום ונקם ישיב לצריו וכפר אדמתו עמו, *The nations will sing songs of praise to His people** for He will be avenging the blood of His servants. He will take vengeance from His enemies and appease His land and His people.* I was shocked. Is it for this—that our enemies will sing our praises—that we hoped our hopes and dreamed our dreams? Rambam for one does not think so.

Rambam (Melachim 12) lists what he believes to be the salient, defining characteristics of אחרית הימים. He sums up his conclusions by quoting Yeshayahu (11:9), כי מלאה הארץ דעה את ה', כמים לים מכסים, *the earth will be filled with knowledge of HaShem [covering the earth] even as water covers the seabed.* Why did he feel the need to cite the prophet when he has the Ribono shel Olam's own description in Ha'azinu? The one phrase that Rambam uses that might be construed as hinting at the Ha'azinu idea (Halachah 4 there) is: לא נתאוו הנביאים והחכמים ימות המשיח לא … ולא כדי שינשאו אותם העמים … , *neither the proph-*

---

* Rabbeinu Bachya's expression in the segment that I cited above.
** This translation follows Rashi. The verse is difficult and there are many other ways in which it can be understood.

ets nor the sages longed for Moshiach in order that the nations of the world might look up to us. It tells us what ought *not* to be considered central to the Messianic epoch. This question has been bothering me for years but, as long as I was not writing on Ha'azinu, I was able to push it to the back burner. As I am sitting now at my computer trying to understand a little something of Ha'azinu, I no longer have that luxury.

We have now seen how the end of the shirah militates against the assumption that, at the level of peshat, Ha'azinu is a survey of the totality of Jewish history. When we really think about it, the beginning is just as problematic. In chapter 14 we will show that the shirah proper begins at verse 7, where it exhorts us to examine our history and, in order to do so, to approach our father's generation and that of our grandparents for guidance. Here is the verse with our comments:

זכר ימות עולם בינו שנות דר ודר, שאל אביך ויגדך זקינך ויאמרו לך. *Remember the distant past; try to understand the experiences of earlier generations. Ask your father and let him tell you; let your grandfather explain it to you.* We had committed the one unforgivable sin. We had forgotten who we are.[2] Our *mesorah* relies on communication between children and their fathers and grandfathers: והודעת לבניך ולבני בניך, *Make our Sinaitic experience known to your children and grandchildren* (Devarim 4:9). We cannot imagine a healthy, self-confident Judaism without our precious *Seder* nights.

The introduction to the actual shirah had begun with the prayer that this shirah should penetrate our hearts as the heavy rains penetrate the earth to loosen it, making it receptive to the seeds that were to be planted in it.* I suspect that this opening salvo of the shirah would have had the desired effect. We tend to be open to voices from the past, particularly to caressing voices from a glorious past.

---

* יערף כמטר לקחי. See R. Samson Rafael Hirsch's commentary.

Verse 8 then informs us that when the Ribono shel Olam, as a result of the *Haflagah*, first established the "seventy nations" into which humankind was divided, He did not choose the number seventy haphazardly. The idea was to have the number of different nations mirror the seventy people who accompanied Yaakov Avinu to Mitzrayim.[3] Here is verse 8 with our comments:

בהנחל עליון גוים בהפרידו בני אדם, יצב גבולת עמים למספר בני ישראל.
When God assigned the lands that were to become their heritage to each of the nations, when He split up mankind (which had up to that time lived as one single homogenous community) into separate identifiable units, He set up the boundaries to accord with the number of Israel's descendants.

Here we have to take a deep breath. It is not too much to say that this verse, together with verse 9, contains the key to the whole of Jewish history. We have to tread very carefully.

Let us defer analysis for a few moments and concentrate on a very general description of what this verse is telling us. It is this: We know that before the Haflagah mankind lived in one area, as a single community served by a single common language. For reasons that need not detain us here, God decided that this would have to change. Seventy* nations would be formed, each living in its own country.** These nations would speak different languages*** and be unable to communicate readily with one another. So much we know from the story in Noach. Our verse in Ha'azinu tells us something new.**** The number seventy did not come about haphazardly. It was

---

* The number seventy is derived from the number of Noach's descendants listed in Bereishis 9:18 and onward.
** Our verse makes clear that when בהפרידו בני אדם took place (*dor Haflagah*), each unit (read *nation*) was given its own country.
*** The concept "שבעים לשון" occurs frequently in Shas. Members of the Sanhedrin needed to be fluent in "שבעים לשון" (Megilah 13b). The stones that were to be erected in Eretz Yisrael were to have the Torah inscribed "ב"שבעים לשון (Sotah 36a).
**** There are other ways to interpret למספר בני ישראל. We have chosen to follow Rashi's second interpretation.

meant to parallel the seventy family members who made their way to Egypt together with Yaakov Avinu.*

We can now begin our analysis. We will begin with the first half of the verse: בהנחל עליון גוים בהפרידו בני אדם.

R. Samson Rafael Hirsch teaches that the second stitch is not simply a parallelism, but describes a natural result from the first. The geography and topography of the different countries that were then established, their climate, their level of fertility, whether neighbor nations were friendly or not, all these and many other factors that differentiate one place from another played a decisive role in creating and defining the differing cultures that developed within their boundaries. *The breaking apart of* mankind, בהפרידו בני אדם, the fact that the ideas that hold sway in one country may be incomprehensible to even a next-door neighbor, was brought about by the בהנחל עליון גוים. The citizens of these early nation-states (the *ur*-states that lent their description [שבעים אומות] to the entire non-Jewish world)** were quite literally sons of their "mother-country."[4]

יצב גבולות עמים למספר בני ישראל, *He set up the (number of) boundaries of these new nations to parallel the number of Israel's (read Yaakov's) descendants.* What can this possibly mean? And, if all it means is what it says, that just as the group that accompanied Yaakov to Egypt numbered seventy, so, too, the number of states that were established as a result of the Haflagah was seventy,*** why is this significant? Let us put the question this way: Ha'azinu has just forty-three verses**** within which to scan the entire history of the Jews. For any piece of information to make the cut as part of this very select group, it must be of really outstanding importance. Why is this congruence between these two sets of numbers so important?

---

* For our purposes it is not necessary to deal with the question of whether Yaakov was included in the "seventy."

** Even though שבעים does not describe the number of nation-states that people our world.

*** Thus, Rashi's second interpretation.

**** Or only thirty-seven if we are right in our contention that the first six verses are an introduction.

Here is why. Let us postulate that the number seventy is somehow special (see endnote 3). In the case of the אומות העולם, the units that together produce that totality are geographically defined nation-states. In the case of Klal Yisrael, they are individual people, unencumbered by being tied to any particular location, bound to one another solely by being the descendants of Yaakov/Yisrael and, at a deeper level, by being the Ribono shel Olam's portion (verse 9).

Taken together with verse 9, כי חלק ה' עמו, יעקב חבל נחלתו, *But His own nation remained God's portion, Yaakov was the lot of His heritage*, everything becomes very clear. The Ribono shel Olam is for the Jewish nation what the homeland is to the other nations. As surely as the Alps leave their unmistakable imprint upon the Swiss, the Ribono shel Olam leaves His imprint upon His *Yidden*.

I would like to examine how verse 8 relates to verse 7. I have always assumed that verse 8 (בהנחל עליון גוים . . .) is a description of what the fathers and family elders would pass on to the younger generation if they were asked for the details of Jewish history. Upon reflection, I do not believe that this is the case. If it were, why would the youngsters, upon seeing this shirah, turn to their elders for information that the shirah itself provides? Rather, it is my belief that from verse 8 onward, the shirah is intent upon explaining the inner workings of the historical facts that they will learn from their forebears. There are the facts of history and there are the dynamics that drive those facts. I believe that Ha'azinu deals with the latter.

What are those dynamics?

They are lodged in the nature of the relationship between the Ribono shel Olam and Klal Yisrael. You will recall* that even when we have fallen to the lowest depths, the Ribono shel Olam is there with us. His face may be hidden but He has never, will never, can never, jettison our relationship and

---

* From the Introduction and then from various chapters (particularly chapter 7A) throughout the book.

leave us to drift. We argued that this eternal bond has its roots in the segulah relationship into which we entered with the Ribono shel Olam at Sinai. Ha'azinu is the song that celebrates not the historical events, but the relationship that determined how those events played themselves out.

→I maintain that if we really want to understand Ha'azinu's message, the first step that we ought to take is to look at the beginning and the end of the shirah together. We will find precisely that which logic suggests we ought to find. The shirah starts with a problem and ends with a solution.

Here is how. Please check the footnotes that I will supply in this presentation. They will help you understand the way that I am setting it up.

ז. זכר ימות עולם בינו שנות דור ודור שאל אביך ויגדך זקניך ויאמרו
לך.* ח. בהנחל עליון גוים בהפרידו בני אדם יצב גבלת עמים למספר
בני ישראל.** ט. כי חלק ה' עמו יעקב חבל נחלתו.*** י. ימצאהו בארץ
מדבר . . .

מג. הרנינו גוים עמו כי דם עבדיו יקום ונקם ישיב לצריו. . . .****

* As mentioned earlier in this essay, verse 7 is the beginning of the shirah proper. It invites the readers to learn the history of their people from their ancestors. If they do as suggested, they will know the facts of their history but will still be missing a true understanding of why the facts behaved and developed as they did. In the next verse, the shirah will help them understand.

** This second verse in the shirah offers the salient fact of world history. It is that Klal Yisrael will always be at the center.

Needless to say, this verse is not good news for the other nations. They can be expected to resent us very much and our interactions with them over the centuries have been fraught and difficult. The body of Ha'azinu describes some of these interactions.

*** This verse is the explanation for God's actions that are described in verse 8. Again, it is not likely to gain much approval among the other nations of the world.

**** →This verse is obviously not a description of אחרית הימים. It simply tells us that in אחרית הימים the nations will make peace with God's choice of Israel as His סגולה, something that over the centuries they had taken as an unfair favoritism. They will recognize both the justice of the punishments that the Ribono shel Olam (the נקמה) will mete out to Israel's erstwhile oppressors, and that of the Ribono shel Olam's original choice of Israel as His special חלק.

Let us sum up the logic of what we have now learned:

1. Verse 7 is the formal beginning of the shirah. It exhorts us to be interested in our history and directs us to our ancestors, who will surely be happy to share their memories with us.

2. Verse 7 stands alone; it is not a part of the following sequence. It exhorts us to find out about our history and that is not the field of the shirah's interest. The shirah wants to deal with the dynamics of that history. It is interested in why things happened as they did. It teaches us that everything goes back to the special relationship that the Ribono shel Olam formed with us at Sinai. It is interested in defining as clearly as possible what is involved in being the segulah of the Ribono shel Olam. Accordingly verses 8 and 9, which belong together, introduce us to a definition of how a "segulah nation" is to be contrasted to the other nations. The ethos of the other nations grows from the land in which they live. Ours grows from our closeness to the Ribono shel Olam. That makes a big difference. Ours will be a lonely trip through history (ה' בדד ינחנו..., *HaShem will lead them in isolation**... Devarim 32:12). The historical imperatives under which our fate will be decided are different from those that govern any other nation. Certainly we must assume that the nations felt this difference and, needless to say, resented it. We will see in a moment that the story that Ha'azinu tells is the story of how, when in אחרית הימים truth fills the world, they will recognize that this, too, was for the best.

3. Verse 10 then begins the description of what happened to us—in our capacity as the Ribono shel Olam's segulah—from our beginnings in the wilderness. This description continues until the end of the shirah that brings us to אחרית הימים.

4. The shirah ends by telling us what will happen to our segulah status in אחרית הימים. With the "true" truth of history being revealed by the Melech HaMoshiach, the nations will be reconciled to the fact that we have always occupied a place closer

---

* The translation follows R. Samson Rafael Hirsch. There are other ways of understanding the phrase.

to the Ribono shel Olam than anyone else. They will see how
it all turned out for the best and the blood-thirsty hatred that,
to a greater or lesser extent, governed their relationship to us
will give way to an admiration that will find concrete expression in the songs of praise that they will sing to us.

This, in brief, is the history that Ha'azinu teaches us.

The Sefas Emes on "Eidus" II

*I*n the previous chapter we worked out what story Ha'azinu is telling us. We found out that it is our segulah status that stands at the center of the drama. The current chapter is going to be a commentary on what we discovered there. We are going to burrow deeply into terrain that most of us do not visit very often.

It is good to be a segulah, is it not? Well, yes and no. Once humanity is divided into nation-states,[1] it is certainly a great merit to be chosen as the one people who made the grade. However, we must not forget that being chosen is never an unmixed blessing. Shabbos 98b wonders why the mountain upon which we received the Torah was called Sinai. Here is its answer: It is because from this mountain hatred (שנאה, *hatred*, sounds very much like סיני) came down upon the idol worshippers. Now, that makes a lot of sense; their rejection of the Torah puts them into a category of being hated. But as we all know too well, people who are hated, hate back.*

Against this background it becomes clear that verse 8 in Ha'azinu, the one that, together with verse 9, we studied in chapter 7A, must be read differently than I have ever thought. Rather than making a simple statement of fact, it is really a lament crashing forth from the depth of Moshe Rabbeinu's heart. Here, more or less, is how I believe it should be read: *When tragically, His hands forced by a rebellious humanity, the Ribono shel Olam found it necessary to create different nations that would have their identity formed by the different lands into which the Most High settled them, He determined that their number would parallel the number of the Israelites who accompanied Yaakov to Egypt.*

There are many different points of departure from which history might be written. As we worked out in chapter 7A, Ha'azinu chooses to describe what happens when a *nefesh*-based segulah comes up against a conglomeration of

---

* Mishlei 27:19.

land-based, rejected nations. It is not a pretty story. It seems that there is no happy medium. When peace reigns, the un-fettered "freedom" of the "unchosen" proves to be attractive and, predictably, always, always, with unfailing regularity, idol worship becomes rampant among our own Yidden. When our relationship with the Ribono shel Olam turns sour, the nations become God's tools to punish our treason.

Let us now try to get some sense of how the shirah approaches its difficult task.

At this point it becomes important to break down Ha'azinu into its various components. It seems to me that if we manage to do this correctly and convincingly, we will pretty much have proved our contention that Ha'azinu traces the vagaries brought about by our standing as the Ribono shel Olam's segulah.

1. Verses 1–6: As shown in chapter 14, these verses are not yet a part of the shirah proper. They of course anticipate some of the frightful tales of suffering that form a considerable part of the shirah and want to help us deal with these in a positive way. These verses anticipate that the דין of the Ribono shel Olam is ultimately subordinated to His רחמים. That is why the shirah will end with our vindication.

2. Verse 7: This verse exhorts us to study our history. The conditions that inform our present are made up of our past and our future. If we do not know our history, we know nothing at all about ourselves. However, important as our history is, the facts alone are meaningless. The study of the dynamics that bring the facts to life will be the subject with which the rest of the shirah deals.

3. Verses 8–9: These verses set the tone for understanding the dynamics of our history. We were literally put into this world, so to speak, to fight the battles of the Ribono shel Olam for His ultimate vindication. The seventy nations are the same people who, while they were still one family, sought to do battle with the Ribono shel Olam by building the מגדל. Splitting them into

seventy nations did not change their craving to rid their world of God. It simply defanged them by making communication between them impossible. The Ribono shel Olam's weapon against them would be an עם נבחר whose national ethos will be determined by being based on seventy נפשות instead of seventy countries. The battle lines are drawn.

4. Verses 10–14: These verses set the stage for what is to follow. They describe all the wonderful things that the Ribono shel Olam did for us, because the more magnanimous His generosity had been, the more heinous the small-minded and small-hearted ingratitude that we eventually displayed. The fact that this survey begins with a glance back at the wilderness where the Ribono shel Olam "found" us is, of course, absolutely appropriate. If, as we claim, the theme of Ha'azinu is to juxtapose the two seventies, "ours" reckoned in נפשות with no dependence upon any real estate; "theirs" expressed in terms of their seventy countries, then the fact that God first "found" us in the desert is vital to the argument. Really, it says it all!

5. Verses 15–18: It was the best of times and yet—or perhaps, and therefore—we rebelled. The Torah appears to simply state the facts but does not appear to offer any explanation.* Verse 18, which speaks of our having "forgotten" the Ribono shel Olam, is also not an explanation. Why did we forget something so obvious? It seems that the secret lies in the use of ב ע ט, *to kick*, particularly when used intransitively.[2] We get the picture of a young child, having spent hours building a magnificent tower with his Legos, getting bored and kicking the whole thing over. He is not really kicking the Legos. He is divesting himself of the care and responsibility that keeping it intact would demand of him. וישמן ישורון ויבעט,** this was rejection on the grandest of grand scales. One does not kick by chance; this was an ugly spurning, a cruel repudiation.

A particular intensification of the pathos of this passage is

---

* Having become fat (וישמן) is not, in itself, a cause for rebellion.

** We cannot ignore another possibility that would explain why no object is provided for ויבעט. It might be an effort to draw a veil of silence over what was actually being "kicked."

achieved by repeated switching from the third person to the second. Thus, שמנת עבית כשית (third person); וישמן ישורון ויבעט (second person) ויטש אלוה עשהו ... (return to third person). The passage continues in third person until the last verse in this section, צור ילדך תשי. ... The impression is of someone doing his best to remain objective in his accusations, but sometimes breaking down because his emotions are bruised too painfully by the brutal betrayal.[3]

6. Verses 19–27: I would argue that the most shattering verse in Chumash is verse 26 in Ha'azinu. It has a horror of its own, way beyond anything contained in the two tochachos in BeChukosai and Ki Sovo respectively, or in any of the many parshios in the Torah that speak of the punishments that will result from transgressing the *mitzvos* of the Ribono shel Olam. All those predictions speak of the severe repercussions that will result from sin. There will be pain, but in the end there will be reconciliation. In verse 26 Ha'azinu speaks of the unspeakable: God determines that He intends to simply let us waste away in our exile. No Moshiach, no redemption, no anything.* In the course of time we will simply disappear. Verse 27 then explains that in fact this will not happen. But that does not alter our terror at the very thought that it was contemplated. Did the Ribono shel Olam really consider such an option?

The answer is yes.

I believe that the opening verse of this section lays the groundwork for this frightening thought: וירא ה' וינאץ מכעס בניו ובנותיו. *HaShem saw and found them to be despicable*** because of the way His sons and daughters had provoked Him. Let us compare this to, let us say, Bereishis 6:5 where we learn how the Ribono shel Olam looked upon the דור המבול: וירא ה' כי רבה רעת האדם, *HaShem saw that Man's capability for evil was very great.* This phrase certainly pulls no punches. The Ribono shel Olam is, in fact, willing to destroy all mankind on

---

* גלותינו בין העמים אננחו יהודה ובנימין שאין לנו זכר בעמים ולא נחשב לעם ואומה כלל, והנה יאמר הכתוב כי היה במדת הדין להיותנו כן בגלות לעולם ....

** Targum renders ג א ץ, *and became extremely angry.* However, Gra, cited by HaKesav VeHaKabalah, uses מאס, a verb describing *disgust* and the like.

the basis of what He had seen. Nonetheless, the assessment is
an objective one. The Ribono shel Olam "saw" the facts on the
ground and drew the requisite conclusions. Here things are
completely different. The effect of what God "saw" is personal.
He becomes "sickened" by what is happening.

The question now arises: Can a segulah standing be termi-
nated? Speaking theoretically, it would seem eminently possible. The special attachment that the king feels toward this
object is not magic. It derives from facts on the ground. It may
be particularly beautiful—but beauty can pall. It may have
particular associations—and associations can sour. Why, after all, would the Ribono shel Olam want to have Klal Yisrael
constantly on His mind if the very thought of them is repul-
sive to Him?

So it appears that the use of נ א ץ in the introductory verse
to this section is the perfect lead into verse 26. It would indeed
have been possible for the Ribono shel Olam to have us wither
on the vine and remain in galus forever.[4]

7. Verses 28–31–36: The way I identified this passage looks a
little strange. The explanation is as follows: I could really have
written simply 28–36. However as I will explain in a moment,
this passage has a character that is unique within the Ha'azinu
text. The meaning of the entire passage is determined by the
way verses 28–31 are to be understood. I indicate this as best I
can by identifying the passage as I did.

Sifrei (Devarim 322) cites a disagreement between R. Yehudah and R. Nechemiah that centers (initially)* upon verses
28–31. These four verses speak of a גוי אבד עצות, *a nation that
has lost its bearings.* Does it refer to the Jewish people last mentioned in verse 26, or to their enemies, last mentioned in verse
27? Both Rashi and Ramban accept R. Nechemiah's idea that
the reference is to our enemies. Rashi points out the possibility of applying the verses to the Israelites in his commentary

---

* I use "initially" in order to indicate what I have just explained. The actual disagreement as cited in the Sifrei is centered upon only verses 28–31. However,
that disagreement will, to some extent, influence the way verses 32–36 are to
be understood.

to verse 43. Ramban identifies his source as R. Nechemiah in verse 28 and leaves it at that.

At this point, my interest in this disagreement between R. Yehudah and R. Nechemiah is as follows. Why, in a composition that sets itself the almost impossible task of telling a vital, huge, and complex story in the space allowed by just forty-three verses,[5] tolerate an ambiguity that can lead to diametrically opposite interpretations? One would suppose that within such a relatively confining space, precision to the very highest degree would be a *sine qua non*. And, if poetry demands a style that allows the reader to have his say, why not choose prose as the medium?

I believe that there can be only one answer to this question. It is that ambiguity, at this point in the shirah, is the message. In a moment we shall explain how this is so.

We have reached the end of this analysis of the contents of Ha'azinu. From here till the end of the shirah looks into the future and tells us of the reconciliation with the Ribono shel Olam that yet awaits us. We will have the chance to think about that later in the book. For now we have a different challenge to meet. We will have to tackle the question of how blatant ambiguity can, in the context provided by Ha'azinu, be the highest virtue.

The late, great Rav Hutner taught that if we want to point out a profoundly significant difference (hereafter D) between A and B, it were best that in all other properties they be as similar to each other as possible. If, besides the D that we want to hold against the light, there are other substantive differences between A and B, then D becomes simply part of a larger picture of dissimilarities, and its significance becomes dulled. It is for this reason that Yaakov and Eisav were born as twins and that the two he-goats that figured so prominently in the Yom Kippur service had to be *alike in color, height, and price* (Mishnah, Yoma 6:1). God's love for Yaakov and hatred for Eisav (הלא אח עשו ליעקב . . . ואהב את יעקב ואת עשו שנאתי, *Was not Eisav the brother of Yaakov . . . yet I loved Yaakov and hated Eisav . . .* [Malachi 1:2 and 3]) has to stand out as being *the D* quality. There were to be no other significant differences between them. Similarly the two goats, one of which was destined *laShem*, the other *leAzazel*, had, otherwise, to be as similar to each other as possible. If not, their diametrically opposite fates—which are the reason for which they are included in the Yom Kippur service—would have been beclouded.

The ambiguity in which the passage that we marked 7 is couched is, of course, deliberate. There can be no more devastating judgment of the level to which we had sunk than this. We will have reached a point at which there is no longer any way to tell whether it is "we" or "they" who is being described. So much for our segulah standing!

And yet . . . and yet . . . there is a difference.[6] The final passage in Ha'azinu is one of comfort and reconciliation. No wonder that Ha'azinu is a song of jubilation!

This has been a long and complicated chapter. Let us make things a little easier by summing up what we have learned. The most salient fact of our Jewishness is that the Ribono shel Olam chose us as His segulah. The implications of such a standing are of course stupendous: אשריך ישראל מי כמוך!

1. This wonderful gift came with a heavy price. Since we pride ourselves that our national ethos (expressed in the number seventy) derives from within ourselves (שבעים נפש) as opposed to theirs, which rests upon the real estate that they control, we are obviously much closer to the Ribono shel Olam. That clearly must arouse their jealousy and ill will. We will have to go through history as a hated pariah.

2. The Ribono shel Olam is clearly willing to shoulder His covenantal obligations. He "finds" us in the wilderness (no real estate there) and coddles us in a series of miracles that enable us to live in an environment that cannot support life. Upon entry into the Land, these luxuries continue. In a manifestation of unstinting love, the Land allows us to live as sybarites.

3. Living as sybarites devastates our Jewish sensibilities. We grow fat and "kick." The use of the intransitive ב ע ט to describe our relationship to the Ribono shel Olam is horrible beyond belief. It describes a free-fall degeneration.

4. Punishments follow, the severity of which are commensurate with the heinousness of our trespasses. But nothing helps. The Ribono shel Olam reaches a point at which He seriously considers breaking off His relationship with us completely. He will leave us in our festering exile until we disappear from the stage of history. He immediately abandons this plan for the reasons articulated in verse 27.*

5. This is followed by a piece concerning the obtuseness of an "עם" that is not identified. R. Yehudah and R. Nechemiah argue in the Sifrei. R. Yehudah interprets the subject to be the Jewish people; R. Nechemiah has it deal with the other nations. We have argued that the very ambiguity of the text is a terrible condemnation of the depths to which Klal Yisrael will have sunk. They are being criticized in language that could just as well have been used concerning the "others." One cannot sink much lower than that.

6. In spite of that, the shirah ends with the prediction that there will be reconciliation at the end and, moreover, that the nations of the world will sing praises to us. This surely means that once the true interpretation of history will be known, they will agree that our segulah status was and is justified.

This is an interpretation of the shirah that does not read Ha'azinu as a survey of general history, but as a survey of the history of our segulah standing.

---

* At this point you might like to revisit chapter 5, where verse 27 is discussed in detail.

The Sefas Emes on "Eidus" III*

*I*t is high time to do some clear thinking about the place that Ha'azinu occupies in *kisvei hakodesh*. We will devote this chapter to that issue. For the material that we will require, we will go to VaYeilech rather than to Ha'azinu.

Verse 19 in VaYeilech reads, ועתה כתבו לכם את השירה הזאת ולמדה את בני ישראל שימה בפיהם, *Now write this song and teach it to the Israelites. Make them memorize it.* This is the first time that the shirah is mentioned. Rashi makes very clear that "this song" refers to *Shiras Ha'azinu*.

Here is a problem. In Sanhedrin 21b we learn:

אמר רבה אף על פי שהניחו לו אבותיו לאדם ספר תורה מצוה לכתוב משלו
שנאמר ועתה כתבו לכם את השירה . . .

Rava taught: Even if someone inherited a *sefer* Torah from his father, it is a mitzvah for him to write one for himself. We derive this from the verse, *And now, write this* shirah . . .**

How can this verse, which has *Shiras Ha'azinu* as its subject, serve as a source for the obligation to write the whole sefer Torah?

Rambam (Hilchos Sefer Torah 7:1) suggests a solution: He writes as follows:

It is a mitzvah for every Jewish man to write a sefer Torah for himself as it is written, *And now, write this* shirah *for yourselves.* This is to be understood as though it

---

* I have retained the "Sefas Emes" title because the issues we are about to discuss are related to those that we touched upon in the previous two chapters.

** I have used an ellipsis in both the Hebrew and the English because the text in the Gemaras that I have examined does not have the word הזאת. It seems to be a strange omission because it leaves השירה dangling. Without הזאת we do not know which shirah Moshe Rabbeinu was commanded to write. The Rambam that we just quoted does have הזאת in his text. Later, in footnote 5, I will have something to say about this matter.

were written, *Write the Torah in which this* shirah *is to be written*. This must be the meaning of this pasuk since it is forbidden to write *sections of the Torah* as separate units (לפי שאין כותבין את התורה פרשיות פרשיות).

It seems to me that Rashi and Ramban in their Chumash commentaries disagree with Rambam's interpretation. Ramban is explicit as we shall soon see; for Rashi we have only his silence. But his silence tells us a great deal. Here is how. On "השירה הזאת" he comments, האזינו השמים עד וכפר אדמתו עמו; on כתבו לכם, nothing. If he would have agreed with Rambam, we would have expected some comment on "כתבו לכם." Rashi's omissions are as eloquent as his commissions. *Write this* shirah means nothing more than *Write this* shirah. The text is to be understood literally. It does not mean, *Write a sefer Torah in order that you may be able to write this* shirah.

We fast-forward to verse 21, כי לא תשכח מפי זרעו, apparently a promise that Klal Yisrael will never forget Ha'azinu. Rashi writes: *This phrase constitutes a promise that Torah will never be completely forgotten*. Apparently, a promise that Ha'azinu will not be forgotten is construed as promising that Torah will not be forgotten. Where does that leave us?

Chazal appear to equate Ha'azinu with the entire Torah. Why?[1]

For Ramban we do not need to do so much sleuthing. His language yields quite clearly the idea that Moshe Rabbeinu wrote Ha'azinu twice: once as a work standing on its own and once within the sefer Torah. Here are his comments with the relevant passages set in bold.

ויתכן, כי **אחרי שכתב השירה** וילמדה את בני ישראל איש איש לשבטיהם שהביאם לפניו אל בית המדרש, **כתבה בספר התורה**, וצוה את הכהנים לקוח את ספר התורה, לומר **שגם השירה תהיה מונחת בארון עם התורה, שהיא מכלל התורה** כי היא שם לעד.

It is also possible[2] that *after he wrote* the shirah and taught it to the Israelites . . . he wrote it *into the sefer Torah* and commanded the Kohanim to take "this" sefer Torah, an indication *that the shirah too is to be placed in the ark to-*

gether with the Torah since, in as much as it serves as "testimony," it *is a part of the Torah.*

Please study endnote 2 carefully. In it you will see that the
issue that concerns the Ramban is the relationship between
verses 24–26, which speak of Moshe Rabbeinu completing
the writing of the Torah, and verse 9, which had already spoken of his having written the Torah. Here is his first explanation. After verse 9, although the lion's share of the Torah
had already been written, it was still missing some text. At
the time, Moshe Rabbeinu did not know what that might be.
After he learned about the shirah, he realized that this, too, belonged in the sefer Torah as part of the "Torah." Immediately,
he wrote it in the sefer Torah that had been awaiting completion since verse 9, thereby bringing it to completion (עד
תומם).* In this first explanation there is no essential difference
between Ha'azinu and any other *sidrah* in the Torah. It just
so happened that Ha'azinu made its appearance after all the
other material had already been committed to writing.

A glance at the section of the Ramban that we quoted
above—the Ramban's ויתכן—will immediately show how radically different this interpretation is from the one that we
have just described. From the very beginning, Ha'azinu very
clearly has a character all of its own. It is to be written down
as a separate entity (not as part of the sefer Torah; that will
be done later) and this entity is apparently to be used to help
Moshe Rabbeinu to teach the shirah to the people up to the
point at which they will know it by heart (ולמדה את בני ישראל
שימה בפיהם).**

After that was done (כי אחרי שכתב השירה . . . כתבה בספר התורה)
Moshe Rabbeinu added Ha'azinu to the Torah. I am choosing

---

* There is the problem of when וזאת הברכה took place and when it was written
in the sefer Torah. Ibn Ezra raises this question and Ramban discusses his solution. This is an interesting topic, but does not impact upon our discussion of
Ha'azinu in any way.

** The Ramban is clearly not troubled by the Rambam's assertion that, אין כותבין
את התורה פרשיות פרשיות. Much has been written concerning this Rambam, but
that discussion falls outside the ambit of this book.

my words carefully. I did not write Moshe Rabbeinu "wrote Ha'azinu in the Torah" as I did in the first of Ramban's interpretations. →͏ I used "added" because a careful reading of Ramban's language yields that Ha'azinu, even after Moshe Rabbeinu wrote it in the sefer Torah, retained an identity of its own.* Let us look at the language together. שגם השירה התורה מכלל שהיא ,התורה עם בארון מונחת תהיה. The first word is "גם"; it is followed later by "עם." Not only the "Torah" belongs in the ארון, but also the "שירה" with the Torah, because שהיא מכלל התורה, because the שירה is in the same category as is the Torah.[3]**

The same two questions that we asked earlier in this essay on Rashi also constitute a problem for the Ramban. How can "... כי לא תשכח" and "... ועתה כתבו לכם." teach us truths about the entire Torah when the subject of these two phrases was the independent shirah, which, at the time when these two statements were made, had not even been written in the Torah?

Beyond these two questions, there is an internal difficulty within the shirah itself, as Chazal interpret it for us. On יערף תורה נתתי לישראל שהיא כמטר לקחי ...(verse 2), Rashi quotes Sifrei, חיים לעולם כמטר הזה.... Further along, in the same pasuk, Rashi remarks on כשעירים, that, ... מה הרוחות האלו מחזיקים את העשבים אף דברי תורה מחזיקים את לומדיהם. Here is the problem: Verse 2 is obviously an introduction to *Shiras Ha'azinu*, and to nothing else. However, Chazal apply the imagery that is used to the supreme gifts that "Torah" confers upon us. But we have just learned, at least as far as Ramban is concerned, that Ha'azinu maintained its own identity even after Moshe Rabbeinu wrote it into the Torah. How could Chazal extend the ambit of these qualities to include the entire Torah?

---

* I imagine that Ramban assumes this independent identity from the fact that, in this interpretation, it had already been written in its own right. It is a matter of this *"megilah"* or whatever other name would be appropriate, being later joined to the Torah because, as Ramban writes at the end of this piece, it had an עדות standing in common with the Torah.

** Please take the trouble of reading endnote 3.

It seems to me that the difficulties I have raised lead, inevitably, to the following conclusion.*

Here, in brief, is my suggestion. It is based on Ramban's comment to Bereishis 5:1. The pasuk begins with the following words: זה ספר תולדות אדם .... Ramban first quotes Rashi's commentary and then offers the following alternative:

ולפי דעתי ירמוז לכל התורה, כי כל התורה כולה ספר תולדות אדם, על כן אמר בכאן "ספר" ולא אמר "ואלה תולדות אדם."

In my opinion, the words זה ספר refer to the entire Torah [not just to what is about to be said in parshas Bereishis, as is the meaning according to Rashi]. [We are being told that] *the entire Torah is the story of "Adam's" history.* It is for this reason** that the text includes the word ספר (זה ספר תולדות אדם) instead of simply writing, ואלה תולדות אדם.

I find it remarkable that some of Ramban's most world-shattering ideas are offered quietly and modestly, in a simple one-liner. There are no accompanying drumrolls or cymbal-crashings, not even a word or two to indicate that great things are happening. We have just heard the Torah *itself* defining *itself* as a *History of Adam* through that of his children.

But, what could this possibly mean? Since all mankind is descended from Adam, it certainly seems to imply that the Torah is a world history. That, of course, is manifestly not the case, at least taken literally. So again, what does this mean?

It means, it *must* mean, it cannot mean anything other, than that the entire Torah, by being what it is, is announcing that אתם קרויין אדם ואין עובדי כוכבים קרויין אדם (Bava Metzia 114b). The entire Torah is no more than an expansion of the concept spelled out in Ha'azinu verses 8 and 9 as we explained them

---

* Please note an amber flashing light here. I cannot guarantee that my suggestion has any merit. Among the *sefarim* that are available to me, I have not seen even a hint that this thought was ever visited by anybody. In the spirit of the Chazal that כל מה שתלמיד ותיק עתיד לחדש כבר נאמר למשה מסיני, I can only hope that my suggestion is not "all new." So, *caveat emptor!* Let the buyer beware.

** It is in order for us to understand that reference is to the entire Torah ...

in chapter 7A.[4] The Torah, read as Ramban evidently thinks it should be read, is the story of Adam HaRishon's spiritual descendants.

Once we have come this far, it becomes no more than a matter of drawing the inevitable conclusions from the given data. We worked out in chapter 7A that Ha'azinu is the story of how the segulah doctrine, or, in Ha'azinu's own terms, the חלק ה' עמו, fared over the centuries. In the light of what we have discovered in the current chapter, does it not follow that Ha'azinu, as we have defined it, is a kind of mini-Torah?

This, then, is the theory that I am suggesting, and concerning which I posted the warning that I have not found any confirmation in the sefarim that are available to me. It is true that, in contrast to the Rambam, both Rashi and the Ramban deal with our shirah as an entity independent of its subsequent role as part of the Torah. Nevertheless, Chazal were able to generalize some of the lessons that are taught concerning Ha'azinu as being applicable to the entire Torah.[5]

The Sefas Emes on "Eidus" IV

S ince I have begun to think seriously about Ha'azinu, I feel more and more like somebody on *bedikas chometz* night who is searching for the small pieces of bread that the kids have spread around the house. I keep on stumbling across bits and pieces of information that show up when least expected, but which turn out to make vital contributions to the total picture. This time it was a Beis Yosef on Orech Chaim 559.*
The issue under discussion concerns the changes that we make in our *davening* on Tish'ah Be'Av. Without any great fanfare, Beis Yosef mentions that in some מנהגים the שירת הים is omitted. It was felt that the cheerful optimism of the song made it inappropriate for Tish'ah Be'Av. He adds that in some congregations it had become customary to substitute שירת האזינו for the שירת הים.[1][2]

That is exciting news. We have a new pairing, שירת הים with שירת האזינו, which seems to open up new avenues of conjecture. The fact that we are dealing with a theoretical issue** hardly matters. There is no reason to suppose that the Ramo referenced in the second footnote below denies the affinity between the two shiros. He simply denies the necessity of making a substitution.[3]

So where do we go from here? We embark on a trip that will teach us that opposites attract.

It seems to me that the circumstances under which *Shiras HaYam* was said and those that were to prevail when *Shiras Ha'azinu* would stand ready to lend us strength and encouragement are diametrically opposite each other. They relate to each other as "seeing all" relates to "seeing nothing."

Here is how. *Kri'as Yam Suf* was an experience that allowed people to "see." I cannot say what they saw or how they saw it, but we all know the Chazal (Mechilta), that ראתה שפחה על הים

---

* Thank you to my good friend, R. Yossy Rabinowich, who drew my attention to this source.

** Ramo in *Darkei Moshe* says flatly that our *minhag* is to retain the שירת הים.

מה שלא ראה יחזקאל וכל שאר הנביאים, *When the Ribono shel Olam split the sea, a simple maid-servant saw sights that neither Yechezkel nor the other prophets ever saw.* To confirm the Mechilta's assertion that some kind of "seeing" took place, we need only recall the introductory verses to the *Shiras HaYam,* ... **וירא** ישראל את מצרים מת על שפת הים. **וירא** ישראל את היד הגדלה אשר עשה יהוה במצרים ..., *Israel saw Mitzrayim die at the seashore and saw the great power that God exerted against Mitzrayim.**

VaYeilech introduces us to Ha'azinu using words that convey the precise opposite. After having described the idol worship in which we would engage and the dreadful consequences that would result from it (verses 16 and 17); having then described our reactions to these troubles (verse 17); verse 18 goes on to describe what would happen as a result of all this. The Ribono shel Olam says, ואנכי הסתר אסתיר פני ביום ההוא ..., *I will surely hide My face on that day.* ... Verse 19 then introduces שירת האזינו, the prophylactic that is to help us over these difficult times.

A "hidden" face can, of course, not be seen. It is as we have said. *Shiras Ha'azinu* will be called upon to work its magic under circumstances that are precisely the opposite of what transpired at the Yam Suf where, as we learned earlier, it was the faculty of sight that held center stage.

The two shiros, *Shiras HaYam* and *Shiras Ha'azinu,* can be viewed as two sides of the same coin. They both sing of the glory of the Ribono shel Olam, the one under circumstances of גלוי פנים, the other under circumstances of הסתר פנים. It is absolutely logical that, were we in a position that necessitates finding a substitute for *Shiras HaYam* on Tish'ah Be'Av, *Shiras Ha'azinu* should be our choice.**

---

* See R. Tzadok, רסיסי לילה p. 118:

ובקי"ס נתגלה זה דרך ראיה כמ"ש ראתה שפחה על הים ... וכמו ששמעתי דמ"ת הוא בקנין מה שהיה בקי"ס בראיה דהראיה אינו קנין בלב....

** We expand upon the affinity between *Shiras Ha'azinu* and *Shiras HaYam* in chapter 19. It might be a good idea to take a quick peek at this point.

ELEVEN

Some Thoughts About VaYeilech

*T*he more I study Ha'azinu, the more I realize that one cannot do it justice without knowing a great deal about VaYeilech. It is in VaYeilech that Moshe Rabbeinu was first introduced to the shirah, and it is there that we need to go for essential background. The context within which that introduction takes place is of particular interest.

The story of Yehoshua's induction as the successor of Moshe Rabbeinu is prominent among the topics with which VaYeilech deals. This formal transference of power took place in two stages: the first performed by Moshe Rabbeinu,[1] the second by the Ribono shel Olam. It is the second one that interests us in this essay since, against all expectations, Moshe Rabbeinu's introduction to Ha'azinu appears to be a part of that induction ceremony.

Here is the text:

יד. ויאמר יהוה אל משה הן קרבו ימיך למות קרא את יהושע והתיצבו באהל מועד ואצונו[2] וילך משה ויהושע ויתיצבו באהל מועד. טו. וירא יהוה באהל בעמוד ענן ויעמד עמוד הענן על פתח האהל. טז. ויאמר יהוה אל משה הנך שכב עם אבתיך וקם העם הזה וזנה אחרי אלהי נכר הארץ אשר הוא בא שמה בקרבו ועזבני והפר את בריתי אשר כרתי אתו. יז. וחרה אפי בו ביום ההוא ועזבתים והסתרתי פני מהם והיה לאכל ומצאהו רעות רבות וצרות ואמר ביום ההוא הלא על כי אין אלהי בקרבי מצאוני הרעות האלה. יח. ואנכי הסתר אסתיר פני ביום ההוא על כל הרעה אשר עשה כי פנה אל אלהים אחרים. יט. ועתה כתבו לכם את השירה הזאת ולמדה את בני ישראל שימה בפיהם למען תהיה לי השירה הזאת לעד בבני ישראל. כ. כי אביאנו אל האדמה אשר נשבעתי לאבתיו זבת חלב ודבש ואכל ושבע ודשן ופנה אל אלהים אחרים ועבדום ונאצוני והפר את בריתי. כא. והיה כי תמצאן אתו רעות רבות וצרות וענתה השירה הזאת לפניו לעד כי לא תשכח מפי זרעו כי ידעתי את יצרו אשר הוא עשה היום בטרם אביאנו אל הארץ אשר נשבעתי. כב. ויכתב משה את השירה הזאת ביום ההוא וילמדה את בני ישראל. כג. ויצו את יהושע בן נון ויאמר חזק ואמץ כי אתה תביא את בני ישראל אל הארץ אשר נשבעתי להם ואנכי אהיה עמך.

Here is a paraphrase. In verse 14 the Ribono shel Olam tells Moshe Rabbeinu that his death is near and that the time has come to pass on the mantle of authority to Yehoshua. Moshe Rabbeinu is to bring Yehoshua to the *Ohel Mo'ed*, there to be inducted into his new position by the Ribono shel Olam. The end of verse 14 tells us that Moshe Rabbeinu did as he was told and we see Moshe and Yehoshua waiting in the Ohel Mo'ed. Verse 15 then tells us that the Ribono shel Olam also appeared in the tent and that a pillar of smoke attended at the entrance. All seems ready for the induction, and we expect the text to take it up right away.

Nothing of the sort happens. In verse 16 the Ribono shel Olam, apparently ignoring Yehoshua completely, turns to Moshe with the bleak news of how the spiritual standing of his people will become eroded after he dies. He describes how Klal Yisrael, once they are comfortably ensconced in Eretz Yisrael, will lose themselves and their sanctity in orgies of idol worship. That will bring about harsh consequences. Suffering will be great. However, the Ribono shel Olam is about to teach Moshe Rabbeinu a new shirah that will help. It will lend us strength and hope during even the worst of times.

Verse 22 reports that Moshe Rabbeinu wrote down the shirah and proceeded to teach it to the people.

Only after all this, in verse 23, does the Ribono shel Olam turn His attention to Yehoshua.

Here is our problem. How are we to understand the function of verses 16–22 within this context? Verse 14 had made it very clear that Moshe Rabbeinu and Yehoshua were to appear at the Ohel Mo'ed for only one reason. The Ribono shel Olam wanted to induct Yehoshua into his new leadership role. Why the intrusion of the Ha'azinu passage that certainly appears to be extraneous to the issue at hand?

It seems eminently clear that the Ha'azinu material must be regarded as a part of Yehoshua's induction. That induction consists of two parts. One part, described in verse 22, was, as expected, communicated to Yehoshua directly by the Ribono shel Olam. The five earlier pesukim, what we have called the Ha'azinu material, although they were also an integral part of the process, *needed to reach Yehoshua by way of a communication made directly to Moshe Rabbeinu.* In that section the Ribono shel Olam was communicating with Yehoshua through what He was saying to Moshe Rabbeinu. [3] [4]

What can this possibly mean?

I believe that I can offer a reasonable explanation. However, as I have done in various other places in this book, I want to point out a flashing, amber light. *Caveat Emptor,* let the buyer beware. The following ideas are my own. I have not seen them in any sefer. By all means adopt them, or parts of them, as your own if you feel that they are true. Reject them mercilessly if you do not. Above all: Think!

The explanation that I am about to offer assumes a special affinity between Moshe Rabbeinu and Ha'azinu. I have discussed that affinity in detail in the latter part of the Prologue. I do not think that anything will be gained by repeating it here. I do recommend that you take the time to reread those passages now. They comprise valuable background material to what we are about to learn.

I propose that the explanation that we are seeking resides in a correct understanding of Yehoshua's leadership vis-à-vis that of Moshe Rabbeinu.

Any contemplation of the nature of Yehoshua's leadership should begin by noting the encouraging חזק ואמץ, *be strong and resolute,* with which Yehoshua is fortified by both the Ribono shel Olam and Moshe Rabbeinu no less than six times.* With the exception of two times that Dovid HaMelech uses this same expression in encouraging Shlomo (I Divrei HaYamim 22:13 and 28:20), these words occur nowhere else in TaNaCh. Let us remember that there are no coincidences in TaNaCh. What does this say about Yehoshua?

I suggest that the key to a solution is contained in the final Rashi to VaYeilech. In verse 29 Moshe Rabbeinu said that אחרי מותי, *after* MY *death* the Israelites would forsake the path along which he had led them throughout the years of his stewardship. Rashi is puzzled since Shoftim 2:7 testifies that

---

* Devarim 31:7, 31:23; Yehoshua 1:6, 1:7, 1:9, 1:13.

the people served HaShem as long as Yehoshua lived among them. Their disloyalty began only after Yehoshua had died. Rashi words his solution as follows: מכאן שתלמידו של אדם חביב עליו כגופו. כל זמן שיהושע חי נראה חי למשה כאילו הוא חי, *We see from here that the love that a teacher feels for his student is such that he sees himself living in his student's life. It seemed to Moshe Rabbeinu that as long as Yehoshua lived, he himself continued living in him.*[5] Moshe Rabbeinu felt that his real death coincided with that of Yehoshua.

I believe that when Moshe Rabbeinu died he left some unfinished business behind him. The conquest, or if you like, the displacement* of the Canaanite nations, fell, strictly speaking, into the ambit of his contribution to Jewish history.

Here is why. Our right to Eretz Yisrael is of course rooted in the numerous promises that the Ribono shel Olam made to the Avos. Still, it seems to me that there must be something more that justifies an aggressive war against people who had been occupying the land for hundreds of years. Ramban to Bereishis 9:26 provides the key. Noach had cursed Canaan and condemned him to eternal *avdus* to Shem.** This implies כי הוא (שם) ינחל ארצו (של כנען) כי מה שקנה עבד קנה רבו, *that Shem (in the person of Klal Yisrael) will be justified in taking over Canaan's land, since the ownership of that which a slave owns is vested in his master.*

This idea, with all its causes and ramifications, could of course fill an entire book on its own. My readers will understand if I take a shortcut here and state simply that our right to Eretz Yisrael is rooted in the segulah standing that we occupy vis-à-vis the nations of the world. That segulah status has its beginnings in the Sinaitic experience.*** Moshe Rabbeinu

---

* See Rashi to Devarim 1:8. Had the *Meraglim* not been sent, no war would have been necessary.
** Ramban is referring to verse 26, where only Shem is mentioned. This is opposed to verse 25, where Cannan is indentured to אחיו, *his brothers*, in the plural.
*** This is another statement that deserves a book to itself. In this case it has one. Some of you may have seen my most recent book, *I Brought You unto Me*, where all this is discussed in detail. If you have the chance, you might want to look at it.

nurtured us into becoming the Ribono shel Olam's segulah. The most vivid expression of that standing should by rights have been in his hands.

It transpires that Moshe Rabbeinu's successor would not function in his own right but would really have to be a stand-in for Moshe Rabbeinu. I believe that this is implied in the language that Moshe Rabbeinu uses when he tells the Israelites that he will not be bringing them into Eretz Yisrael (Devarim 1:38). יהושע בן נון **העמד לפניך** הוא יבא שמה אתו חזק כי הוא ינחלנה את ישראל, *Yehoshua,* HE WHO STANDS BEFORE YOU [AS A TALMID], *he will come there, give him your encouragement, for it is he who will bring Israel to its inheritance.* Do you, dear Reader, not agree that the words "העמד לפניך" seem superfluous? The people did not need to be told which Yehoshua bin Nun was meant here. Clearly this phrase has the function of explaining why Yehoshua and nobody else was the chosen one. Only the lifelong, loyal talmid could be the "Moshe Rabbeinu" of the next generation.*

It is small wonder that Yehoshua required the constant encouragement of חזק ואמץ. It is not easy to fill Moshe Rabbeinu's shoes.

You may recall from chapter 7A that, from evidence we mustered there, we concluded that the message of Ha'azinu centers upon just the segulah status of our people. Yehoshua, who, standing in Moshe Rabbeinu's shoes, was about to actualize that status by conquering Eretz Yisrael, had to hear *Shiras Ha'azinu* as Moshe Rabbeinu heard it, directly from the Ribono shel Olam. It has become clear why verses 16–21, although addressed to Moshe Rabbeinu, were a significant part of Yehoshua's induction.

---

* I venture to guess that the well-known statement from Bava Basra 75a that while Moshe's face shone like the sun, Yehoshua's face, moonlike, projected only the reflected light that reached it from the sun, has this idea in mind. Yehoshua's entire being shone with only a reflection of Moshe Rabbeinu's light.

תמה זכות אבות

*H*a'azinu predicts that history will end on a high note.
There *will* be a *ge'ulah*, no ifs and no buts!*
Let us jog our memory by quoting a few lines from Ramban
as he winds up his commentary to Ha'azinu.

וזה דבר ברור כי על הגאולה העתידה יבטיח, כי בבנין בית שני לא הרנינו
גוים עמו, רק לעגו עליהם (נחמיה ג לד) מה היהודים האמללים עושים,
והיו גדוליהם עבדים בהיכל מלך בבל וכולם משועבדים לו, ובימים ההם
לא השיב נקם לצריו ולא כפר אדמתו עמו. והנה אין בשירה הזאת תנאי
בתשובה ועבודה, רק היא שטר עדות שנעשה הרעות ונוכל, ושהוא יתברך
יעשה בנו בתוכחות חימה, אבל לא ישבית זכרנו, וישוב ויתנחם ויפרע מן
האויבים בחרבו הקשה והגדולה והחזקה, ויכפר על חטאתינו למען שמו
אם כן, השירה הזאת הבטחה מבוארת בגאולה העתידה ...

It is perfectly clear that Ha'azinu's promises speak of the
future. It cannot refer to, let us say, the return to Zion after the Babylonian exile [since its predictions were not
fulfilled at that time]. For example, the nations of the
world certainly sang no praises to Israel (as is predicted in
verse 43). On the contrary, as is reported in Nechemiah
3:43, they mocked the returnees. . . . Again, at that time
the Ribono shel Olam certainly did not avenge all that
had befallen us in our exile . . . [In the absence of any fulfillment of Ha'azinu's predictions at any earlier occasion
it is clear that] this shirah makes an absolute commit-
ment to a future redemption.

We still have some work to do before we can put this topic
to rest. Let us go to Ramban in Bereishis 22:16 and listen to the
mal'ach speaking to Avraham immediately after the *Akeidah*.
The verse reads, *He (the mal'ach) said, "I swear by My own
Being—the words of HaShem—that because you have done this*

---

* Chapter 5 contains much material that, in one way or another, impacts upon
the issues that we will discuss in this chapter. If you have the energy, the effort
that you would expend in rereading this chapter now would be well invested.

thing, and have not withheld your son, your only one, that I will surely bless you and greatly increase your offspring like the stars of the heavens and the sand of the seashore; and your offspring shall inherit the cities of their enemy."

Ramban makes the following comments.

... והנה הובטח שלא יגרום שום חטא שיכלה זרעו, או שיפול ביד אויביו ולא יקום, והנה זו הבטחה שלימה בגאולה העתידה לנו.

... It turns out that we have here a guarantee that no sin will ever wipe out Avraham's descendants,[1] nor will they ever fall into the hands of their enemies and be lost there to all eternity. *In short, this is an absolute promise that we can anticipate a full redemption in the future.*

Apparently, the promise that we identified as one of the central themes of Ha'azinu is really an old, old story. That creates a problem for us. What then does Ha'azinu add to what must have been a part of Jewish tradition from Avraham's time? What is so central about the shirah if it merely[2] repeats that which had always been a significant part of Jewish tradition, passed down through the *avos*?

I believe this to be a serious question. However, as Ramban does so often, he provides an answer if we but read him as carefully as he deserves to be read. I believe that in just a few words he tackles the problem and provides an answer.

Here is a section of the Ramban to verse 26 that we have not yet considered.

אשביתה מאנוש זכרם גלותנו בין העמים אנחנו יהודה ובנימין, שאין לנו זכר בעמים ולא נחשב לעם ואומה כלל והנה יאמר הכתוב, כי היה במדת הדין להיותנו כן בגלות לעולם, לולי כעס אויב ויורה זה, כי בגלותנו עתה תמה זכות אבות ואין לנו הצלה מיד העמים רק בעבור שמו ... אשביתה מאנוש זכרם.

This passage has in mind the exile of the two tribes Yehudah and Binyomin—our current exile—during which we, as an independent nation in our own land, have been totally forgotten by the nations of the world. This text is telling us that were the faculty of Justice in play, we would be condemned to an eternal exile . . . *for the "merit of our fathers" has been entirely used up,* and our hope for ultimate salvation is pinned solely on His great Name . . .

I have bolded the phrase that concerns us here.

The issue of whether or not תמה זכות אבות, *the merit of the avos has been used up,* is a complicated one and is discussed in Shabbos 55a.* Now, I have learned this Ramban very often, but never asked myself seriously why, in the present context, he has to involve himself in that *sugia*. It seemed to me that he could simply have said that our Jewishness had simply shriveled to the extent that we do not anymore deserve to be redeemed even with the aid of our forefathers' merits. There have been enough occasions in our long and often unstable history in which the Ribono shel Olam considered destroying us. For example, at the חטא העגל He certainly contemplated such a step. To the best of my knowledge, neither Ramban nor the other commentators resorted to תמה זכות אבות on that occasion. It seems to me that they simply had no pressing need to do so. The issue of תמה זכות אבות is a question of an absolute ending (at least for a time) of the concept of זכות אבות. There seems to be no need to invoke such a radical break in every situation in which the merit of the Avos was not considered by the Ribono shel Olam. There could be, and almost certainly were, situations in which our failings were so heinous that זכות אבות was simply not enough to help us. That could happen easily enough without postulating or contemplating the cosmic concept of "תמה."

Why does Ramban require it here?

I have not seen the following proposal discussed by any of the Ramban's commentators. But I suggest that Ramban may simply be borrowing the phrase from that sugia without formally invoking the concept as it is used there. He is simply saying that the point in history at which the Ribono shel Olam would consider that it was time for אשביתה מאנוש זכרם would

---

* For a better understanding of some of the issues, please see Tosafos there, s.v. ושמואל אמר.

be one at which the promise that He had made to Avraham at the Akeidah would have ceased to be relevant. That promise, as we will explain in a moment, assumes a measure of connection to the Avos. That connection would have to be one that could persuade our forefathers that they would wish to be associated with us, would be unashamed to acknowledge us as their children, and would be moved to intercede on our behalf. Those conditions would simply not obtain at that point.

Rav Dessler (*Michtav MeiEliyahu* 2:278) teaches that "זכות אבות" is to be read as "זַכּוּת אבות". The "merit" of the Patriarchs can help only those children in whom there are still traces of their parentage and in whom the *purity* ("זַכּוּת") of their forefather can still be discerned. זכות אבות is the kind of consideration that a judge might apply to a youngster who has turned delinquent and whose fate he must decide. Should he be sent to a reformatory or should he be permitted to go home to his decent and caring parents? If the judge determines that the lines of communication between parents and child are still open, if the child is still conversant with his parents' language because their ways have not yet been completely discarded, the judge might well incline toward a path of mercy.

We now understand why Ramban needed to preface his remarks to the second half of verse 26 with his assessment that this would happen only when תמה זכות אבות.* If we are correct in our interpretation, this would be a point in history when the promise that the Ribono shel Olam had made to Avraham at the time of the Akeidah would no longer be effective. That promise had been predicated upon the assumption that we would still be considered to be זרעך, (Avraham's) *offspring*. At the time in history now being discussed, that assumption would no longer accord with the facts.

We have made a good beginning in coming to grips with verses 26 and 27. We will continue our explorations of these two verses in the next chapter. Come! We have much to learn.

---

* As noted above, the use of this phrase in the present context is not meant in the technical sense, but is to be taken metaphorically.

Some Thoughts on the Structure of the Shirah

*A*gain and again we are drawn inexorably to verses 26 and 27.* The juncture between these two verses can be viewed as the critical point at which the nonnegotiable guarantee that Moshiach will come and find us ready for him[60] comes into being.

Here is how.

What we really have here is a conversation between מדת הדין and מדת הרחמים.

DIN'S VOICE:** In verse 26 it occurs to the Ribono shel Olam that it would be best to simply forget about us and leave us to wither away in our exile. Our history had been so full of lapses, betrayals, wrongheadedness, and stubborn self-assertion; it had revealed so little gratitude or true faith that there did not seem much point in continuing. Of course if the זְכוּת אבות*** could still be detected, it would have been another story. For true scions of Avraham, Yitzchok, and Yaakov there would be an inexhaustible fount of patience. But even their influence had left no trace. The kindest fate for a rootless, goalless, floundering mass of failures would, so it would seem, be utter oblivion. Thus, verse 26.

RACHAMIM'S VOICE:**** Verse 27 says, "No!" We have examined Ramban's understanding of the whys for this adamant refusal in chapter 5; we will now have the opportunity to consider them once more. We will not need to go into all

---

* From this point on we will be basing our thoughts on the way that Ramban understands these two pesukim. We have resorted to this Ramban many times in the past chapters.

** See Ramban 26 under ואשביתה מאנוש זכרם. He writes: והנה יאמר הכתוב כי היה **במדת** **הדין**. . . .

*** See previous chapter.

**** See Ramban 26 under ואשביתה מאנוש זכרם. Much further toward the end, when he explains the argument in verse 27, he writes: . . . . שיזכיר מהם **ברחמים** כי הם "עמו" מאז ויזכור כי הם עבדיו . . .

the details of his argument, but we do need to ponder the implications. In chapter 5 we learned how God's fate and ours are inextricably woven together, that God "needs" us even as we need Him. Only through us, or, to be more precise, through the memories that our history keeps alive, can God realize His plans for mankind. Destroy us and He will be forgotten; grant us reprieve for our shortcomings, and there is a chance. It is as simple as that.

It sounds pretty presumptuous, does it not?
→Who, after all, are the people of whom verse 26 speaks? We recall that they are a generation cut off from our avos.* [1] These would barely acknowledge them as their children. They are bereft of even vestiges of זְכוּת אבות, a people so far removed from the Jewish ideal that we cannot even recognize them as the ones whose ancestors are described in Chumash. Can a people so twisted out of shape that even the avos give them up as lost really guarantee that God's universe will be shown to have been a worthwhile project? Does the Ribono shel Olam really want such as these to bear the most significant testimony in history to a cynical world?

And against all expectations the answer to all these weighty objections is a resounding yes! Apparently once the faculty of Rachamim becomes an active player, it precipitates a fundamental difference in the Ribono shel Olam's perception of things. It seems that *din* and Rachamim do not only influence actions; they define the way things are perceived. Din, so it seems to me, is concerned with the facts on the ground. It asks what is happening in the real world. By contrast, Rachamim (a close cousin to רחם, *the womb*) takes a motherly interest in all aspects of Jewish life. It registers matters that do not at all show up on din's screen.

At this point you might want to reread chapter 6 where we worked out that after the Ribono shel Olam's decision that the world ought not to run on din alone, but that din would be

* Recall that Ramban said that for the generation concerning whom the Ribono shel Olam said, אמרתי אפאיהם, it was תמה זכות אבות.

partnered with Rachamim, the partnership was not to be an equal one. Not only does the שם הויה, the name of the Ribono shel Olam associated with Rachamim, precede Elohim, the name associated with din, but it stands much higher in the hierarchy of the divine names. The שם הויה is the שם העצם, describing as far as that is possible the Ribono shel Olam Himself, while אלהים describes what the Ribono shel Olam *does*, not what He *is*.

In the context of our concerns in the present essay, where we are trying to understand why qualities that matter deeply to Rachamim are completely absent from the concerns of din, we might word what we have learned in chapter 6 and paraphrased briefly here as follows. We *live* in a world of Rachamim, a world within which, for reasons understood by the Ribono shel Olam, din is occasionally *exercised*. The concept "world" obviously encompasses more than do gestures that occasionally occur within it. It stands to reason that Rachamim will pick up vibrations that are totally unnoticed and therefore completely unknown to din.

What causes those vibrations?   →It is Israel's unbending and fierce loyalty to the Ribono shel Olam, at times and under circumstances when simply moving with the tide would have been much the easier choice.[2]

Take a good look at that last sentence, the one brought to your attention by that heavy arrow. There is a good reason why that arrow is there. What is described in that sentence touches upon the very fulcrum on which the Ribono shel Olam and Klal Yisrael forged their eternal bond.

Of course we are going to have to explain why just loyalty is of such cosmic significance. We will get to that before the end of this chapter. But before we deal with that, let us first demonstrate that the thesis is correct, that it is indeed loyalty that stands at the center of Rachamim's concern.

Here, once more, are Ramban's words in his commentary to verse 26.

ועל כן ראוי מדין הרצון שהיה בבריאת העולם, שיהיה רצון מלפניו להקים לו לעם כל הימים, כי הם הקרובים אליו והיודעים אותו מכל העמים.

וזה טעם כי ידין ה' עמו ועל **עבדיו** יתנחם (פסוק לו), **שיזכור ה' ברחמים**
כי הם **עמו מאז**, ויזכור **כי הם עבדיו שעמדו לו בגלותם כעבדים לסבול
הצרות והשעבוד**, וכענין שנאמר (ישעיה סג ח) ויאמר אך עמי המה בנים
לא ישקרו ...

Therefore it is appropriate as a consequence of the
[Divine] will that existed at the creation of the world, to
establish for Himself a people for all time that are nearer
to Him and who know Him more than all the other
peoples.

And the meaning of the verse *For HaShem will judge
His people and for His* SERVANTS *He will reconsider* is that
God will remember in mercy that they are *His people*
of old, and He will remember *that they are His servants,
for they stood by Him in their exile like servants to suffer the
troubles and bondage,* as it is written, *Surely they are My
people, children who will not deal falsely.**

The phrase that I set in italics certainly does the job that
I assigned to it. It speaks of the fact that we *stood by Him . . .
[unperturbed by] troubles and bondage.* Clearly, it is our loyalty that God will remember. However, before we go on, I
just want to point out the significance of the italicized phrase,
and the Yeshayahu verse with which Ramban buttresses his
argument.

It is certainly no coincidence that Ha'azinu begins by describing Klal Yisrael as *children* of the Ribono shel Olam,** but
ends with picturing us as *servants.**** Why the switch? Here
is what strikes me as a possible explanation. It seems clear to
me that the parent/child relationship begins with the parent,
while the master/servant relationship begins with the servant.
We need only think of the well-known and well-loved passage
from our Rosh HaShanah *Machzor* to bear this out.

---

* Most of this translation is taken from R. Chavel's *Ramban*. The last quote is
from Yeshayahu 63:8.

** לא בניו (5), אביך קניך (6), בניו ובנותיו (19), בנים לא אמון בם (20).

*** ועל עבדיו יתנחם (36), כי דם עבדיו יקום (43).

אם כבנים אם כעבדים ...

אם כבנים רחמינו כרחם אב על בנים

אם כעבדים עינינו לך תלויות ...

[As You sit in judgment over us, You could regard us in
one of two ways;] as children or as servants.

If [You regard us as] children, have mercy upon us as a
father would show mercy to his child.

If [You regard us as] servants, [know that] our eyes look
to You, hoping always that You will give us freely of Your
kindness.

Parents love their children; that is simply a given. In a normal family, children reciprocate that love, particularly as
it is manifest in all the things that parents do for them. The
first part of Ha'azinu describes the many gifts with which the
Ribono shel Olam showered us and then (beginning at verse
6) castigates us for our lack of reciprocation, evidenced by an
absence of any meaningful gratitude. Within such a context,
it would be natural to think of Klal Yisrael as God's children.

At the end of the shirah, once the Ribono shel Olam is persuaded that Rachamim must play an active role if our rehabilitation is to be assured, the focus shifts to *loyalty*. Earlier we
demonstrated *that* this is so; very soon we will attempt to explain *why* it is so. In the meantime we will examine why, *if it
is so*, the shirah uses the metaphor of servant to describe the
protagonist, when it began by describing him as a son.

The reason is simple. Loyalty is the forte of the servant
more so than of the child. A child remaining loyal to his parents under difficult circumstances is acting as nature bids
him act. To do otherwise, he would have to struggle against
his instincts. By contrast, the servant has no intrinsic reason
to feel anything particular for his master. At best the master
is a buyer, purchasing the servant's production against a reasonable price; at worst he is a despot robbing the servant of
his freedom by imposing slavery upon him. Either way, at bottom, the condition of servitude is objective rather than subjective. Personalities need not be involved. If they do become
involved, if the servant feels loyalty toward his master, that

would constitute a voluntary gesture of submission, one generated by the "man" hiding beneath the guise of the servant.

Why is this difference between child and servant significant?

In order to give a reasonable answer to this very reasonable question, I am going to quote myself from my book on Tish'ah Be'Av and the Meraglim, *Tear Drenched Nights*. In chapter 19 of that book I discuss BeMidbar 14:8 where Yehoshua and Kaleiv are trying to persuade the people to reject the undertones of defeatism that seemed to energize the report of the Meraglim. They said, אם חפץ בנו ה' והביא אתנו אל הארץ הזאת ונתנה לנו ארץ אשר הוא* זבת חלב ודבש, *If HaShem really wants us, then He will bring us to this Land and will give it to us, a Land that is flowing with milk and honey.* We wondered at the strange phrase, אם חפץ בנו ה', *If HaShem really wants us.* . . . In what way would the Ribono shel Olam "want" us? We use *want* only for something that we do not own. I can want your car; I cannot want my own. I can love it, I can feel possessive toward it, but I cannot *want* it. Here is what I wrote there.

> Let us examine to what extent the idea of "wanting" anything is applicable to the Ribono shel Olam, the Omnipotent.
>
> A good place to consider is BeMidbar Rabba 10.
>
> שוקיו עמודי שש וגו' שוקיו זה העולם שנשתוקק הקב"ה לבראתו כמה דתימא ועלי תשוקתו ומנין שכן הוא אומר שנאמר (בראשית ב) ויכלו השמים והארץ וגו' אין ויכלו אלא לשון תאוה שנאמר (תהלים פד) נכספה וגם כלתה נפשי.
>
> שוקיו (in Shir HaShirim 5:15, lit. *His thighs*) can hint at שקק, to crave. Thus, the word refers to . . . this world, which God craved, as it is written, ועלי תשוקתו, *His craving is centered upon me* (Shir HaShirim 7:11). Now, from where would we know that the Ribono shel Olam craves this world? We can derive it from the word ויכלו in the phrase, ויכלו השמים והארץ. . . . The root כלה (from which

---

* Please note that the word is vocalized, הִוא.

ויכולו is formed) implies desire. This can be shown from Tehilim 84, נכספה וגם כלתה נפשי, My very being craves and longs for...

Apparently, there is one thing that even an omnipotent God lacks. He lacks the voluntary obeisance with which a creature, full of love and awe, turns to its Creator. A cosmos infinitely full of infinite possibilities nevertheless lacks that one, infinitely important, element. For that, God needs puny, fallible, imperfect man. There is no way around that. God longs for man because only man can provide the one thing that omnipotence cannot deliver.

Our wholehearted services, freely offered in love and submission, is the one thing, by definition the only thing, which the Ribono shel Olam can "want" from us. Without us He cannot have it.

So it is loyalty, specifically the loyalty of a servant to his master, that ultimately tips the scale. Once the Ribono shel Olam permits Himself to act with Rachamim, He becomes overwhelmed by the fierce determination that lent constancy to our hearts and rigidity to our spines, which infused us with a stiff-necked stubbornness to remain true to ourselves and to our God when logic and common sense sorely tried such faithfulness. When this becomes the thought mode, the picture really changes. Somber blacks that speak of abject failure give way to the bright colors that sing of hope; winter gives way to spring and the קול התור נשמע בארצנו.

We have given the Ribono shel Olam the one thing that He craves. The Ribono shel Olam is well pleased that he subordinated דין to רחמים.

This chapter is ending on such a positive note that it seems almost sacrilegious to finish with a question. But ask we must if we want to understand. Earlier in this essay I quoted a Ramban that starts with the words ועל כן ראוי מדין הרצון. This is the Ramban who draws our attention to the idea that the Ribono shel Olam's determination that we are not to be destroyed as a nation is based upon the fact that throughout our exiles we always remained loyal servants. Ramban buttresses his argument with a quote from Yeshayahu 63:8, which reads ויאמר אך עמי המה בנים לא ישקרו ....

The problem is clear. Why would Ramban quote a pasuk that identifies us as בנים לא ישקרו when the entire logic of the shirah as we have interpreted it revolves around the change from בנים in the beginning to עבדים at the end? I do not believe that this is a major, major problem, but it certainly could use some thought. We will try to tackle this issue in chapter 16. Come, we have much to do.

Analyzing Verse 3, or How Did
Birkas Hatorah *Find Its Way into Ha'azinu?*

*I*n this chapter we will concentrate upon verse 3, which reads:

כי שם ה' אקרא הבו גודל לאלהינו

If I were to follow the system that I have used throughout this book, I would now provide a translation and then follow up with an analysis. That sounds simple enough; here is the translation:

When I proclaim the name of HaShem, [I call upon you all] to ascribe greatness to our God.

It sounds simple, but in the present instance it misses the mark completely. We are going to find out very soon that "שם ה' אקרא" is an idiomatic expression and, as we all know, rendering idioms into different languages is a tricky business. All we can say for certain is that a literal translation of the words will *not* do. All else is, at this point, conjecture.

After this brief introduction, we are ready to plunge into the task that we have set ourselves. What, in this all-important sentence, are we called upon to do?

In the previous chapter we began to examine the structure of Ha'azinu. In the current chapter we will continue with this project. I will argue that the shirah proper does not begin until verse 7. The first six verses are to be viewed as an introduction.* Further along in this essay I will cite a Rashi that appears to support this contention. In the meantime, in order

---

* In an earlier draft I wrote that these six verses are in fact not part of the shirah, which really begins with זכור ימות עולם. I think now that there is no need to express things quite so radically. The poetic idiom in which they are cast and the fact that in the sefer Torah they are written in the same form as is the rest of Ha'azinu indicates that they are an integral part of Ha'azinu. We should word our contention as follows: The actual message of Ha'azinu begins with verse 7. The first six verses are an introduction to that message.

to forestall objections, I quote S'forno to verse 7: אחר שהשלים הקדמת השירה.... Even before I cite the Rashi that I am about to discuss, it is clear that I am in good company.[1]

I suggest that this introductory passage is to be broken down into four sections, as follows.

1. Verse 1: This verse invites heaven and earth to be witnesses to the truths that the shirah is about to reveal.
2. Verse 2: Moshe Rabbeinu expresses the hope that just as the rain and the dew, by loosening the earth, ready it to receive the seeds, so, too, should his words penetrate to the hearts of the people, making them receptive to his teachings.
3. Our analysis of verse 3 will yield that *Shiras Ha'azinu* can be described as a "קריאה בשם השם" that should be received on our part with a reaction that can be described as "הבו גודל לאלהינו".
4. Verses 4–6 constitute the required "הבו גודל לאלהינו".

What precisely is verse 3 asking of us? What is it that the pasuk describes as "כי שם ה' אקרא," and how do we go about the "הבו גודל לאלהינו" that is required of us in reaction to this קריאה?

We cannot begin our analysis without first noting the Gemara in Berachos 21a.

מנין לברכת התורה לפניה מן התורה שנאמר כי שם ה' אקרא הבו גדל לאלהינו

We learn that we are required to recite a berachah before beginning to study Torah, from verse 3 in Ha'azinu: כי שם השם אקרא, הבו גדל לאלהינו.

To this Gemara, Rashi remarks:

כי שם ה' אקרא כשבא משה לפתוח בדברי שירה* אמר להם לישראל אני אברך תחלה, ואתם ענו אחרי אמן, כי שם ה' אקרא בברכה, אתם הבו גודל לאלהינו באמן.

---

* This is the Rashi to which I referred earlier. Rashi says כשבא לפתוח ..., which implies that in verse 3 he had not yet begun the shirah. Apparently we are still in an introductory phase. Presumably he would agree that the shirah proper would begin with זכור ימות עולם. See endnote 1.

כי שם ה' אקרא . . . : As Moshe Rabbeinu was about to begin the shirah, he said to the Israelites, "Before I begin
this shirah I am going to recite a berachah. Make sure
that you answer אמן after my berachah." The words כי שם
ה' אקרא refer to the recitation of a berachah. The words,
הבו גדל לאלהינו refer to the response, אמן.

In his Chumash commentary, Rashi offers a different explanation.

. . . כשאקרא ואזכיר שם ה', אתם הבו גדל לאל-הינו וברכו שמו. מכאן
אמרו, שעונין ברוך שם כבוד מלכותו אחר ברכה שבמקדש.
When I proclaim the ineffable Name, ascribe greatness
to our God and bless His Name. From this we can learn
that we are to answer ברוך שם כבוד מלכותו when we hear a
berachah in the Beis HaMikdash.

Both explanations that Rashi suggests seem very technical
and do not appear to belong in a shirah. I feel intuitively that
if we are going to understand the Gemara as does Rashi, we
are dealing with a *d'rashah* rather than the *p'shuto shel mikra.*
Ramban's offering* seems to me to fit more comfortably into
the simple meaning of *Shiras Ha'azinu.*

שנצטוינו להודות לשמו יתברך, בכל עת שנקרא בתורה, על הטובה הגדולה
שעשה לנו בתתו תורתו אלינו והודיענו המעשים הרצויים לפניו שבהם
ננחל חיי העולם הבא.
[The fifteenth mitzvah that Rambam should have men-
tioned] is that, whenever we read in the Torah, we are
bidden to give thanks to the Ribono shel Olam for the
great favor that He has done us in giving us His Torah,
thus letting us know what actions are pleasing to Him
and will therefore guarantee us a place in *olam haba.*

As the source for this mitzvah, Ramban, in accordance
with the Gemara, cites our pasuk in Ha'azinu. The implica-

---

* ספר המצוות להרמב"ם, מצוות ששכח אותן הרב ממצות עשה, ט"ו.

tions are very broad. We are commanded to react to any experience that can be described as a קריאה בשם ה' by ascribing greatness to the Ribono shel Olam. Birkas HaTorah need be no more than one application of this universal rule.

What would Ramban believe qualifies as a קריאה בשם ה'? Is this phrase to be taken literally, or idiomatically?

I begin with the assumption that "proclaiming the name of HaShem" is an idiomatic expression. The words, in themselves, do not convey anything that we are able to pin down. Luckily this formula occurs in a number of other contexts, and if we approach the matter as a sugia that requires elucidation rather than as simply an exercise in translating words, we will soon begin to experience the satisfying heft of solid understanding.

So what does כי שם ה' אקרא mean to the Ramban? He is silent here, but not because he has nothing to say. Ramban had the right to assume that we would do our homework, and that includes checking around to see whether there is perhaps some other place where he deals with this idiom. The answer is of course that there is. We go to Bereishis 12:8, where we learned that shortly after he arrived in Eretz Canaan, Avraham built an altar, ויקרא בשם ה'. That phrase is a fraternal twin to our כי שם ה' אקרא, and we will know beyond doubt or cavil that whatever Ramban said there will help us here. Here is Ramban's commentary.

> והנכון שהיה קורא בקול גדול שם לפני המזבח את שם ה', מודיע אותו
> ואלהותו לבני אדם, כי באור כשדים היה מלמדם ולא אבו שמוע, ועתה
> כשבא בארץ הזאת שהובטח בה "ואברכה מברכיך," היה למוד ללמד
> ולפרסם האלהות וכן אמר הכתוב (להלן כו כד) ביצחק כאשר הלך אל
> נחל גרר והובטח אל תירא כי אתך אנכי, שבנה מזבח "ויקרא בשם ה'"
> **כי בא במקום חדש אשר לא שמעו את שמעו ולא ראו את כבודו והגיד**
> **כבודו בגוים ההם ולא נאמר ביעקב כן מפני שהוליד בנים רבים כלם עובדי**
> **ה', והיתה לו קהלה גדולה נקראת עדת ישראל ונתפרסמה האמונה בהם,**
> **ונודעה לכל עם,** וגם כי מימי אבותיו נתפרסמה בכל ארץ כנען וכך אמרו
> בבראשית רבה (לט טז) מלמד שהקריא שמו של הקב"ה בפי כל בריה.

[Ramban began by quoting Ibn Ezra, who reads the phrase as an idiomatic expression standing for *prayer*. In this passage Ramban disagrees and suggests his own interpretation.] Rather, the phrase means that Avraham loudly proclaimed God's name (or fame) to all the people, *introducing them to concepts about which they had never heard.* He taught them that a Divine Being existed, and what the quality of Godliness might involve. . . . This interpretation of the phrase finds support in Bereishis Rabba (39:16) where we read "He called" (ויקרא, in the simple active form, ק ר א, *to call*) really means that "he caused others to call." (הקריא, in the causative voice, ה ק ר י א, *to bring about that others should call.*) God became a familiar topic of conversation among the Canaanites.

At this point we may conclude that the phrase is used when, through "calling בשם ה'" previously unknown, or perhaps completely unanticipated, ideas become the stuff of general discourse.

We are already at a point at which we can begin gathering in the fruits of our labors. For example, we can understand Shemos 31:2 better than most of us have understood it in the past. Let us put ourselves in Moshe Rabbeinu's position when, in Terumah and Tetzaveh, the Ribono shel Olam first told him about the infinitely intricate *mishkan* and kohanite vestments that he would be expected to produce. He must have wracked his brain, wondering whom among a slave population, unschooled in the finer points of silver work and needlepoint,* he could find to execute these tasks. Certainly it would not even have occurred to him to think of the youngster, Betzalel ben Uri, who was all of thirteen at the time.**

At Shemos 31:2 the Ribono shel Olam appears to Moshe Rabbeinu and says, "ראה קראתי בשם בצלאל בן אורי בו חור . . . ," and suddenly there was no more problem. That which the Ribono shel Olam announced could not have been known to anybody

---

* See Ramban to Shemos 35:21. You will find it endlessly rewarding.
** See Sanhedrin 69b for the mathematics.

before then. The conditions that Ramban laid down for the use of this formula were all fulfilled.

We have almost reached the point at which we can safely return to our parshah. We are very close to where we need to get. However, there is one more stop to make before we are completely ready.

What must surely have been among the greatest moments in Moshe Rabbeinu's leadership of the people came when he needed to elicit forgiveness from the Ribono shel Olam for the *Cheit HaEigel*. We read with bated breath as Moshe Rabbeinu step by hard-won step manages to roll back the dreadful distancing between the Ribono shel Olam and ourselves that this almost unforgivable lapse had precipitated. As success appears to be within his grasp, Moshe Rabbeinu is emboldened to beg for the most profound of all graces. He entreats the Ribono shel Olam, הראני נא את כבודיך, "Show me, I beg You, the full reach of Your *kavod*." Let us listen in to the Ribono shel Olam's answer.

ויאמר אני אעביר כל טובי על פניך **וקראתי בשם יהוה לפניך** וחנתי את אשר אחן ורחמתי את אשר ארחם.

He answered, "I will permit the full extent of My goodness to pass before you *and will proclaim the name of HaShem before you*, showing grace to whom I shall show grace, and mercy to whom I shall be merciful."

Here we have it again. Moshe Rabbeinu had begged for something that no human being had ever before requested. The precise degree of the *chaninah* and *rachmonus* that could be expected under the "כל טובי" rubric was, until this moment, completely unknown. The proclamation of the Ribono shel Olam's name would bring it into the range of the knowable.

And, now, after having gone so far afield, we are finally ready to return to Ha'azinu and birkas HaTorah.

Here is my contention.

I believe that the כי שם ה' אקרא of pasuk 3 is the exact parallel of the . . . וקראתי בשם ה' לפניך of Ki Sisa that we have just discussed. There it was a matter of revealing to Moshe Rabbeinu the extent of chaninah and rachmonus that could be expected from the "כל טובי" mode that the Ribono shel Olam chose to reveal at that moment. Here we are interested in the other aspect of the Ribono shel Olam: the faculty of משפט, of God's *stern justice,* that we would be experiencing at those times in history for which the Ribono shel Olam was giving us *Shiras Ha'azinu.** For Klal Yisrael entering Eretz Yisrael after the forty years of desert wandering embraced in the Ribono shel Olam's loving arms, learning about משפט would be a terribly frightening experience. It would be sufficiently unknown to warrant the expression כי שם ה' אקרא as we have now come to know its meaning.

And that is why our reaction to discovering this side of the Ribono shel Olam's stewardship is supposed to call forth the obligation of הבו גודל לאלהינו. Here is how Rashbam understands these words.

> **כי שם ה' אקרא** כאשר אספר לכם גבורות שעשה לכם הקב"ה והטובות שגמל לכם וגם שהוא צדיק במה שיעשה לכם גם אתם הבו גודל לאלהינו היו מודים על האמת.

When I tell you all the mighty things that the Ribono shel Olam did for you, and all the favors that He granted you, and that also when He punished you He was fair and righteous in what He did (כי שם ה' אקרא), it is your duty to acknowledge all this as the truth (הבו גודל לאלהינו).

All this, I firmly believe, is the פשוטו של מקרא of this difficult sentence. The obligation to recite birkas HaTorah is an application of the general principle that is derived from this pasuk, but by no means exhausts it. It is a part of a potentially limitless set of fresh insights that can be learned concerning significant truths about the Ribono shel Olam and the way He runs the world. Each of these can oblige us to react with an appropriate הבו גדל לאלהינו. The particular form in which this requirement is fulfilled in Ha'azinu is the subject of the next two chapters.

---

* Remember that Ha'azinu was given us for times כי תמצאן רעות רבות וצרות.

הבו גודל לאלהינו א'
Analyzing Verse 4

*I*n the previous chapter we dealt with the first half of verse
3, כי שם ה' אקרא. We are now ready to move on to the second
half of that verse, הבו גודל לאלהינו. You may recall that we used
Rashbam's interpretation for that second phrase. "Ascribing
greatness"* in *Shiras Ha'azinu* means being מודה על האמת, *ac-
knowledging that nothing happened to us that we did not deserve.*
In the present essay, it will be my contention that verses 4, 5,
and 6 are designed to express our acquiescence to this truth.
They affirm God's unwavering integrity and declare that the
fault for all the tragedies that have dogged us throughout our
history lies squarely at our own door. We, and only we, have
sent history veering from the perfectly straight line from
conception to realization that the Ribono shel Olam had
intended.

Only once all this has been firmly established does the
shirah proper begin with verse 7.

Let us first note a significant fact. The Ribono shel Olam is
described as צור, *a rock*, no less than six times in the forty-three
verses of this song. Here is a shock for you. *Never once* in the
entire Chumash does this descriptive name for the Ribono
shel Olam recur. Never once. Things like that just do not
happen by coincidence. Here is what I believe we are being
told. The Ribono shel Olam appears to us in many different
roles. Chazal tell us that at the Yam Suf we experienced Him
as a youthful, energetic warrior; at Sinai He seemed to us a
teacher imbued with the wisdom that only old age can confer.
Ha'azinu tells us that the God of history is a "rock," firm and
resolute, determined that history will end up at precisely the
point at which He has determined that it will.**

Let us read carefully. The text itself will get us where we
need to go.

---

* גודל is, of course, *greatness*, hence, הבו גודל = *ascribe greatness.*

** See the language of the final Ramban to Ha'azinu: אם כן השירה הזאת הבטחה
מבוארת בגאולה העתידה בע"כ של מינין.

Here is verse 4:

הצור תמים פעלו כי כל דרכיו משפט אל אמונה ואין עול צדיק וישר הוא.

And here are Ramban's remarks:

הצור תמים פעלו רמז למדת הדין, ואמר "תמים פעלו," כי הפועל הבא ממנו
תמים ושלם לא ימוט ולא ישתנה לעולם "כי כל דרכיו משפט [הרחמים
[הם]," ולא תבוא בפועל חסרון אך במשפט, כי המשפט לאל אמונה, ואין
עול בצור, והמשפט צדיק והצור ישר.

We are nowhere near ready for a translation. Instead we
will roam around a bit within the text, tapping a little here,
feeling a little there, and in general attempting to get a sense of
the direction toward which Ramban seems to be taking us.

Ramban begins his comments by telling us what this verse
is up to. It will tell us something about the מדת הדין. Although
the text does not announce in so many words that its interest is focused on מדת הדין, what it does say points (רמז)* in that
direction.

EXCURSUS

We need to add a few lines simply in order to understand
where we are heading. I will offer a list of what we already
know and how what we are about to learn in the current
chapter is built on those assumptions.

1. We already know from chapter 14 that when something
new and significant is about to be proclaimed, the Torah describes the event as "declaring" (ק ר א) the "name" or "fame"
(שם) of the Ribono shel Olam. That expression was used in
כי תשא when the Ribono shel Olam was about to introduce
Moshe Rabbeinu to His מדת הרחמים, and it is used here in verse 3
(כי שם ה' אקרא) when we are about to be introduced to the
workings of His מדת הדין.

---

* I am not sure whether רמז is to be taken as a noun, רֶמֶז, or a verb, רָמַז.

2. Verse 3 demands that a "קריאה בשם ה'" be met with "הבו גודל
לאלהינו." We are assuming that the "הבו גודל לאלהינו" in Ha'azinu
will be expressed in verses 4, 5, and 6. After that we will be
ready to begin the shirah proper with verse 7.

3. Together with the Rashbam, we are assuming that we fulfill the obligation of "הבו גודל לאלהינו" by being מודה על האמת, *ac-
knowledging that we were at fault* in the suffering that was our
lot throughout our galus.

4. In effect, we will be making that acknowledgment by af-
firming that whatever happened to us under the rubric of
מדת הדין was fair. That is really what verses 4, 5, and 6 are all
about.

5. From Ramban's language we have established that Ha'azinu
is a celebration of מדת הדין. That seems a little problematic in
as much as throughout these essays we have discovered again
and again that from verse 36 onward מדת הרחמים appears to
be taking over. How are we to make peace with this seeming
contradiction?

6. That is the issue with which we are about to deal in this
essay. We will find that in contrast to humanly administered
justice in which mercy may play no role at all, in the justice
that the Ribono shel Olam metes out, mercy is very much a
part of the equation. His "משפט" is a "משפט הרחמים."

We are now at a point that we can begin this very important
chapter.

Ramban sets out to teach us the nature of actions (פעלו)
that are taken under the rubric of מדת הדין. These are both תמים,
perfect, and שלם, *complete.*[1] This description is later amplified
by אין עול, an assertion that in these actions there is never any
miscarriage of justice because the actions that are undertaken
in the actualization of the מדת הדין are in the hands of an אל
אמונה, a God Who can be totally trusted, a God, moreover,
Who is both צדיק and ישר.*

---

* In the last few words of his comment, Ramban says something about "צדיק"
and "ישר" that I do not understand. The way he words it makes me suspect that
sisrei Torah might be involved. I have chosen to translate these words according to their simple meaning.

This description of the way that מדת הדין works in the real world could really stand on its own as the introductory verse of the הבו גודל לאלהינו requirement. It would certainly be an adequate fulfillment of Rashbam's demand for an admission that the fault for all that has happened to us must lie with ourselves and not with the Ribono shel Olam. Still, there is another phrase in this verse that we have not yet examined. It will turn out to lie at the very center of Ha'azinu's message.

So let us turn our attention to the phrase כי כל דרכיו משפט.

We will first try for a general meaning of the word משפט as Ramban to Shemos 15:25 understands it, and move on from there.

First, then, let us define what משפט is *not*. It is *not* "law." "מצוה" (from צ ו ה, *to command*) is law (that which is commanded) and the simple economics of language development decrees that different words do not describe the same thing.[2]

Let us then listen to Ramban (Shemos 15:25) on משפט.

ועל דרך הפשט, כאשר החלו לבא במדבר הגדול והנורא וצמאון אשר אין מים שם להם במחייתם וצרכיהם מנהגים אשר ינהגו בהם עד בואם אל ארץ נושבת, כי המנהג יקרא "חק," כענין הטריפני לחם חקי (משלי ל ח), חקות שמים וארץ (ירמיה לג כה), ויקרא "משפט" בהיותו משוער כהוגן, וכן כה עשה דוד וכה משפטו כל הימים (ש"א כז יא), כמשפט הראשון אשר היית משקהו (בראשית מ יג), וארמון על משפטו ישב (ירמיה ל יח), על מדתו. או שייסרם בחקי המדבר, לסבול הרעב והצמא, לקרוא בהם אל ה', לא דרך תלונה, ומשפטים שיחיו בהם, לאהוב איש את רעהו, ולהתנהג בעצת הזקנים, והצנע לכת באהליהם בענין הנשים והילדים, ושינהגו שלום עם הבאים במחנה למכור להם דבר, ותוכחות מוסר שלא יהיו כמחנות השוללים אשר יעשו כל תועבה ולא יתבוששו, וכענין שצוה בתורה (דברים כג י) כי תצא מחנה על אויביך ונשמרת מכל דבר רע.

וכן ביהושע נאמר ויכרות יהושע ברית לעם ביום ההוא וישם לו חק ומשפט בשכם (יהושע כד כה), אינם חקי התורה והמשפטים, אבל הנהגות ויישוב המדינות, כגון תנאים שהתנה יהושע שהזכירו חכמים (ב"ק פ:), וכיוצא בהם.

The simplest explanation of חק is as follows. As the Israelites entered the foreboding desert, Moshe Rabbeinu enacted certain usages (מנהגים) that would facilitate efficient communal desert living pending the time when they would once more reach inhabited land. There is ample precedent for the use of "חק" for "מנהג" . . . and the word "משפט" is also appropriate since these usages were structured in a way that would guarantee that everything would be measured appropriately. This use of משפט occurs in sentences like I Shmuel 27:11, *This is what David would do and this was his* mishpat *always*. . . .

Alternatively, חק ומשפט might mean that Moshe Rabbeinu disciplined them in the rules of desert travel, how they should deal with hunger and thirst . . . that they should be kind to one another and listen to the advice of the elders, that they should act modestly in their tents . . . so too when Yehoshua gave the people חוק ומשפט (Yehoshua 24:25), this does not mean the laws and ordinances mentioned in the Torah, but rather usages that would promote peaceful community relations . . .

So משפט does not mean "law." Endnote 2 deals expansively with the issue of what it does mean and I ask you to go through that note as carefully as you would have read it if it had been a part of the text of this essay. Important though it is, I have relegated it to a note because I did not want it to deflect attention from what we are about to discover.

We are about to enter the arcane world of משפט as it is practiced by the Ribono shel Olam. Our source will be Rabbeinu Bechaya to Shoftim[3] (Devarim 16:18).

There the Torah defines the duties of the judges that are to be appointed in every city. They are to dispense משפט צדק. Rabbeinu Bechaya explains that this term defines a justice unsoftened* by mercy.** Now the need to modify משפט with צדק implies that the word משפט standing on its own would convey a more nuanced concept. Indeed he makes the point that the

---

* In contrast to the feminine form צדקה, which implies a soft kindness, the masculine צדק is a strong, uncompromised justice.
** His expression is שיהיה המשפט ענין נחתך. The expression conveys the idea of sharp lines with no fuzziness around the edges. Nothing may impinge upon the law in its pristine glory.

word משפט describes the midpoint* between two extremes,** which when the word is used in the sense of justice, would presumably be absolute justice softened by touches of mercy. That, Rabbeinu Bechaya teaches, is in fact the משפט practiced by the Ribono shel Olam.[4] [5]

Earlier in this essay, when I first quoted the Ramban to verse 4, we maintained that we were nowhere near ready to be able to offer a translation. I think that after all that we have been through together in these last few pages, we have reached a point at which we can try our hand. I will intersperse the translation with explanatory remarks. That way you will easily be able to decide whether you agree with what I have to say.

So here once more is this very short but very difficult Ramban.

הצור תמים פעלו רמז למדת הדין ואמר תמים פעלו, כי הפועל הבא ממנו תמים ושלם לא ימוט ולא ישתנה לעולם כי כל דרכיו משפט משפט הרחמים הם, ולא תבוא בפועל חסרון אך במשפט, כי המשפט לאל אמונה, ואין עול בצור, והמשפט צדיק והצור ישר.

"הצור תמים פעלו" is the phrase that introduces us to a contemplation of the Ribono shel Olam's מדת הדין. "תמים פעלו" describes the actions that the Ribono shel Olam undertakes under the aegis of the מדת הדין. These actions are "לא ישתנה לעולם" and "לא ימוט," "שלם," "תמים".

Ramban uses four adjectives. We have discussed the first two, תמים and שלם, *perfect* and *complete*, in endnote 1 and there is no need to examine them once more. However, we have not had the opportunity to think about the next two, לא ימוט ולא ישתנה לעולם, *[those actions] are immutable. They will never be*

---

* משפט הוא המצוע וענין בינוני.

** Rabbeinu Bechaya adduces a number of proofs that this is the base meaning of the word. Among them is Tehilim 112:5 where a sensible householder is described as one who is יכלכל דבריו במשפט, one *who handles his possessions prudently*; he will be openhanded but not wasteful.

toppled, never be changed. These qualities need a little thought.*
Why would we have supposed that they might change?

Moreover, does not *Shiras Ha'azinu* itself belie Ramban's assertion? Again and again in the previous chapters** we have
noticed that the מדת הדין that controlled events as they un-
folded throughout the shirah ultimately subordinates itself
to the exercise of רחמים that enables the Ribono shel Olam
to recall our loyalty to Him throughout the dreadful galus
years. The change from דין to רחמים at verse 36 is the very crux
of Ha'azinu's presentation of our history as Ramban himself
portrays it in his commentary to verse 26. So situations that
came about through the exercise of מדת הדין *do* change, and
change radically. What can Ramban possibly mean?***

The secret lies in the phrase, "כי כל דרכיו משפט הרחמים הם."

This phrase causes Ramban commentators major problems. Exactly what does "משפט הרחמים" mean?**** The two
terms seem to be mutually exclusive; we seem to have before
us a classic oxymoron. R. Chavel quotes *Kesef Mezukak,* who
resorts to emendation. Instead of "הרחמים," he reads "דתמים,"
punctuating as follows: כי כל דרכיו משפט, דתמים הוא ולא בפועלו
חסרון.[6]

For the reasons explained in endnote 6, I will try to show
that the reading that all editions have is the correct one. Once
we accept that, we will be able to answer the question that
we posed earlier concerning Ramban's assertion that where
מדת הדין is exercised there will be no change in what was decreed. Ha'azinu itself seemed to us to patently contradict that
assertion.

---

* It is not clear to me from which word in the text Ramban derives these
qualities. I am inclined to think that it is the word צור that prompts Ramban
here. Rocks do not change, nor will God's פעולות. However, it is also possible
that תמימות also precludes transience.

** Particularly, chapters 5 and 6.

*** See the top footnote above that the immutability of usages that were generated through the exercise of מדת הדין is implied in the appellation צור and possibly by the description תמים. That, however, just makes things harder. We have
just demonstrated that things do indeed change. So what is the solution?

**** Rav Chavel notes that some manuscripts read "משפט רחמים," leaving out the
letter ה.

Earlier in this essay we began to look at the Rabbeinu Bechaya to Shoftim.* Perhaps it has already struck you that the differentiation that he establishes between human and divine משפט points to the answers to all our remaining problems.

In a word, we can state with a reasonable certainty that we have hit the right solution. The phrase "משפט וה[ה]רחמים" is a perfectly legitimate way of counterpoising the Ribono shel Olam's משפט in which רחמים plays a decisive role, to human משפט, "משפט צדק," in which it plays no role at all. Once we have established that simple idea, we have answers to the weighty problems that we raised earlier. We had seen that the third and fourth adjectives that Ramban uses to describe the Ribono shel Olam's מדת הדין deal with immutability. Whatever would be done under the aegis of the Ribono shel Olam's מדת הדין would neither stumble nor change. Why would we need to be convinced of this? What would have caused us to suspect otherwise?

The answer, of course, lies in the weakness that would inhere in a system of justice that knows only pure דין. At the very beginning of Creation the Ribono shel Olam saw that our world cannot exist without רחמים playing a role, indeed, playing the controlling role.** So almost by definition, an unbending "דין" system must ultimately founder. How then can Ramban claim that מדת הדין functions with immutability? The answer lies in the Ribono shel Olam's "משפט הרחמים." In contrast to human justice (משפט צדק), God's דין functions in tandem with רחמים and can therefore be nuanced precisely as the situation demands.[7]

We have suggested that verses 4, 5, and 6 have the task of fulfilling the obligation stated in verse 3. The "שם ה' אקרא" that would consist of *Shiras Ha'azinu* was to elicit an expression of "הבו גודל לאלהינו." These three verses do just that. As we have explained in verse 4, it makes an ideal introduction to such a passage. It extols the righteousness of the מדת הדין and leads

---

* There is really no help for it. I have to suggest you take a quick glance at endnotes 3, 4, and 5. Each of these could be helpful here.

** See Rashi to Bereishis 1:1 and our discussion in chapter 5.

logically into the next verse. We shall consider that verse in the next chapter.

We are not yet quite home. Near the beginning of this essay we noted how, throughout the shirah, the preferred name for the Ribono shel Olam is צור, a name that does not occur, even once, in the rest of the Torah. We suggested a reason. Ha'azinu is the story of our history, and the God of history is rocklike, unbending, unchangeable, and determined that the goal that He has set for history will somehow be reached.

Still, it seems to me that for people who were nearing the end of a forty-year trek through the wilderness, the mention of "צור," while serving as a metaphor for stern immutability, must also have carried another message, this one quite different from the first. For forty years this mighty nation of some two million people had quenched its thirst by the unstinting plenitude of the cool, sweet water gushing forth, willy-nilly, from tightfisted, sullen rocks.[8] Can there be any doubt that, when here, for the first time in history, we heard the Ribono shel Olam compared to a צור, the picture conjured up by the word carried a dual message?[9]

What are the implications? Is the choice of צור as the name of the Ribono shel Olam for parshas Ha'azinu a natural one? From all that we have learned in this chapter, it would certainly appear so. We recall that Ramban identified Ha'azinu's message as introducing us to the Ribono shel Olam's מדת הדין. We recall further that our own researches found that רחמים is an integral part of the Ribono shel Olam's משפט. It stands to reason, does it not? צור, the unbending symbol of מדת הדין, from within the inner recesses of its own being, finds the big-hearted bounty to dispense life from its own sparkling waters. For *Shiras Ha'azinu*, the celebration of the God of history as the God of דין, there really is no other name by which the Ribono shel Olam ought to be described.

הבו גודל לאלהינו ב'
Analyzing Verse 5

*B*efore we begin our analysis of verse 5, let us remember that, based upon what we worked out in the previous chapter, we contend that verses 4, 5, and 6 are of one piece. Together they constitute the "הבו גודל לאלהינו" to which verse 3 summoned us. Accordingly, we will expect verse 5 to follow smoothly from what verse 4 had said, and to lead smoothly into verse 6.

Verse 5 is extremely difficult. Our discussion is going to be based upon Ramban's interpretation. Nevertheless we will also present Rashi's interpretation simply in order to see the range of possibilities that this strangely worded pasuk offers. Here is how Rashi (based upon Targum) reads the verse. In the following diagram the top line running from right to left presents the pasuk as it is written in the Torah. The second line shows how Targum renders the pasuk. The third line translates the Targum into English. You will notice that the Targum takes liberties with the Torah text, adding words that have no parallel in the text (column two); leaving a word that appears in the text untranslated (column six); and again, in column seven, adding words that have no parallel in the text. More details follow below.

	מומם	בניו	לא	לו		שחת
דפלחו לטעותא	[מומם]	בניו	ליה	לא	להון	חבילו
In that they served idols.	[but have become blemished]	They were once His sons	Him.	not	them-selves	They have hurt

Herewith an analysis of what the Targum, followed by Rashi, has done.

1. He changes the singular שחת (*he has hurt*) to the plural, חבילו (*they have hurt*).

2. He adds להון, *themselves*, which has no parallel in the text.

3. He changes the text לו לא (the pronoun before the negative), which is almost impossible to translate, to לא לו (the negative before the pronoun), which translates readily.
4. He offers no translation for מומם, and instead adds the words דפלחו לטעותא, *in that they served idols.**

Apparently, he did all this for the following reasons: He believed that the subject of שחת is בניו, a plural noun that requires a plural verb. Hence he substitutes חבילו for חביל. The words "לו לא" belong together and to make good sense their sequence must be changed. בניו has two functions: It serves as the subject of שחת as we have just explained, but it is also the first word of a second sentence. At this stage of my thinking, I do not understand why Targum offers no translation for מומם.[1]

Ramban is completely at odds with this rendering.[2] The subject of שחת is מומם, the *blemish* mentioned at the end of the phrase.** In contrast to Rashi, who has the pasuk teach us that no השחתה attaches to the Ribono shel Olam (לא לו), Ramban, by detaching "לו" from "לא," *** has the pasuk say the exact opposite: שחת לו, *[The blemish (*מום*) (of the sons) has caused Him damage. How so?* לא בניו, (by making Klal Yisrael) *"non-children"****(of the Ribono shel Olam)]*, thereby separating the Ribono shel Olam from His beloved people.

As Ramban reads verse 5, it is a direct continuation of the previous verse. There we had learned that no fault of any kind attaches to the Ribono shel Olam's מדת הדין. Our verse confirms this by laying the blame for all the tragedies that we have

* If you have access to the נפש הגר on the Targum, you might want to examine his ideas concerning the Targum's justifications for offering a "translation" that, in many aspects, seems contradicted by the syntax.
** Obviously, taken thus, the singular form of שחת does not create any problem.
*** He has the לו and לא in the correct sequence. He splits them from each other. The first phrase reads, שחת לו, the second one reads, לא בניו. For explanation, please see within.
**** The end of the verse explains: דור עקש ופתלתול. The previous verse had taught that God was both צדיק and ישר. Ramban maintains that "עקש" is the opposite of ישר and "פתלתול" the opposite of צדיק. We cannot be viewed as the children of the Ribono shel Olam if we are the very opposite of the qualities (צדיק וישר) that define Him.

had to suffer squarely at our door. It was *our blemish*—our *crookedness* (עקש) and *twisted ways* (פתלתול)—that separated us from our Father to the extent that we can only be described as "לא בניו," non-children. The victim of our abject failures is first of all, כביכול, the Ribono shel Olam Himself. Bereft of His children, He had no option but to harness His מדת הדין.

Very clearly, in this view, this verse is a part of the הבו גודל לאלהינו of which we have spoken so much in our discussion of the previous verses.

In chapter 13 we noted that Ha'azinu begins with Klal Yisrael being described as the Ribono shel Olam's בנים, His *children*, and in the end discards that description in favor of regarding us as עבדים, His *servants*. We had some ideas that, we thought, might be able to explain that switch. We ended that chapter with a question on the Ramban.

Here is the question as we worded it there.

> Earlier in this essay I quoted a Ramban that starts with the words ....ועל כן ראוי מדין הרצון. This is the Ramban which draws our attention to the idea that the Ribono shel Olam's determination that we are not to be destroyed as a nation is based on the fact that throughout our exiles we always remained loyal servants. Ramban buttresses his argument with a quote from Yeshayahu 63:8, which reads ....ויאמר אך עמי המה בנים לא ישקרו.
>
> The problem is clear. Why would Ramban quote a pasuk that identifies us as בנים לא ישקרו, when the entire logic of the shirah as we have interpreted it revolves around the change from בנים in the beginning to עבדים at the end?

Before we venture an answer to this nagging difficulty, we should realize that the Ramban that we paraphrased above confirms, and therefore strengthens, the data upon which we based our question. Ramban reads the "לא" of verse 5 as being joined to בניו, creating a phrase that we have not met before, "לא בניו," *His non-children.* Somewhere along our turbulent history something snapped. The loving parent/child relationship that had bound us to the Ribono shel Olam and Him to us* was sundered. Probably, at the time that it happened, we were not even aware of what we had lost. An icy detachment had demoted us from children to servants. It was surely a national tragedy of epic proportions!

So we were right about the assumptions that we had made. At some point in our history we turned from children into "non-sons." But that is very small comfort. Where do we go now with our question? Where can we turn?

I cannot vouch for the correctness of the following suggestion; I offer it to you for what it is worth. It may not be sufficiently convincing to make it, if judged in terms of pure מדת הדין. If you will permit entry to a small measure of רחמים, perhaps it will pass muster.

There is another thought that I want to share before I attempt to answer the question. I cannot claim to have sufficient knowledge of the Ramban's methodology to insist that the following question is justified. Nevertheless, it is my sense that Ramban would not suggest an interpretation of a passage in Chumash where that interpretation stands in direct contradiction to a Chazal,** without pointing out that "על פי פשט," the verse might be read differently. To say that we reached a stage of being "לא בניו," apparently simply ignoring R. Meir in the Sifrei who says specifically אף על פי שהם מליאים מומים קרוים בנים, seems strange.[3]

The structure "לא בניו" as denoting "non-children" is very familiar to us from Hoshe'a,*** but, outside Ha'azinu,**** does

---

* בנים אתם לה' אלהיכם (Devarim 14:1).

** In this case, R. Meir in the Sifrei that we shall soon quote. As we shall see, R. Meir insists that even when we have reached the lowest possible ebb, we remain the Ribono shel Olam's "children."

*** Hoshe'a (1:6 and 9) was told by the Ribono shel Olam to call a daughter "לא רוחמה" to indicate that God would no longer have mercy on us, and a son "לא עמי" because we no longer acted toward the Ribono shel Olam as would be becoming to "His" nation.

**** Verse 20 has בנים לא אמון בם, and verse 21 has לא אל for idols and לא עם to describe a degenerate nation.

not occur in the Torah. Why? I think that this is a reasonable question. If a certain grammatical form appears four times within a shirah that spans just forty-three verses and never once anywhere else, it seems to me that this tells us something. Well, what is it telling us?

I suggest that the לא ... formula expresses a radical negation. It tells us that the object of this assessment is entirely bereft of even the slightest residue of the indicated virtue. Its formulation suggests that, relative to this particular quality, the object shouts out an emphatic no!

I further suggest that this radical formulation is appropriate only under a מדת הדין, unsoftened by the more forgiving מדת הרחמים. Once מדת הרחמים enters into consideration, judgments can change substantively.

If all this is correct, then we have good and sufficient answers both to the question that we left open at the end of chapter 13 and to the problem that we just raised.

Herewith the solutions offered על ראשון ראשון ועל אחרון אחרון. As we explained in chapter 13, the change from מדת הדין to מדת הרחמים that is augured in Ha'azinu's verse 36 becomes effective when the Ribono shel Olam recalls the loyalty that Klal Yisrael, His servants, demonstrated during the long and terrible years of galus. Now it is true that, as we explained there, it is the loyalty of servants, not of children, that plays the decisive role. However, once מדת הרחמים is in play, there is no reason why the Father/child relationship cannot also be resurrected. We just now argued that the fateful "לא בניו" that denied that bond was a function of מדת הדין. Once that has receded into the background, leaving center stage to מדת הרחמים, that fearful assessment becomes moot. There is nothing to prevent the Ribono shel Olam from rejoicing in His בנים לא ישקרו.

Perhaps this is also the reason why Ramban seems to have ignored R. Meir's opinion* that even the burden of terrible מומים will not get in the way of the Parent/child relationship. Quite possibly, Ramban felt that R. Meir's reading does not

---

* Recorded in the Sifrei.

stand in contradiction to his own. His own reading was correct when מדת הדין alone held sway. R. Meir's softer approach revealed the possibilities of the verse's words after the revelation in the latter part of the shirah that ultimately מדת הרחמים prevails.

SEVENTEEN

הבו גודל לאלהינו ג'
Analyzing Verse 6

*W*e are by now familiar with the concept that verses 4, 5, and 6 in Ha'azinu should be viewed as a fulfillment of the obligation הבו גודל לאלהינו that is mandated by the כי שם ה' אקרא of verse 3.* The title of the current chapter announces that we are about to analyze verse 6. I am going to have to ask your forgiveness, because on the basis of how I now read verse 6, I am going to have to back down a little. I am going to argue that verse 6, although loosely tied to verses 4 and 5, is not completely congruent with them. I will demonstrate that although verses 4, 5, and 6 are all indeed spoken in fulfillment of הבו גודל לאלהינו, verse 6 plays a role in this exercise that is not identical with that played by verses 4 and 5.** Sorry for the complication! I hope that when we are done you will agree that handling things as I did was a good idea.

It became clear to me that I would have to rethink the nature of verse 6 when I noticed that, while verses 4 and 5 are written in the third person (נסתר), verse 6 switches to the second person (נוכח). There must be a reason.*** ¹ What might that reason be?

And that question, dear Reader, is the wrong one to ask at this point. Here is why. Before we seek to understand how a given sentence fits in with its neighbors, we need to understand it on its own terms. I suggest that logic demands that we ask three questions in sequence—a sequence in which the question that we posed in the previous paragraph comes in a distant third. Here are the questions:

---

* Try looking back at chapter 14. The current essay really deals with the proposals that we made there. You will stand on more solid ground here if you feel at home with what we said there.

** I left the wording that I used in chapter 14 intact. This way you can, if you so wish, read what I wrote there together with what I am about to write here and, by contrasting the two passages, have a clearer picture of what I am doing here.

*** Endnote 1 is going to be long and a little complicated. You can skip it if you like—you do not need it for understanding the current chapter—but if you can summon the required energy, I think that you will find it rewarding.

130

1. What is being said?
2. Could the author have conveyed the same idea by using a different style? If he could, why did he choose as he chose?
3. What is the function of this sentence within the context in which it appears? How does it relate to what went before and to what is to follow?

I think that we will all do better if we have the pesukim in front of us. Here they are.*

ד. הצור תמים פעלו כי כל דרכיו משפט אל אמונה ואין עול צדיק וישר הוא. ה. שחת לו לא בניו מומם דור עקש ופתלתל. ו. ה'** ליהוה תגמלו זאת עם נבל ולא חכם הלוא הוא אביך קנך הוא עשך ויכננך.

4. The Rock! All that He initiates is wholly good [and will be seen through to the end], for the paths that He follows are always harmoniously balanced [between justice and mercy]. He is a mighty God Who can be fully trusted. He is both righteous and trustworthy. 5. The ugly behavior of His sons caused Him great damage because in its wake they became His "non-sons." They are an evil and twisted people.*** 6. What? Is it to HaShem that, through stupidity, you repay kindness with evil?**** Are you not aware that He is your Father Who made you and fashioned***** you?

Let us remember that we are interested in verse 6. If we

---

* As is to be expected in a poetic work, these verses are difficult to translate. I will paraphrase and, as much as is possible, will weave Ramban's ideas into my rendering.

** R. Samson Rafael Hirsch points out that this "הַ," which is essentially a question mark, is written by itself in the Torah. It stands alone, unattached to any question. If I understood him correctly, he reads this as an amplification of the sheer problematics of such foolish behavior. The shadow of a question mark hangs over the entire enterprise.

*** My rendering of this verse is based upon my analysis of Ramban's ideas in chapter 16.

**** The rendering of נבל as *ingrate* follows Ramban.

***** See below where we explain this rendition based on Ibn Ezra to Tehilim 119:73.

are to follow the sequence that we suggested above, we should ask ourselves what this pasuk wants to convey to us. That, of course, is not difficult. The pasuk makes an observation (in the form of a rhetorical question) that one who ignores all the favors that he has received from the Ribono shel Olam and acts contrary to the Ribono shel Olam's will reveals himself to be a disgusting person (= נבל [נבלה is a *disgusting act*], in this case by his ingratitude) and a fool (ולא חכם).

Could the author have conveyed the same message using a different style? Of course he could. He could either have addressed the people using a declarative statement instead of a rhetorical question: "You are boors and fools for being ingrates!" Alternatively he could have simply made a statement without addressing it to the people: "Lack of gratitude reveals a boorish and stupid personality!"

Why, given these other possibilities, did he choose the rhetorical question? It seems to me that we have here a lesson in effective תוכחה, the obligation to reprove a sinner rather than remaining passive, hating him for the evil that he does, without helping him to improve.* It is no easy task to fulfill the mitzvah of *Tochachah* in the best possible way. Two needs have to be weighed very carefully against each other if the thing is to be done correctly. Obviously the arrow of reprimand must be aimed true. If what you say is not going to be effective, it were better left unsaid. At the same time, the Torah stresses that the sinner is not to be embarrassed. A very fine balance must be struck.

By simply learning Chumash, we can pick up some valuable pointers. A question, even if rhetorical, can be a very effective tool. A statement, "You were wrong to do this or that!" triggers a defensive reaction: "Who are you to arrogate to yourself the role of the all-knowing arbiter of right and wrong? You are trespassing into my private zone, a place in which strangers, particularly strangers with holier-than-thou pretensions, are not welcome. Please see yourself to the door and do not bother to come again!" By contrast, a question makes no de-

---

* See VaYikra 19:17 and Rambam, Dei'os 6:7 and onward.

mands. It invites your interlocutor to think things through together with you and to get to the bottom of the issue. It does not, in and of itself, threaten. Yosef HaTzadik knew this secret. He knew that the moment he revealed himself to his brothers he would have to address the matter of their guilt. He did not avoid his responsibility. But all he did was to ask a question (Bereishis 45:3): "[After all that has transpired] can my father really still be alive?" That was all that it took. Those three words (העוד אבי חי?), couched in the form of a question, penetrated all the defenses in which the brothers had sought shelter all those terrible years.*

We can understand why Moshe Rabbeinu chose to use the rhetorical question in verse 6.

We are finally ready to approach the matter of context. Does verse 6 follow logically upon verses 4 and 5? Does it lead smoothly into the shirah proper, beginning at verse 7? It seems to me that it fares poorly on both counts. Verses 4 and 5 describe the integrity and the blamelessness of the Ribono shel Olam. Verse 6 is a Tochachah addressed by Moshe Rabbeinu to the people, personally (he uses the second person) and passionately (see the second footnote on page 131 on the alone-standing הַ). It cannot, in any sense, be seen as a smooth-flowing continuation from the theological thesis (held at arm's length by the use of the third person) propounded in verses 4 and 5.

It is also not a part of the shirah proper that, as we have worked out many times in previous chapters, begins with verse 7.

So verse 6 stands alone and must be understood on its own terms. These comprise both text and positioning. Let us see what we can work out.

I would like to be able to pin down the mood of this pasuk. Is its entire message one of harsh criticism, or can we catch glimpses of encouragement and hope? Looking at the relevant page of a Mikra'os Gedolos Chumash is an exercise in

---

* Bil'am's donkey used the same strategy (BeMidbar 22:30). "Think things over," he said to Bil'am, "have I ever acted this way before?!"

frustration. There seem to be as many different ways of learning as there are commentators. How am I supposed to pick
and choose?

For reasons that will become clear as we move along, I have
decided to go with the Targum while, at the same time, drawing upon some of the Chazal that Rashi quotes. I think this
will leave us with a coherent understanding of verses 4, 5, and
6 as a single unit. In order to understand Targum's rendering
we will go to Ramban, who has something to say about it.

Here is Targum's rendering of עמא דקבילו אורייתא ולא חכם:עם נבל ולא חכם
ולא חכימו, *a people who received the Torah but failed to become wise*
[through its study]. Now, obviously this is not a word-for-word
translation since the text says nothing about receiving the
Torah. From where did the Targum draw his ideas? Ramban
tells us. The root word, נ ב ל, can have two meanings. The first
is *to wilt like a flower that has lost its freshness*. The second is *to*
act in an offensive manner. Ramban suggests that the Targum
took נבל in the first sense. Now *wilting* is a close relative to acting apathetically, or allowing oneself to become bored. The
Torah occasionally borrows the term in order to use it in that
sense. Thus, when Yisro advised Moshe Rabbeinu to appoint
assistant judges, he told him that, if he continued trying to do
everything on his own, נבל תבול, *you will exhaust yourself, losing*
the cutting edge of your brilliant mind with all that that entails.
The work was simply too much for one man.

It is with this meaning in mind that Targum understood
our pasuk. You did not become wise (ולא חכם) because you
lacked enthusiasm for your studies. You were lethargic when
you should have been excited, bored when you should have
been borne high upon the energy generated by your creativ-
ity (עם נבל).

How terrible is that? If we were to make a graph plotting
the severity of various sins, where would studying the Torah
lackadaisically come in? Is it really so important to be a חכם?

The answer is an unqualified "Yes!" And that is so particularly in the context of Ha'azinu. You surely remember that,
in chapter 7C, we worked out how, after the Haflagah, the
Ribono shel Olam decided to make us His segulah, the nation

that would carry the message of His glory through history. We, with our "seventy" vested in our persons, were to be pitted against the nations whose "seventy" was to be vested in the countries that they would occupy.* That is all very well, but on what was the Ribono shel Olam's expectation of our ultimate victory based? Our secret weapon was our חכמת התורה.** To have failed to appreciate what the Torah has to offer us, to have attended the Beis HaMidrash as dilettantes, blind to the implications, is to have dropped the ball[2] in the game of history.

Let us assume that we have understood the first half of verse 6 correctly, at least as Targum sees it. What do we do with the second half? How do we read it? I believe that there are two ways in which this could be handled, and I believe that both of them are true! In essence, there is an intended ambiguity.

Here is what I mean. It is true that the second half of verse 6 can easily be read as a continuation of the Tochachah begun in the first. Its thrust is to harden and sharpen the criticism that the first half articulated. The fact that the Ribono shel Olam is a loving father who had moved mountains to place success within our grasp underscores the heinousness of our uncaring attitude. The Ribono shel Olam had not asked much of us. Why could we not have tried harder?

However, there is also another possibility, and, as I mentioned earlier, I believe that it, too, as much as the first, inheres in the text.

I base my contention upon an apparent textual irregularity in the first half of verse 6. It occurs to me that there seems to be no very good reason to express תגמלו in the future tense. Surely the criticism leveled at us concerns what has already transpired. We are *now* an עם נבל ולא חכם because we had frit-

---

* If you do not remember all this from chapter 7C, I urge you to at least skim through it once more now. It is crucial that you should be comfortable with what I am writing in the current chapter, and that cannot happen without chapter 7C.

** ושמרתם ועשיתם כי הוא חכמתכם ובינתכם לעיני העמים אשר ישמעון את כל החקים האלה ואמרו רק **עם** חכם **ונבון הגוי הגדול הזה**.

tered our time away *in the past.** So why not גמלתם instead of תגמלו?

I want to argue that verse 6 speaks in two voices. The harshness of its criticism (voice 1) is tempered by intimations of a better, more productive future (voice 2). Unrelieved reproach can go only so far. Hope, and only hope, is the sugar that makes the medicine go down.[3] And the second voice offers hope aplenty. In view of the unexpected future tense of תגמלו, we can suggest the following paraphrase of the pasuk: *Are you going to continue upon the dead-end practices of your past? Look at yourselves in a mirror. Are you not disgusted by what you see? An* עם נבל ולא חכם*! Can you not dream of something better? Remember Whose love you are spurning. It is the father Who has nurtured you and always provided you with your every need. Can you not see how happy He would be to stretch out a helping hand were you to initiate a change of direction?*

I believe that Rashi's treatment of "קנך" אביך is directed to this second, entirely positive reading of the verse. Let us look at how much movement toward reconciliation he finds there.

הלא הוא אביך קנך: I do not feel adequate to the challenge of translating this phrase correctly. The root ק נ ה is generally (though I believe incorrectly[4]) translated as *to acquire.* I believe that translations such as *the One Who acquired you* or *your Master* do not fit comfortably with the subject אביך. I am going to settle for R. Samson Rafael Hirsch's rendering, *Your father Who claims you as His own.* I imagine that he believes this to be the idea expressed by Targum who offers את דיליה. I feel that Rav Hirsch's rendering fits snugly into the spirit of this passage as I read it. You can make up your minds as we go along.

In the present context, my interest focuses more on how Rashi sets about expanding the meaning. He continues, [or] שקננך, *Who provided you with a nest* (ק נ ן, *to build a nest*) *of boulders in a strongly fortified land,* [or] שתקנך, *Who provided you with all things that you would consider to be necessary for your*

---

* Compare verses 15 and 16: וישמן ישורון ויבעט uses the conversive וי"ו to create the past tense from the future, and שמנת עבית . . . is in past perfect. It seems to me that that, not the future tense, is the handling of the material that logic demands.

comfort (ק ן ת, *to effect an improvement*). Rashi is clearly going for superlatives. The phrase seems to be saying, "Look how forthcoming and generous the Ribono shel Olam has been in all His dealings with you! Think how eager He would be to help if you demonstrated an interest in making your way back home!"

For הוא עשך ויכוננך I am going to go to Tehilim 119:73. That verse reads, ידיך עשוני ויכוננוני ואלמדה מצותיך, *Your hands made me and fashioned me; grant me understanding so that I may learn Your commandments*. Ibn Ezra (there) renders ויכוננוני, *You have made me a vessel ready to be filled with understanding*. If we assume the same meaning for the two words in our verse, everything in the verse, as we have interpreted it, ties together very well.

Well, we have done what we have set out to do as far as the translation of verse 6 is concerned. Now we come to our final task. What can we say about the positioning of the verse?

So, what is this verse doing here?

I think it is Moshe Rabbeinu himself, translating the הבו גודל לאלהינו of verses 4 and 5 into a final מוסר שמוע to his potentially wayward children.* The last *shiur* that he is going to deliver as he ends his career of forty years as *rosh hayeshivah* to the דור המדבר and to all subsequent generations is going to be on the sugia of הבו גודל לאלהינו. It is not to be merely a formal pronouncement. The וידעת היום must be translated into a והשבתה אל לבבך. All else is commentary.

Before we leave this topic behind, we will need to revisit chapter 4, where we discussed how Chazal thought of Ha'azinu as שירת משה, as somehow related to Moshe Rabbeinu more than the שירת הים and the שירת הבאר. There is some heavy thinking to be done. Come, join me in a voyage of discovery in the final essays of this book.

---

* כל המלמד את בן חברו תורה, מעלה עליו הכתוב כאלו ילדו (סנהדרין יט:).

137

שירת משה א'
The Thesis Developed in Chapter Four Revisited I

*T*he detailed analysis of verse 6 that we offered in the previous chapter was made possible by the fact that it was Moshe Rabbeinu who spoke the six introductory verses* in the first person, thus, apparently, in his own name. What precisely is Moshe Rabbeinu's relationship to Ha'azinu? The time has come to revisit the ideas that we first discovered in chapter 4.** There we found a number of midrashim that use the name "שירת משה" to describe Ha'azinu. That was an exciting find and we tried to make the most of it in that chapter. However, we have never yet discussed the parameters that set the limits to the implied "ownership"*** of Ha'azinu that, in some form, was apparently granted to Moshe Rabbeinu. The time has come to examine that very difficult topic. In what sense is Ha'azinu Moshe's shirah?[1]

Shiras Moshe (Ha'azinu) is the fifth in a series of ten שירות of which midrashim speak.**** It occurs to me that in at least two very significant ways שירת משה, or, as we know it, Ha'azinu, is unique among the ten שירות.

The first noteworthy difference is in the impetus for reciting the shirah. Maharal (Netzach Yisrael 43) defines the cir-

---

* See chapter 14 where I first introduced the idea that the first six verses in Ha'azinu are to be viewed as an introduction to the shirah proper. I have made reference to this assumption in a number of other essays.

** The Prologue with which this book begins was written after I had already written chapter 4. In that Prologue I discuss the affinity between Moshe Rabbeinu and Ha'azinu. What I wrote there was based upon the research I had done when writing chapter 4. The ideas I am about to develop in this and the coming chapters should be viewed as a continuation of what I wrote in the Prologue and in chapter 4.

*** The "ת" at the end of "שירת" puts שירה into the construct or סמיכות form. Thus it is the shirah of Moshe Rabbeinu. Our challenge is to find out in what sense the possessive voice is meaningful in this context.

**** Please take the time to glance at endnote 1.

cumstances that, all being equal, would coax a שירה out of a community or an individual.*

והאדם כאשר הוא בשלימות הגמור, אז נותן שירה ושבח למי שממנו השלימות. והפך זה הוא האבל, שהגיע לו ההפך, שהוא ההעדר והמיתה, הוא יושב ודומם, ולא יפתח את פיו. אבל כאשר הוא בשלימות, והוא בפעל הגמור, אז מוציא גם כן הדבר אל הפעל, ונותן שירה ושבח אל השם יתברך, שממנו השלמות.

Shirah is a concretization of appreciation and gratitude that may be said to burst forth from a person when he finds himself entirely fulfilled. It can be said to be an instinctive urge to repay in some appropriate way the goodness of the Ribono shel Olam in allowing ourselves to luxuriate in the fullness to which our potential has been realized.

I noted in the first footnote below that it is difficult to understand Maharal even in the original, and translating him correctly is almost impossible. I am not particularly enamored of my paraphrase, but it will have to do. The point that Maharal is making seems to be clear enough. We might say that he defines shirah as the palpable joy of fulfillment[2] evinced in song. Now, I believe that to be true of the other nine shiros. It is most certainly not true of Ha'azinu.[3] So in what sense is Ha'azinu a shirah?

The other difference between Ha'azinu and the other nine shiros is equally troubling. As far as I can tell, the texts of the nine other shiros were composed by the people who sang them. The Torah (or, in some of the shiros, TaNaCh) records what the people sang as it records many of the other actions that they took or words that they spoke. However, from all appearances, the text of Ha'azinu was given by the Ribono shel Olam** to Moshe Rabbeinu to teach the people. If, as

* We will not expect to understand this Maharal fully. Maharal's ideas are very profound; his language is largely idiosyncratic. Without a solid acquaintanceship with the entire Maharal corpus, it is practically impossible to really grasp what he is saying. For our purpose, even a simplistic reading will suffice.
** וטעם השירה "הזאת" השירה אשר אגיד לך עתה (Ramban to Devarim 32:19).

Ramban in Devarim 32:19 maintains, this was to be a song that the Jews would always be singing,* that would not be a spontaneous shirah welling up inside them.**

It almost seems to me that שירת משה is a kind of interloper in the list of ten shiros with which we have been dealing. It strikes me that it can hardly be called a שירה in the same sense that that name is appropriate to the other nine.

So where do we go from here?

I think that I can suggest a reasonable answer to these questions, but I feel myself on shaky ground. Here is why. When we set out to understand a parshah in Chumash, the most direct path, which at the same time offers ironclad protection against getting things very wrong, is to read it through the eyes of the meforshim who, over the centuries, have become accepted by Klal Yisrael as the arbiters of acceptable *parshonus*. If you have read this book up to here and have perhaps read some of the other volumes in this series, you will have noticed that I have tried to be guided mainly by Rashi and Ramban. That system has served me well. It cannot serve me in the present instance since, as far as I can tell, neither of them has asked these questions*** nor offered remarks (except for one very small one in the Ramban—see below) that would have indicated that they were grappling with these issues.

Please accompany me on my search and let us see where it will lead.

I would like to begin with some thoughts about the term "השירה הזאת[4] that occurs no less than five times (in VaYeilech) between Devarim 31:19 and 31:30. In addition, it occurs once more in Ha'azinu at Devarim 32:44. In a moment I will ex-

---

* ‏(Devarim 32:19) ויקראה שירה כי ישראל יאמרוה תמיד בשיר ובזמרה. . .‏

** As I was sitting in front of my screen waiting for inspiration, the following contrast suddenly occurred to me. At the שירת הים we have משה ובני ישראל לך ענו שירה (*siddur*), in VaYeilech we have וענתה השירה הזאת לפניו לעד (Devarim 31:21). That is a big difference, is it not?

*** I can just hear some of you saying that, on the contrary, they have guided me very clearly. By their silence they have indicated that there is no room for asking these questions. That argument does not work very well for me. תורה היא וללמד אני צריך.

plain why even the first usage of the word seems to me to be difficult. Certainly the following five times seem problematic. Here is why. "This" is a "determiner," the function of which is to separate a particular unit from others like it that were in the running: "I would like *this* suit" [not any of the others]. It would seem to me that once that suit has been "determined" by "this," there is no reason to reiterate the fact that it, and none other, was chosen. We would find nothing strange if the customer at the clothing store, after having determined which suit he wants, and having made this clear to the salesman, would then say, "Please be kind enough to put the suit [clearly, the one that I determined earlier] in a bag." Why did "הזאת" have to be repeated each time that השירה was mentioned?

In the case of Ha'azinu, even the first use of הזאת is difficult. Let us first note that according to the mesorah of Chazal the words הזה and הזאת are more than simple determiners. They are said to indicate an actual presence, sometimes physical, sometimes less than actually physical, of the object that is being determined. It can be seen and it is possible to point a finger at it.*

The first time that השירה הזאת appears in VaYeilech is in verse 19. Let us show verses 18 and 19 together and we shall immediately be struck by the difficulty.

יח. . . . . ואנכי הסתר אסתיר פני ביום ההוא על כל הרעה אשר עשה כי פנה אל אלהים אחרים. יט. ועתה כתבו לכם את השירה הזאת ולמדה את בני ישראל שימה בפיהם למען תהיה לי השירה הזאת לעד בבני ישראל:

I will completely hide My face on that day because of the evil that they will have done in that they turned to idol

---

* This story begins at Shemos 12:2, החדש **הזה** לכם ראש חדשים . . . where Rashi remarks: הראהו לבנה בחדושה. Maharal in Gur Aryeh there writes, מלשון "זה" הוא דמפיק דמילת זה מוכח על דבר הרמוז. . . . (See Rav Hartman there on רמוז.) Rav Hartman cites Menachos 29a, שלושה דברים היו קשין למשה עד שהראה לו הקב"ה בעצמו, ואלו הן, מנורה, וראש חדש ושרצים. He points out that in each of these three cases the word "זה" appears. Now it is clear from Rashi that this interpretation of זה or זאת is a דרשה rather than פשט, since immediately after he brings the Chazal that the Ribono shel Olam showed Moshe Rabbeinu לבנה בחדושה he continues, ואין מקרא יוצא מידי פשוטו, על חדש ניסן אמר לו זה. . . .

worship. So now, write for yourselves this shirah and teach it to the Israelites, make them learn it by heart, in order that this shirah might serve Me as testimony for the Israelites.

Verse 18 is the last verse in a series of pesukim in which our perfidy is described in detail. Verse 19 introduces the Ribono shel Olam's reaction to all this evil. He commands Moshe Rabbeinu to write השירה הזאת and to teach it to the benei Yisrael thoroughly, until they know it by heart.

What can "הזאת" השירה possibly mean in this context? The text of the shirah is not given here, so it is not comparable to שירת הים and שירת הבאר. There is certainly no indication that the Ribono shel Olam showed Moshe Rabbeinu anything at this point, or, indeed, that Moshe Rabbeinu had any idea what might be the subject of this shirah. In what sense is there any specificity that would justify the "זאת"?

I mentioned earlier that there is one very small Ramban from which it appears that he felt called upon to explain the use of "זאת." He writes, וטעם השירה הזאת, השירה אשר אגיד לך עתה. Now, if Ramban feels that this would justify the "זאת," that is something that we must accept.* However, I personally still feel very far out at sea since nowhere in either VaYeilech or Ha'azinu do we actually hear that the Ribono shel Olam told the shirah to Moshe Rabbeinu. As the story unfolds it is suddenly simply there.** There is no indication at all of how it was passed from the Ribono shel Olam to Moshe Rabbeinu.

If you have kept up with me, we are all in this together. All

---

* Although it is a vastly different situation from שירת הים and שירת הבאר, where we are given the text immediately. Right after God's words, those shiros actually appear.

** The Ribono shel Olam's speech runs from verse 16 through verse 21, with verse 19 being where He tells Moshe Rabbeinu that he and Yehoshua are to write down השירה הזאת. Without any pause, verse 22 then starts, ויכתוב משה את השירה הזאת ביום ההוא. . . . Ramban is silent. I imagine that had he written something it would have been, ". . . Moshe Rabbeinu wrote the shirah that he had now been told." Ramban to Shemos 34:27 makes the point that occasionally the Torah does not spell out the obvious: אבל לא חשש הכתוב להאריך לאמר ויעש כן משה, כאשר הראיתיך במקומות רבים.

of us are now faced with three questions that I have not found anywhere else.

1. The situations under which we are to make use of Ha'azinu וְהָיָה כִּי תִמְצֶאןָ אֹתוֹ רָעוֹת רַבּוֹת וְעָנְתָה הַשִּׁירָה הַזֹּאת לְפָנָיו לְעֵד, certainly do not qualify under Maharal's description* of the conditions under which singing a shirah would be appropriate.

2. The texts of the other nine shiros were composed by the people who had attained the שלימות of joy of which Maharal speaks. Let us look at his language once more: אבל כאשר הוא בשלימות, **והוא בפעל הגמור**, אז מוציא **גם כן הדבר אל הפעל**, ונותן שירה ושבח אל השם יתברך, שממנו השלמות. The language of the Maharal makes clear that the composition of the text is a spontaneous outpouring of love and gratitude growing from a person's sense of inner fulfillment. He has, so to speak, found in himself a persona that he had not met before. He feels the need to give that heady experience a concrete expression. Ha'azinu, a shirah that was handed down ready-made to the people, does not carry that character at all.

3. Then there is the matter of the ubiquitous הַשִּׁירָה הַזֹּאת that we discussed earlier.

In order to get where we need to get, we are going to have to do some very basic thinking about *Shiras Ha'azinu*. We will need a new chapter for that.

---

* וְהָאָדָם כַּאֲשֶׁר הוּא בִּשְׁלִימוּת הַגָּמוּר, see the full quote above in this essay.

שירת משה ב׳
The Thesis Developed in Chapter Four Revisited II

*W*e are going to have to study Ha'azinu's status as a shirah more closely than we have done till now. In what sense can Ha'azinu be said to qualify as a shirah? We are standing within sight of the end of this book, and it took us till now to ask this most fundamental of questions in quite the way that we are asking it now. That stands to reason. In almost every chapter in this book we learned something new, often something unexpected. We are better informed now than we were when we started. We can be a little more sophisticated.

Clarity sweeps clean. We are on the way to discovering some very basic truths. Everything is going to work out just fine.

Let us check our inventory of facts and questions; look at them with fresh eyes, and just stand back.

Here is what we have:

1. In contrast to other shiros that were made up on the spot, Ha'azinu's text is provided.
2. Where other shiros are bursts of irrepressible joy, much of Ha'azinu sounds very much like an elegy. And still the Ribono shel Olam calls it a shirah! How can that be?
3. The Torah goes out of its way to stress that somehow, in some way, Ha'azinu must always be regarded as השירה הזאת.

There now. Once we break things down clearly, they do not look so threatening.

We will find that these three givens are inextricably bound up together. And together they produce a truly wonderful picture.

THE SHIROS OF THE NIGHT

In the excursus to endnote 3 of the previous chapter, we came upon a concept that was completely new to me. Among the heavenly choristers there are those who sing praises to the

Ribono shel Olam by day and those who do it at night. Of the two, the night singers are looked upon as an aristocracy. It is not difficult to fathom the reason. The night is a time of worry (אמונתך בלילות) and trepidation (שמדת הדין שולטת בלילה). It cannot be an easy task to dredge its secrets for that which might yield a *shir*. By contrast, the day (בבקר חסדיך) is a natural environment for song.

The passage that we quoted there goes on to say that the gates of wisdom swing open for those who understand the songs of the night. Small wonder! Those songs will be understood only by those who are able and motivated to dig beneath the surface, who are citizens in the world of essence rather than in that in which form reigns supreme.

Can there be any doubt but that Ha'azinu, with all the hurt and disappointment that fill its forty-three pesukim, is a "night song"? Does it not stand to reason that a song that is designed to give courage when *they are beset by many evils and distresses* (Devarim 31:21) would require superhuman talent to find the right words, to hit upon the perfect mix between stricture and comfort that would enable it to do its job? When we get right down to it we are no longer surprised that the text for Ha'azinu was prescribed by the Ribono shel Olam Himself. It was really the only way.

In this section I was really only aiming to deal with the issue that I labeled #1. However, without even trying, we have also solved #3. I am convinced that the ubiquitous הזאת that gave us so much trouble in the previous chapter can also now be readily explained. When I broached the issue in the previous chapter, I had mistakenly thought that all the uses of "הזאת" are, so to speak, created equal. I unsuccessfully attempted to force our הזאת into companionship with החדש הזה and the other examples that we cited there. In those instances the object for which the "this" is the determiner is said to be an almost tangible presence, something at which one can point. That, of course, was not going to work here, and most certainly it was not helpful in explaining the seemingly unreasonable number of times that it was repeated.

In light of what we have now learned, the matter seems to

me to be self-explanatory. The function of הזאת in השירה הזאת is not at all related to the function of the determiners in those other cases. Here its purpose is to insist that in times of trouble, *this* SHIRAH and none other is to be recited. It is as we have just said. "Songs of the Night" are different.

INTRODUCING A THREESOME

We are not doing badly. The first and third items in our inventory seem to have been tackled successfully. We are going to have to work a little harder on the middle one, but everything will work out fine in the end.

Here is the strategy that I am going to follow. I will argue that Ha'azinu does not stand on its own. The irregularities that seem to engrave a hovering question mark over the whole experience of Ha'azinu as a shir will be neutralized once we judge Ha'azinu in the context of a group. I will suggest that Ha'azinu is part of a threesome consisting of itself, the *Shiras HaYam,* and מזמור שיר ליום השבת, which, for the rest of this essay, we will identify as *Shiras HaShabbos.*

HA'AZINU AND SHIRAS HASHABBOS

In this essay we will not have to expend any effort in tracing the relatedness of these two shiros. The entire issue is treated in the Introduction. Please do go there and read it. There really is no point in repeating everything here.

HA'AZINU AND SHIRAS HAYAM

This is a matter upon which we have not yet touched in this book. Let us begin with a Rambam in Hilchos Tefilah 7:13.

יש מקומות שנהגו בהן לקרות בכל יום אחר שמברכין ישבתח שירת הים
ואחר כך מברכין על שמע ויש מקומות שקורין שירת האזינו ויש יחידים
שקורין שתי השירות הכל לפי המנהג.

There are communities who, every day after they have said *Yishtabach,* recite the *Shiras HaYam* and then continue with the recitation of the kri'as Shema blessings. There are other communities who substitute *Shiras Ha'azinu* [for the *Shiras HaYam*]. There are also individuals who recite both shiros. Everybody follows their own custom.

I had no idea that this Rambam existed and certainly had not realized that in some communities, vestiges of these customs are alive and well, at least on Tish'ah Be'Av. My good friend R. Eliyahu Hakakian brought the following Ben Ish Chai (already noted in endnote 1 to chapter 10) to my attention.

גם עוד המנהג פה עירנו בגדא"ד לומר האזינו במקום שירת הים וגם בדבר זה לא שניתי מנהגם של הציבור, ורק אני אומר שירת הים כמו כל יום ושירת האזינו אני אומר אותה אחר העמידה, וכן עושים החכמים ויראים ואנשי מעשה.

In our city, Baghdad, it is the custom to recite Ha'azinu instead of the *Shiras HaYam*. I decided not to make any changes in that custom as far as the community is concerned. However, for myself, I recite *Shiras HaYam* as I do every day and leave the recitation of Ha'azinu to the end of prayers. Many great and pious sages do just that.

We have reached a point at which we will have to do for *Shiras HaYam* here what we did for *Shiras HaShabbos* in the Introduction. We will have to find the central theme of *Shiras HaYam* and try to understand its affinity to both Ha'azinu and *Shiras HaShabbos*.

Those of you who still delight in the Sefas Emes to whom we devoted chapters 7–10 will be pleased that for *Shiras HaYam*, too, his will be the shining light that we will follow.

Here is the Sefas Emes. It is taken from BeShalach תרל"ה.

ענין קי"ס אחר יצ"מ. כי יצ"מ הי' לצורך גאולת ישראל בלבד. אבל לא נתברר עדיין כבוד מלכותו ית' אשר היא בכל משלה. להודיע שגם כח פרעה וחילו וכל כח הסט"א הכל ע"פ השגחה עליונה. ובקי"ס נתברר זה [והוא מ"ש יתרו עתה ידעתי כו' כי בדבר אשר זדו עליהם]. וזה ענין השירה מה

שבוררו בנ"י כי כל הבריאה היא המשכה אחת מרום מעלות עד תהום רבה.
וזהו כי גאה גאה. כי מלך ב"ו המתגאה על מלך אחר. גאותו מבטל גיאות
השני. אבל גיאות הקב"ה הוא בעוד קיים גיאות המלכיות שבארץ. וע"ז
הוא נורא עלילה עליהם. ועושה בהם כרצונו. וז"ש סוס ורוכבו רמה כו'.

[Kri'as Yam Suf has much to teach us even after all the miracles that accompanied the Exodus. This is so because] the process by which the Israelites won their freedom from Egypt had been set in motion for one reason only: it was time for the Jews to be emancipated. Nothing that happened as part of this process was directed toward illuminating the full glory of the Ribono shel Olam in that He is in absolute control of all that happens in this world. But that glory needs to be taught. Whatever Pharaoh in his awesome might had been able to accomplish, all the insidious evil that the powers of evil, the סט"א, are able to perpetrate, succeeded, and succeed only because God wishes it to happen. . . . This truth is the subject of the *Shiras HaYam*. It glories in the insight that all that takes place in our world, from the highest spheres to the most bottomless depths, is one fully integrated whole, set in motion by nothing other than the Ribono shel Olam's will.

That is the significance of the doubled גאה גאה. The fact is that a king who sets out to subdue a rival must first undermine that rival's triumphs; he has first to "unseat" his intended victim from his "horse." The Ribono shel Olam has no such needs. The king whom He seeks to conquer may be at the very peak of his glory—riding, as it were, unfettered, upon his horse—the Ribono shel Olam can still do with him whatever He wishes. . . .

It is interesting that when Miriam gathered the women to dance and to jubilate, she chose only this one verse—אשירה לה' כי גאה גאה סוס ורכבו רמה בים—to give voice to their hearts' promptings.

The mightiest monarch does nothing, can do nothing, that is not already willed by the Ribono shel Olam.[1] No *auto da fe* was ever forced upon us by the bloodthirsty inquisitors, no

crematorium ever spewed our ashes heavenward, no whip-
lash swished upon our poor defenseless bodies, but that the
Ribono shel Olam brought it about for our and the world's ultimate good.[2] It is that knowledge, not the litany of miracles
of which *Shiras HaYam* then begins to sing, that stimulated
the shirah. אשירה לה' כי גאה גאה סוס ורכבו רמה בים. Note the "כי." The
deep understanding that lies in those simple six words is the
essence of *Shiras HaYam*. It is this that places *Shiras HaYam*
right next to Ha'azinu and *Shiras HaShabbos* to form the threesome of which we spoke.

THE TRIUMVIRATE OF SHIRAS HASHABBOS, SHIRAS HAYAM, AND HA'AZINU

Here is my thesis. I argue that this threesome, *Shiras
HaShabbos, Shiras HaYam,* and *Shiras Ha'azinu,* are in a class of
their own, can in fact be considered like a single shirah with
three installments. *Shirim,* as a group, focus on the event that
they seek to celebrate. These three focus on the Ribono shel
Olam. They salute the "All," the Ribono shel Olam, His world
and the yichud, the coherent "oneness" that breathes life into
it all.

These three shirim span history. Adam sang *Shiras
HaShabbos* on the Shabbos of Bereishis. Moshe Rabbeinu
sang *Shiras HaYam* at the Yam Suf as we took our first uncer-
tain steps into history as the Ribono shel Olam's people. The
Ribono shel Olam handed us Ha'azinu as we were about to
enter Eretz Yisrael. It would be our companion on the long
hard road to *Acharis HaYamim.*

World history runs its course against the background music of these great songs, "one" mighty song celebrating the one
Mighty Ribono shel Olam.

WE RETURN TO THE SECOND ITEM ON THE INVENTORY, DEFINE THE REAL PROBLEM, AND FINALLY OFFER WHAT I BELIEVE TO BE AN ACCEPTABLE SOLUTION

Please read how I worded the second item in the inventory of problems earlier in this essay. We can harden the difficulty considerably by returning to the rule formulated by the late Brisker Rov, which we quoted in endnote 2 of the previous chapter, this time together with a paraphrase. Here is the quote:

ואני בחסדך בטחתי יגל לבי בישועתך אשירה לה' כי גמל עלי. ובשם הגר"ח. דיש לעיין ממתי אפשר לומר שירה על הנס, האם רק אחר שקרה כבר הנס, או גם אם יהא לבו בטוח שיקרה נס, וכגון שנביא שיאמר לו כן, יכול כבר לומר שירה על הנס. וזהו דמבואר בפסוק הנ"ל "ואני בחסדך בטחתי" היינו דבטוח רק בחסדך אזי רק "יגל לבי בישועתך," יש לי שמחה ע"ז, אבל מתי "אשירה לה'," דאומר שירה הוא רק "כי גמל עלי," כשקורה ונהיה הנס כבר.

R. Chaim Brisker wondered whether it is permissible to sing shirah in gratitude for a miracle that has not yet happened, but which the person involved feels certain will happen. An example would be a case in which a true prophet has prophesied that salvation will certainly come about.

He adduces Tehilim 13:6, ואני בחסדך בטחתי יגל לבי בישועתך אשירה לה' כי גמל עלי, *As for me, I feel certain of your kindness, my heart rejoices in [the anticipation of] your deliverance. I will sing a* SHIRAH *to HaShem for He has [already] dealt kindly with me.* David is certain that God will deal kindly with him and his certainty permits his heart to rejoice in anticipation of that deliverance. However, shirah will only be possible after *He has [already] dealt kindly.* Feeling happy is one thing; singing shirah is another. For that, the anticipation is insufficient. The *kindness* must already have occurred.

The rule seems clear enough, but it appears to constitute a devastating problem for much of what we have written about Ha'azinu as shirah. Throughout the book, but particularly in chapters 7–10 where we discussed the ideas of the Sefas Emes, we have grappled with the difficult problem of why Ha'azinu, full as it is with descriptions of dreadful suffering, should be considered a shirah. All the explanations that we offered defended Ha'azinu's shirah status by discovering something wonderful that the horrors could never hide lurking beneath the surface.

If we take Sefas Emes's ideas as an example, he maintains that there was always the redeeming feature that the Ribono shel Olam's presence is with us in even the most difficult moments. That certainly makes us feel warm and loved and can engender much comfort while we drag along under the often heavy yoke of our destiny. There were also other ideas, scattered throughout the book, that, each in its own way, found gold under the rubble of history's black holes.

There is no doubt that all this thinking turned up silver linings to many dark clouds. However, *none* of these helpful sparks seem adequate to deal with the כי גמל עלי requirement. At the end of the day, the Ribono shel Olam still told Moshe Rabbeinu that Ha'azinu was to be our help when *they will have been beset by many constricting troubles*. Under any definition, such a time can never have risen to the Brisker Rov's criterion. Ha'azinu seems simply not to measure up.

This is the *real* problem. At this point it seems rather hopeless, does it not?

I am ready to offer my solution. It is this:

I believe that once we accept the idea of a triumvirate consisting of *Shiras HaShabbos, Shiras HaYam*, and Ha'azinu, each of which is focused not upon a particular event but upon the yichud of the Ribono shel Olam, the problem simply disappears. The requirement that things must have developed to a state of "גמל עלי" is applicable only when a shirah is called forth by the roiling forces of a particular event. When that is the case, it is possible to ask at what stage in the developments a shirah would be appropriate. When the shirah is unattached to any particular event but is an exaltation of the Ribono shel Olam, then the stage of "גמל עלי" has been reached countless times since the very first moment of Creation. There is never a moment in anybody's life at which the adoration expressed in Ha'azinu is any less than totally appropriate.

A Fond Look Backwards

The time has come to bring this long and difficult book to a close. If you have stayed with me from the beginning, you will know what I mean when I say that what we have left unsaid far exceeds what we have discussed. That is just the way it is. The book is already much larger than the others in the series of which it is a part. That admitted, I still hope that it will prove useful by providing a coherent framework within which further learning and analysis can take place.

And take place it should. Most of us know far too little about this precious gift that the Ribono shel Olam gave us.

In this final chapter I would like to revisit an old question that has dogged me throughout the book and also to broach one that I have not mentioned before. I will deal with the second one first.

By now we are all familiar with the Ramban to verse 16. It is in that verse that he contends, apparently intuitively, that the fierce criticism that Ha'azinu levels against our national behavior throughout history is limited to our having served avodah zarah. No other transgression makes the cut.* The time has come to examine why this should be so.**

To make things easier, I will quote myself from chapter 7A, where I argue that the story that Ha'azinu tells centers upon our status as a segulah treasured by the Ribono shel Olam. The confrontation between us and the "seventy nations" (augured in verse 8) is the stuff of which the history that interests Ha'azinu is made. It is because of this that Ha'azinu ends with

---

* Verse 16 mentions that we had often angered the Ribono shel Olam by engaging in "תועבות." Rashi suggests that this word refers to practice of the occult (כשפים) and deviant relationships, both of which are called תועבה (the former at Devarim 18:12, the latter at VaYikra 20:13). Ramban argues that "תועבות" in verse 16 must refer to idolatry, since no other transgressions are mentioned in Ha'azinu.

** Ramban cites no source for his contention. If anything, he notes that Rashi seems to be supported by Sifrei, which has תועבות חומר refer to deviant relations. None of the Ramban commentaries available to me make any attempt to work out what Ramban's assertion might be based on.

הרנינו גוים עמו ..., the acceptance of the reality of our special status by the nations of the world. Here is the quote:

> ... The shirah [deals] with the dynamics of [our] history. It is interested in why things happened as they did. It teaches us that everything goes back to the special relationship that we formed with the Ribono shel Olam at Sinai. It is interested in defining as clearly as possible what is involved in being the segulah of the Ribono shel Olam.... Certainly we must assume that the nations felt this difference and, needless to say, resented it. We will see ... that the story that Ha'azinu tells is the story of how, when in אחרית הימים truth fills the world, they will recognize that this too was for the best ...

If we accept this premise, it is easy enough to understand why, of all possible transgressions, it is only avodah zarah that attracts Ha'azinu's attention. No sin other than avodah zarah militates directly against our segulah status. Other shortcomings are of course bad, but have no place in Ha'azinu's particular approach to our history.

If this answer is not a particularly exciting one, it nevertheless seems adequate.[1] However, it raises a very serious question. From the time that the exiles returned from Babylon to found the Second Commonwealth, avodah zarah ceased to be a problem for us.* According to the Ramban's thesis, Ha'azinu should have lost interest at that point. However, in his concluding remarks to Ha'azinu, Ramban himself states unequivocally that Ha'azinu takes our history all the way to Moshiach's coming. What are we to make of a hiatus lasting two thousand years?

We are going to have to get used to the idea that avodah zarah is a concept that encompasses more, much more, than bowing down to graven images. We will seek guidance from the late, great R. Shlomo Wolbe in his המצוות השקולות, the

---

* See Arachin 32b, דבעי רחמי על יצר דעבודה זרה ובטליה, and Rambam, Hilchos Avodas Yom HaKipurim 1:7, בבית שני צץ המינות בישראל....

book that was his final legacy to us before his death. He cites Avodah Zarah 14b, where we have the strange statement that Avraham Avinu's Tractate Avodah Zarah comprised four hundred chapters, in contrast to ours, which has just five. R. Wolbe wonders with what those four hundred chapters might have dealt.

R. Wolbe introduces us to a whole new world of what he calls עֲרָכִים (from עֶרֶךְ or עֵרֶךְ), which we might translate as "values": things like democracy, health, food, music, sports, visiting the sick, and myriads more, that we regard as significant aspects of our lives. He postulates that every person has an ערך עליון, a *highest value* to which all his other ערכים are subordinate. In Judaism that ערך עליון would be the Ribono shel Olam.* His value to us would be absolute. All other ערכים would be relative, in the sense that they have a role to play in making us the kind of person who can ultimately relate to the Ribono shel Olam in a certain way. They could be imagined as the rungs of a "value" ladder leading from one to the next, with the Ribono shel Olam occupying the peak.

Now, let us imagine that a person would stop at a certain "value" on his way upward toward the Ribono shel Olam and decide that this value is going to be his ערך עליון. Let us postulate that he is so taken with music that he regards it as end rather than means. He feels that music satisfies his creative stirrings, lends meaning to his life, fulfillment to his soul. For this person music would cease to be a rung on the ladder leading toward the Ribono shel Olam; it would have become self-validating, standing outside the continuum of the ascending, relative values.

That, says Rav Wolbe, would in Avraham Avinu's lexicon be considered avodah zarah. No wonder that he needed four hundred chapters! In any life there are so many weighty values vying כביכול with the Ribono shel Olam for centrality. Each needs its own chapter, each its own strategy, if it is to be successfully pummeled back into its nonthreatening place among the ascending rungs.

* ....אין כערכך ה' אלהינו בעולם הזה

Ha'azinu is needed today as much as it was ever needed. The returnees from the Babylonian exile touched upon only the crass, outer surface of idolatry. It is true that we no longer have the urge to bow down before idols, but there are still multitudes of "strange"* gods** jostling for our attention.

This of course leads us straight to our first question, the one that has been bothering us from the very beginning. If Ha'azinu is still so important in our lives, why does it seem so unimportant? What has happened to us? What has happened to Ha'azinu? Why do most of us not turn to it anymore in times of trouble?

I have a solution to suggest, but feel diffident about offering it. It seems to me to be much, much weaker than the question.

For better or worse, here it is.

Let us recall that it was only Avraham Avinu's Tractate Avodah Zarah that comprised four hundred chapters. Ours has five. What does that mean? It means that Avraham experiences "value transference" as avodah zarah; we do not. Our spiritual antennae are too gross to pick up the "strangeness" vibes that are involved. We do not recognize our "idols" as idols; we do not seek out "idol medicine."

There you have it. It is the best that I can do. Perhaps, if you put your mind to it, you can do better.

In this essay I have taken care of some housekeeping and that is no trifling matter. Still, I ask myself whether there is not something more appropriate with which to end this contemplation of Ha'azinu. This is the thirteenth in the series of books that I began thirteen years ago with *A Pearl in the Sand*,*** and I do not recall that any one of the earlier twelve took over

---

* Let us remember that the "זרה" in the term *avodah zarah* translates as "strange."

** Rav Wolbe lists חכמה among the relative ערכים that might, if we are not careful, compete for the position of ערך עליון. If I understand him correctly, he means to include even Torah learning, if that is allowed to become an end in itself, divorced from the Ribono shel Olam.

*** On Shevu'os and Megilas Rus.

my life with the same fierce proprietorship that this one has exercised. I suppose that this was brought about by a sense of urgency that seemed constantly to spur me on, the feeling that I was doing something important that needed to be done. This, as we have seen in the Prologue and in many other contexts throughout the book, is *Shiras Moshe!* The least that we can do is to listen, first intelligently and then with rapture, to what he wanted us to know.

On reflection, I believe that I can turn the issues that we discussed in the earlier part of this essay into the kind of closing material for which I am looking.

What have we discovered about Ha'azinu in the current chapter that we did not know before?

It is this: Ha'azinu lives in an esoteric world of its own. It is a world in which it is deemed idolatry to raise values like music, which would be appropriate as "means," to inappropriate "end" status.* It is a world in which the most dreadful suffering can be celebrated in song. It is a world in which distance from the Ribono shel Olam is never more than illusory, where every "הוא" is really "אני." It is a world in which questions turn into answers, where the obverse side of the tapestry is what we get to see. In short, it projects a view of Acharis HaYamim to us who live as denizens in our own prosaic world.**

So what is it—an interloper if ever there was one—doing here?

That is a good question and calls for a good answer.

It requires us to give some thought to, of all things, oil. That sentence is a bit of self-indulgence. It felt like fun to shock you into wakefulness. What on earth does oil have to do with anything? The truth is that I am deadly serious and it is indeed oil that will lubricate our way out of our difficulties.

From TaNaCh we know that oil had a significant function. It was used to anoint people or objects, making it possible for them to enter into some more exalted position or use.

---

* Avraham's מדרגה.

** Each of the points made in this paragraph has been carefully and lovingly discovered and described in one of the earlier chapters. I do hope that they became friends to accompany you along the way.

What is it about oil that makes it particularly suited to the task of conferring the sanctity, responsibility, or privilege of special standing upon people or objects?

The late, great Rav Hutner offers an explanation. He postulates that oil is an otherworldly substance that, in its own right, has no place in our physical world.* If its presence here cannot be explained by its own needs, it follows that its purpose must inhere in that which it can do for others. Hence שמן becomes שמן המשחה, *the oil that anoints*, or as we might well put it, the "otherworldly entity that has come here for no other purpose than that it might anoint (read: *touch the purely physical with intimations of sanctity*) people or objects that are destined to rise beyond their current status."

I wish to contend that Ha'azinu is the שמן המשחה of the Torah.[2] As we have shown earlier in this essay, its ideas and standards are not of the present but of the future. If nevertheless the Ribono shel Olam permitted it—oil-like—to become part of our present lives, it can only be—again oil-like as in שמן המשחה—with the purpose of taking us by the hand and leading us out of the morass into which our propensity toward idol worship[3] had immersed us.

At this point I am going to quote myself from the Prologue. It is a short paragraph that asks a question and opens the possibility of finding an answer. In the Prologue I suggest an answer. I stand by that answer; I have no intention of backing down from it. Still, with the maturing of my understanding of Ha'azinu that I hope came to me by bringing this difficult

---

* Our goal in this essay is to discover why this otherworldliness makes it the ideal substance to use for anointment. The question of why oil is to be considered "otherworldly" lies outside our concerns. Here I will note only briefly that Rav Hutner believes that this standing is implied in the name שמן ש. מ נ is of course the root word from which שמונה, *eight* is built. In the number system worked out by the Maharal, six stands for our physical world, seven, for the physical world endowed with a spiritual center, and eight for the otherworldly. There is also, of course, the fact that oil does not mix with water. In the Maharal's system water is typical of the physical world (Moshe Rabbeinu *splits* the waters of the sea); oil apparently stands above that world and does not integrate into it.

book to a close, I want to suggest another answer. Both are possible; neither contradicts the other.

Here is the paragraph. It refers to the passage in VaYeilech where the Ribono shel Olam tells Moshe Rabbeinu of a poem that He is about to hand him. It is to be learned by heart and sung frequently, in effect becoming a part of the people's lives. It will stand them in good stead when the terrible suffering triggered by their obstinate cleaving to idol worship will crash down upon them.

Here is the paragraph.

To us it sounds almost bizarre. What is a poem going to do to alleviate stark tragedy? But you know, dear Reader, you and I live in times in which we ought to be as leery of glib questions as we surely are of glib answers. We have lived through times and places in which there was little more than a stubborn clinging to a half-remembered Torah to see us through. Words pack power. Moshe Rabbeinu was not shocked by what the Ribono shel Olam told him; neither should we be.

The salient phrase is the one that asserts that words pack power. What volcanic rumblings lie quiescent in Ha'azinu waiting to be released, waiting floodlike* to inundate a despairing humanity in the healing light and warmth of understanding?

We will now bring this chapter and this book to a close by quoting a passage by R. Pinchos Horowitz (the Ba'al Hafla'ah) taken from the introduction to his Kesubos commentary.

אך האור הגנוז ומופלא הזה שיאירו עינים הטהורים השכליים לא ישיגוהו האדם בהיותו עכור ומלובש בחומר הגופני כי עיני הגשמיים הם מתנגדים ומחשיכים עיני השכל . . . וכמו שכתב הרמב"ם ז"ל בחטא אדם הראשון שנתגשם בגופו ונפקחו עיניו הגשמיים אז נחשכו עיניו הרוחניים. ובתחלה קודם החטא שהאירו עיני השכלים לא היה מכיר כלל בעניני הגשמיים ומאפס ותהו נחשבו לו . . . כי העולם הזה נקרא עלמא דשקרא . . .

---

* ומלאה הארץ דעה את ה' כמים לים מכסים.

However this hidden, supernal light that was created so that it might light up the pure eyes that deal only with the spiritual cannot be apprehended by man as long as his sight is distorted by his physicality. This is so because the physical eyes not only perceive things differently than do the spiritual eyes, but actually darken the eyes of the spirit ... as Rambam writes concerning Adam's sin in eating the forbidden fruit. *As a result of this transgression his physical eyes were opened, resulting in the darkening of his spiritual sight.* Originally with his spiritual eyes he did not even see that which was purely physical; it held no interest for him. He knew that this, our physical world, is an עלמא דשיקרא, a world of falsehood ...

Ha'azinu allows us a peek into a world for which, as yet, we do not have a visa. We see what we have never seen before and all the familiar landmarks that once inveigled us into deifying the physical sink into the shadows. It beckons us to the mountaintops from where panoramas akin to those revealed to Moshe Rabbeinu atop Mount Nevo invite our scrutiny.* Ha'azinu, if we but allow it to enter our hearts, can be our "Moshe Rabbeinu" whose presence always saved us from ourselves. Ha'azinu can be the flame by whose light we may once more find ourselves among the shambles that galus has made of us. Ha'azinu calls out to us:

---

* For our discussion of Moshe Rabbeinu's experiences atop Har Nevo and how this ties in with Moshe Rabbeinu's connection to Ha'azinu, please see the latter part of the Prologue.

A Fond Look Backwards

הזיו לך

THE LIGHT THAT PERMEATES ALL
IS TO BE TRACED TO YOU*

---

* In case you have forgotten our discussions of הזיו לך, please take the time to reread the Introduction. Reflections concerning this term recur in various chapters throughout the book.

PROLOGUE

1. A careful reading of VaYeilech makes clear that Yehoshua had a personal involvement with Ha'azinu.

Please take the time to read the entire piece from verse 14 through verse 23. Verse 14 makes very clear that what follows is to be a part of Yehoshua's formal induction to leadership at the hands of the Ribono shel Olam (קרא ואצונו...את יהושע). Verse 14 goes on to say, וילך משה ויהושע ויתיצבו באהל מועד.

To our intense surprise, from verse 15 through verse 22 Yehoshua is completely ignored. The Ribono shel Olam speaks to Moshe Rabbeinu (only; the second person singular is used throughout), apprising him of the rampant idol worship that would spread among the people some time after his death, the terrible punishments that would follow, and the fact that he was to be handed a shirah that, in some form, would be a support for the people during their dreadful travail. All this runs through verse 21. Verse 22 then tells us that Moshe Rabbeinu wrote the shirah (with Yehoshua in attendance). (See Ramban in the footnote.) Only in verse 23 are we told that (after all that) the Ribono shel Olam inducted Yehoshua into his new role.

How are we to understand this strange passage?

It seems to me that it permits only one interpretation. *As part of his induction, it was essential for Yehoshua to hear Shiras Ha'azinu handed to Moshe Rabbeinu by the Ribono shel Olam.* As the leader who was, so to speak, to stand in for Moshe Rabbeinu in the next generation, it was necessary for him to hear the shirah straight from the Ribono shel Olam's mouth to Moshe Rabbeinu's ear (not as *Torah she'be'al peh* from Moshe Rabbeinu).

This idea underlines the enormous significance of *Shiras Ha'azinu.* I hope that in the course of this Prologue we will come to understand at least a part of its significance. However, that is not the focus of our interest in the present endnote. Here we are simply concerned with ascertaining that we are justified in asking why Moshe Rabbeinu felt that he could not leave the invitation to heaven and earth to become witnesses in Yehoshua's hands.

2. The facts on the ground make it very clear how deeply the allure of avodah zarah had burrowed into the *Yiddishe neshamah.* Sanhedrin 64a makes a shattering observation: It is true that Jews cleave to the Ribono shel Olam; they cling to Him as do two dates which, because of their viscous surfaces, adhere to each other. Then comes the shocker. They cling to even the most depraved idolatry like a צמיד פתיל, the *twisted ring* (Jastrow) that attaches the lid to an earthenware vessel. The latter (dare we say it?) is stronger than the former.

How could this possibly have happened?

The truth is that it is not too difficult to understand.

Later on in the book we will be thinking about the fact that the "seventy nations" are all "at home" in this, the gorgeous, very physical world that the Ribono shel Olam prepared for mankind. So much beauty! So much power!

Such an overwhelming range of pastels on its pallet; so many tricks in its bottomless bag! It is a seductive place. For all the problems that often attend life down here, we all love it and do not want to let go of it. Nobody wants to die.

I said that the nations feel at home in this world—and so they should. It is their natural element; it is—and here we come to the touchy subject of idol worship—their truth. It is what Devarim 4:19 makes very clear; the heavenly bodies are that which the Ribono shel Olam *apportioned to them*.

The phrase אשר חלק ה' אלהיך אתם is difficult from many standpoints and that difficulty is reflected in Chazal and the meforshim. However, it seems clear to me that the פשוטו של מקרא accords with העמק דבר who writes: אשר חלק ה' אלהיך אותם לכל העמים. שמתנהגים בטבע תחת יד אמצעים בלי השגחה פרטית מה' המסדר אותם ברקיע. אבל כאשר אתם מן המזל אינכם צריכים לטובתם אפי' לפי המחשבה שיש בהם כח להיטיב או להרע מדעת עצמם ח"ו. The phrase means quite simply that the nations are denizens of the physical world and, bereft as they are of השגחה פרטית, are subject to vagaries of its blind but exquisitely balanced forces.

That truth is certainly the impetus toward the idol worship that was universally practiced among the ancient peoples. To understand that there was another truth beneath their truth, to allow oneself to suspect that maybe the obvious reality was less than really real, that required a degree of sophistication and energy that they neither had nor wished to muster. Even if there were among them individuals who had it within them to intuit that there was a Ribono shel Olam, it seemed more convenient and less demanding to deal with the local authorities.

But what can be said for us? Where did our own טייערע יידען lose themselves? Whence our fatal attraction to all this nonsense?

I am quite sure that there are depths beyond depths that are involved here and I am not privy to any of them. But I feel quite certain that there are accessible surface truths that can help us at our level. I suspect that it is the very human disinclination to be the eternal stranger that is at work here. The deal that Yaakov Avinu, while still in the womb, had cut with Eisav left us with a very heavy yoke to bear. We are tolerated here, but have no rights. We would always be bereft not only of privileges that in "*olam hazeh*" currency were not important to Yaakov, but also of the most basic rights. There is no need to rehearse here what that pariah state has cost us throughout the ages. There is no doubt that, as Klal Yisrael, we have learned to treasure our fate and would spurn any offer to trade it in. But there is also no doubt that not all of us under all circumstances were able to maintain our justified pride. Convincing ourselves that we were olam hazeh people, rather than unwelcome guests from a different world, must sometimes, perhaps frequently, have appeared attractive.

3. The fact that only three thousand out of a total of six hundred thousand were actively involved in the worship cannot be a great comfort to us. Just this past Shabbos I came across a quote from the Chasam Sofer. He wonders why Moshe Rabbeinu became angry when he had brought

down the *luchos* and saw the people dancing. He had, after all, been fore-warned by the Ribono shel Olam about what was happening, and knew exactly what he would find. The Chasam Sofer is said to have answered that, on the contrary, he had anticipated an entirely different scene. True, he knew that there would be people worshipping the calf, but he expected to see the "Neturei Karta" in full action. Stones would be flying; the po-lice would be in action defending the rights of people to worship as they saw fit. He would surely come upon a major *balagan*. Sadly enough, we all know the truth. Nothing of the sort occurred. Here was the picture: three thousand frenzied dancers and 597,000 *nebbiche Yidden* standing around watching.

4. Initially this essay included an analysis of Ramban together with that of Rashi. Eventually I reached the conclusion that such detail would drag out this Prologue beyond any reasonable length. In this endnote I will simply quote Ramban and point out the very real problems I had with what he says. For the interested reader I will just point out that the ideas that I pre-sented in this essay to explain Rashi can also be drafted to answer my objec-tions to what Ramban says. Please follow up on this suggestion. I think that you will find it rewarding.

Here is the Ramban and one paragraph to note my problems.

וטעם המראה הזאת אשר הראהו, בעבור שהיתה הארץ מלאה כל טוב צבי לכל הארצות, ומאשר היה גלוי לפניו רוב האהבה שהיה משה רבינו אוהב את ישראל שמחו ברבות הטובה בראות עיניו.

The Ribono shel Olam permitted Moshe Rabbeinu to see this vast panorama, because He wanted him to see how very good, how vastly more beautiful than other lands, it was. The Ribono shel Olam knew well how much Moshe Rabbeinu loved the Israelites and so decided to make him happy by allowing him to see the abundant goodness that lay in store for them.

When I saw this Ramban, I was truly shocked. Just hours earlier, Moshe Rabbeinu had recited Ha'azinu to the people. It had stated unambiguously that the delight now spread before him would soon enough turn into a cancer gnawing away at the spiritual vitality of the people. This friendly, generous land would be dotted with idolatrous shrines on every hill; the re-freshing breezes would be befouled by fires fueled by the writhing bodies of *Yiddishe Kinderlach*. Would Moshe Rabbeinu really have been able to take delight in a beauty and fertility that must have seemed to him to be no more than a ghoulish grin hiding filth and sorrow beneath its leer? Was it this vi-sion that was supposed to make him happy?

5. At Devarim 34:5 Rashi writes that Moshe Rabbeinu died "בנשיקה," *by means of a kiss*. What is a kiss? What do people seek to express when they kiss each other?

It seems to me that a kiss signifies a removal of barriers, the creation of oneness to the extent that such a fusion is possible within a physical world.

That is how Chazal appear to have understood it. They use the term השקה

(from נשק, "to kiss") to describe the halachic fusion of two bodies of water into a single entity through simply touching each other. There is no need for the waters to intermingle physically. The touching itself, the "kissing," is sufficient.

I believe that a מיתת נשיקה is a death that is no more than a final removal of the final barriers. Moshe Rabbeinu, while he was still alive, had come as close to the Ribono shel Olam as it is given a human being to come. But, withal, he was still human and subject to the לא יראני stricture. In the final moments of that life, he had broken through even that last barrier. Now, nothing, nothing at all, stood in the way of an absolute fusion, except the simple fact of his still being alive. The divine kiss removed that final obstacle. Moshe Rabbeinu had come home.

6. Some of you intrepid readers may want to make use of the following suggestion. Even those of us who do not know much about *sefer Iyov* know that he had serious theological issues to thrash out with the Ribono shel Olam. After a long, complex, and in many ways futile debate with his three friends, followed by the sudden appearance of a fourth protagonist, Elihu, the Ribono shel Olam appears to him.

An endnote to a Prologue introducing a study of Ha'azinu is not the place to discuss how this appearance of the Ribono shel Olam finally untangles Iyov's problems. However, it is clear from just the simple text of God's speeches that He really does little else but describe some of the wonders that we can observe in the animal world. Somehow these descriptions seem to set Iyov's mind at rest. It seems to me that what is happening in sefer Iyov is very close to what we are discussing here. "Heaven and earth" seem to contain some very effective answers to theological conundrums.

I believe that this is a rich and promising vein to follow.

INTRODUCTION

1. Certainly the questioner would have assumed that, whatever the answer, it would be incorporated into our Musaf service on Shabbos. We, of course, all know that that is not the case. The only shir that we recite is שיר מזמור ליום השבת, the *chapter* assigned by the Gemara to the Shabbos morning *Tamid*.

The *Aruch HaShulchan* (Orech Chaim 133:3) is sorely puzzled why the recitation that the Gemara assigns to Shabbos Musaf has fallen into disuse. He remains with a צע"ג.

2. I have described the system as the Gemara works it out and as it is codified in Rambam, Temidim UMusafim 6:9.

3. זיו describes something that shines, something that is luminous. It is interesting that the word appears only twice in TaNaCh, at I Melachim 6:1 and 6:37 where it is used as the name of a month. The meforshim explain that the second month (Iyar) is meant and that it was called the month of "Ziv" because at that time of the year the fields and gardens glisten with the new growth that pushes its way to the surface in the springtime. We should,

however, note that in that passage וו is spelled without the י. That may mean that it is not the same word at all.

4. I would love to know, but cannot even think where to look, when we dropped that gorgeous name and traded it in for our prosaic "Ha'azinu." I think that we can all agree that very much was lost in translation.

5. When I told a good friend of this find, he demurred. He felt that I am reading too much into this Chazal. He felt that it is possible, perhaps even likely, that turning the various introductory letters into real words may simply have been a mnemonic device that slipped into the language without any profound meaning in its own right. I suppose that my certainty that my treatment is the correct one derives from the fact that Rav Elie Munk, in the commentary that first made me aware of this Gemara, presented the facts as I have described them here.

I do stand by what I wrote. As the late great Rav Hutner never tired of teaching, there are no coincidences in the Torah. You will have to make up your own mind.

6. השירה הזאת Ramban to VaYeilech (Devarim 31:19) writes, יקראה שירה, כי ישראל יאמרוה תמיד בשיר ובזמרה, וכן נכתבה כשירה, כי השירים יכתבו בהם הפסק במקומות הנעימה, *Ha'azinu is called a* SONG *because, as a song it is meant to accompany Klal Yisrael through the generations. Moreover, the form in which it is written in the Torah suggests a musical composition since it is customary to leave a space in the text to indicate that it is there that the harmonies are to be inserted.*

ONE

1. You may find some repetition in this chapter from points that we already covered in the Introduction. You may recall that I wrote that Introduction after I was already halfway through the book. I decided to leave this chapter as is. There are no contradictions, so no harm will be done. Everything fits together pretty well as it stands.

2. If you are interested, it was mid-January of 2008. The second President Bush was casting around desperately to salvage something of his battered presidency and had apparently decided that it was in the Middle East that he would leave his mark. It was a time to remember Mishlei 21:1, פלגי מים לב מלך ביד ה' על כל אשר יחפץ יטנו.
Please look at Ramban to Shemos 7:3.

3. Ramban to BeMidbar 23:5 interprets the "שימה בפיהם" of VaYeilech, verse 19, in the following comment: שילמדם ויגרסוה עד שתהא שגורה בפיהם. [Moshe Rabbeinu] was commanded to teach this shirah to the Israelites in order that they should practice it until they would know it by heart.

4. Else, why would He have insisted that we learn it by heart and sing it constantly (תמיד) (see endnote 4)? Why would He insist that we put it to music if not to endear it to us and thereby persuade us to carry it around in our hearts?

TWO

1. When I refer to the shirah as *testimony* and use the phrase *to bear witness*, it should be understood that that is not the only way to translate עד, and may not even be the best. Even in the Torah, and certainly in TaNaCh, the root ע ו ד is used in contexts in which the concept of bearing witness is simply not appropriate. Thus in Bereishis 43:3 Yehudah tells Yaakov that העד העד בנו האיש לאמר לא תראו פני בלתי אחיכם אתכם. The Egyptian viceroy did certainly not bear witness to the brothers. We might say that he *warned* them or *admonished* them and the like. Similarly at Shemos 19:23 Moshe Rabbeinu told the Ribono shel Olam that there was no reason to fear that anybody would attempt to approach the mountain too closely, כי אתה העדות בנו לאמר הגבל את ההר וקדשתו.

At the end of parshas Ha'azinu Moshe Rabbeinu tells the Israelites, שימו לבבכם לכל הדברים אשר אנכי מעיד בכם היום (Devarim 32:46). Here, once more, עוד is used together with Ha'azinu but not in the sense that the shirah itself is testifying, but Moshe Rabbeinu—in telling them the text of the shirah—was testifying to them. What does that mean? He could hardly have been testifying that all the events predicted in the shirah had come about, because at this time none of them had yet happened. In this context it seems certain that taking עוד as a warning or admonishment would be much the best.

This leads me to suspect that עוד as used in VaYeilech and Ha'azinu is to be understood as a serious and profoundly meaningful message rather than as actual testimony. Nevertheless, I retain *testimony* and *bearing witness* in the text since readers will probably feel more comfortable with the more common usage. The words are close enough in meaning to assure that nothing terrible will happen as a result of this minor inaccuracy.

THREE

1. We can take Bereishis 31:44, ועתה לכה נכרתה ברית אני ואתה והיה לעד ביני וביניך, as an example. Rashi thinks that the subject is the Ribono shel Olam while Ramban believes that the subject is the ברית as made tangible by the pile of stones that Yaakov and Lavan erected. In either case neither God nor the stones were called upon to testify to anything at this point. They were, so to speak, on call, to be summoned to render testimony when this might be required.

FOUR

1. Commentators point out that the betrayal of which these few verses speak did not occur *immediately* after Moshe Rabbeinu died. It began only after Yehoshua also died. I have tried to reflect this in my translation.

2. There appear to be two ways in which this pronouncement can be understood. Ramban sees it as the significant beginning of a teshuvah process. Sin is most gruesomely evil only as long as the sinner does not even realize that he is sinning. The realization that the Ribono shel Olam Who had been in their midst had now departed is a major step in the right direction. Since, in

this view, the people were already *Ba'alei Teshuvah*, Ramban wonders why, as verse 18 clearly states, this would lead to an apparent intensifying of the הסתר פנים. Ramban's discussion can be found in his commentary to verse 18.

R. Samson Rafael Hirsch reads the passage differently. The people's pronouncement that their suffering is the result of God's departure from their midst, far from being any kind of teshuvah, is a ratcheting up of their disloyalty. Instead of blaming themselves for their suffering, instead of admitting that only after *they had forsaken God* did the Ribono shel Olam bring these punishments upon them, they pass the blame on to the Ribono shel Olam, claiming that He had not kept His part in the covenants that they, the people, had made with Him. Verse 19 is understood as the Ribono shel Olam's setting the people right. Nothing had happened because He had forsaken the people, for the very good reason that He had never forsaken them. Never, ever, would He forsake His beloved people. However, precisely because He is so close to them, He knows intimately the extent of their treason and therefore hides His Presence from them. He is there, but has denied them His guardianship.

At this point I will quote another excerpt from the Sefas Emes to VaYeilech, this time from page 132 from the year תרל"ט.

. . . אנכי הסתר אסתיר, פרשנו שיהיה נסתר ההסתר ויאמרו כי אין אלקי בקרבי כו' ושמעתי בשם הרה"ק מפרשיסחא ז"ל שזה הוא נחשב לחטא כי צריכין להאמין כי השי"ת עמנו בצרה וע"י התורה ושירה הזאת יכולים לברר זאת כי השי"ת עמנו . . .

This approach appears to me to be identical with that of R. Hirsch. Note particularly the phrase שיהיה נסתר ההסתר. Once more I suggest that it would be very rewarding to learn the entire passage in the original.

3. Here is what Ramban says on "נחנו מה":

אבל הוא כמו מה אנוש כי תזכרנו (תהלים ח ה), מה אדם ותדעהו (שם קמד ג), כי במה נחשב הוא (ישעיה ב כב) וזאת דרך ענוה, כי מה אנחנו שתליתם עלינו שהוצאנו אתכם מארץ מצרים, הן אנחנו אין ופעולינו הבל, ולא עלינו תלונותיכם כי על ה', הוא המוציא אתכם מארץ מצרים לא אנחנו ובמכילתא (כאן) וכי מה אנחנו ספונים שאתם עומדים ומתרעמים עלינו:

The "מה" is not at all a question but is simply a rhetorical device, as is, for example, מה אנוש כי תזכרנו (Tehilim 8:5). "נחנו מה" expresses extreme modesty. Its meaning in the present context is as follows: "Why mention us as though it were we who took the people out of Egypt? We ourselves, as well as any action that we might have taken, are nothing at all. Your complaints should not be directed to us. Rather you should turn to God (Who is really the One Who took you out) . . ."

4. The following could have fitted very well into the essay. However, I relegate it to a note in order to leave the essay itself as uncomplicated as possible.

The main point of this essay is to show the affinity that exists between Moshe Rabbeinu and *Shiras Ha'azinu*. Another aspect of this affinity can be discovered from the connection that exists between Ha'azinu and Shabbos, something that we discussed at length in the Introduction. Perhaps it would be a good idea to glance back there and jog your memory. Here, I feel that it is necessary to make the point that Moshe Rabbeinu seems to have been a

Shabbos-dicker Yid. This is not something that normally I would know any-thing about, but I asked a wise colleague who is much better informed than I am whether there is any truth to this assertion.

He immediately drew two *sugios* to my attention. (I have the feeling that he knew a lot more but felt that these two were sufficient for my purposes.) The first is the fact that our Shabbos morning Shacharis is specifically built around Moshe Rabbeinu and his relationship to Shabbos (ישמח משה במתנת חלקו . . .). The second is Berachos 7a where Moshe Rabbeinu seeks an answer to the problem of the righteous who suffer and the wicked who prosper. You surely recall from the Introduction that this is the precise issue where Shabbos and Ha'azinu meet. Moshe Rabbeinu and Ha'azinu both, so to speak, equal Shabbos. The well-worn axiom that two things that both equal a third also equal each other holds true in Torah as well as in mathematics. Moshe Rabbeinu and Ha'azinu belong together!

FIVE

1. זו היא שיעור במתן החרות של כח הבחירה. כי מתן חרות מוחלט היה מחייב שיקול הכוחות של הטוב ושל הרע. והלא מובנה של ההבטחה הזו היא, כי אע"ג שניתנו כוחות לרע להתנגד לצד הטוב, ולהלחם בו ולהכשילו, וארץ ניתנה ביד רשע, מכל מקום נמנעת היא ממנו האפשרות להחריב את צד הטוב, וסוף סוף יחזור הכל לקדושה . . .

2. This will serve as an all-purpose translation, eliminating the need to dwell on the subtle differences between the various options offered by the commentators for the difficult אפאיהם. However, even at this point it is worth noting that Ramban's opinion, which we will cite and discuss in chapter 12, differs substantively from this translation. This will not affect us in any way in the present context.

3. See Yechezkel 20:9, and 41.

4. I am aware that RaMChaL's answer requires further explanation. However, that falls outside the ambit of this book.

In the meantime I have realized that ambits sometimes expand. See the next chapter.

5. Rambam in Sanhedrin 17:8 cites an exception to this rule but, as explained by various *acharonim*, that exception would not in any way affect our use of this principle.

6. Perhaps accompanied by an escalation of the harshness of the exile experience such that a degree of equivalence can be attained. This would be analogous to the Egyptian experience where, according to some commentators, the unsparing cruelty of the task masters made it possible for the Ribono shel Olam to telescope a four-hundred-year duration into a mere two hundred and ten years.

7. One of the peculiarities of Ha'azinu is that it begins by describing Klal Yisrael's relationship to the Ribono shel Olam as that of children to their father (הלא הוא אביך קניך . . .) and ends with our *eved* status (ועל עבדיו יתנחם . . . כי דם עבדיו יקום . . .). Two possible explanations occur to me. It could be that the two expressions are context driven. When being censured for a lack of

gratitude, it is the son who is more at fault than the servant. When the topic is loyalty during the trying periods of exile, perhaps the servant mode is the more impressive.

I suppose that there is also the possibility that we may perhaps have failed as sons (the censure at the beginning of the שירה) but succeeded as servants (the praise at the end). At this moment I have no knowledge of any source that might be said to confirm or contradict either of these two theories.

SIX

1. I have just used the phrase "change of perspective" because my point of departure was Rashi who, in the passage that we quoted above, uses the phrase שעלה במחשבה, *originally it was intended*, which certainly implies a "change of mind." Obviously the concept of the Ribono shel Olam having intended one thing and then changing His mind is completely beyond us. Maharal in Gur Aryeh in fact disagrees with Rashi's formulation, אמנם דבר זה הוא עיקר סוד סדר העולם . . . ולא כמו שפירש רש"י ש"עלה במחשבה. From this point onward we will be guided by Maharal, not because I feel capable of having an opinion in a disagreement between him and Rashi, but simply because it will help us to keep things as simple as possible.

SEVEN A

1. This assertion is not quite as simple as it sounds; it seems to be open to challenge. To my mind the wording in the Yisro passage, in which the Ribono shel Olam promised to make us His segulah, seems to be conditional. It appears to be predicated on our adherence to our covenant with Him (אם שמוע . . . תשמעו בקולי **ושמרתם את בריתי**). Since the Ribono shel Olam (in VaYeilech) describes the sins of which Ha'azinu speaks as a forsaking of their covenantal obligations (. . . ועזבני והפר את בריתי . . .) (Devarim 31:16), it would seem that against the background that Ha'azinu describes so vividly, our segulah standing would no longer be operative.

I have spent many hours of deep thinking on this problem and have written down reams of apparently possible, and certainly complicated, solutions, only to erase them all. It all seemed to be beyond me. None of the solutions that I contemplated left me with a solid sense of accomplishment. There were always some loose threads that needed to be tied, and that is never a good sign.

All this happened on a Friday and I entered Shabbos in a dark mood. My entire thesis, so carefully and lovingly prepared for this chapter, seemed in danger of collapsing. Today is Sunday and I feel a whole lot better. What happened? It was Shabbos parshas Balak and, of all people, Bil'am handed me a simple and, I believe, satisfying insight.

Here is the process by which I reached my conclusions.

In Bil'am's second attempt to curse us, we have the following verse (BeMidbar 23:21): לא הביט און ביעקב ולא ראה עמל בישראל ה' אלהיו עמו ותרועת מלך בו, *He (the Ribono shel Olam) does not look upon the wrongdoing that Yaakov might undertake, nor does He see any vice in Israel. HaShem their God is with them and they enjoy His friendship.* Rashi to the phrase, *HaShem their God is with them,* caught my attention. He writes: *Even when they arouse His anger and rebel against Him, He does not move away from their midst.* Initially, it simply struck me that here we have a confirmation for the Sefas Emes from Rashi himself, and, of course also from the Midrashic source (Tanchuma 14 to Balak) from which he draws.

Then I recalled that Ramban shows that Bil'am's first prophecy against us was undertaken under the rubric of מדת הדין (ויקר **אלהים** אל בלעם [chapter 23:4]), but the second one, the one from which our verse is taken, was under the rubric of מדת הרחמים (ויקר ה' אל בלעם [chapter 23:16]). Immediately, it struck me that this might be the solution to my problem. The conditional segulah standing in Yisro might have its provenance in מדת הדין, while Bil'am's absolute statement draws its viability from מדת הרחמים.

Baruch HaShem I had the good sense to check, and, of course, saw my mistake immediately. The Yisro parshah uses the שם הויה throughout, and my theory was stillborn. It appears that even within מדת הרחמים the segulah standing is no more than conditional. Once more I was left without a solution.

As I took one more look at the Balak verse, the solution jumped out at me. The phrase immediately preceding עמו אלהיו ה' is לא הביט און ביעקב ולא ראה עמל בישראל, *He (the Ribono shel Olam) does not look upon the wrongdoing that Yaakov might undertake, nor does He see any vice in Israel.* To this expression Rashi remarks: *When they sin the Ribono shel Olam does not look too closely at their falsity and perversity.*

The place to examine the theological import of a Ribono shel Olam Who, so to speak, looks away from the dreary failings of His spiritually limping people is not an endnote. Certainly it has to do with the fact that sin is not endemic to Israel. Even when they sin, it does not touch their essence. (See Maharal, *Gevuros HaShem,* chapter 8: כי ישראל מעלתם שהם נבדלים מן הפחיתות לגמרי, והחטא שמקבלים אין זה רק מקרה ודבר שהוא מקרה בלבד אפשר הסתלקות.) However, be that as it may, I believe that we have the answer to our problem. The conditionality of our segulah standing is only theoretical. When there would be a danger of its being no longer operative, the Ribono shel Olam "looks away" and does not allow the cumulative disappointments to rise to a level at which that could happen.

SEVEN B

1. ... אשירה נא לידידי שירת דודי לכרמו (Yeshayahu 5:1) might have read: *There was once a man who owned a vineyard. He loved it very much and decided to sing it a song. I will now sing this song to you.* Both versions contain essentially the same information. Nevertheless, they press very different buttons in our minds. What in "informing" prose sounds ridiculous becomes beautiful and touching in "moving" poetry. Emotions create a world in which singing songs to vineyards is the stuff of which normalcy is made.

2. My rather sympathetic description of what might have persuaded our forefathers to be caught up in the travesties of idol worship is not designed to gloss over the palpable evil of avodah zarah. The ideas that I describe are proscribed for even their non-Jewish neighbors. I am not excusing but explaining. We see, from the opening verses that we are just now discussing, that the problems are laid at the door of a myopic, nonhistorical view of life. The shirah obviously assumes that once the people would be brought face-to-face with their antecedents, they would realize the error of their ways. It seems to me that this assumption can hold true only if theirs was not a rebellious turning away from the Ribono shel Olam.

Our forefathers seem simply to have forgotten that they were different. It seems to have been our old nemesis, the magnetic pull of assimilation, that was at work here. Life is easier if we just forget our uniqueness and become one of the crowd. We might profitably think about this tendency to the extent that it describes ourselves, who do not express our smallness in overt idol worship!

SEVEN C

1. This appears to be a very strange question. Why not just read Ha'azinu and draw conclusions? I am confident that a book on American history could be identified as such even if the title were missing. So why does Ha'azinu not make itself clear?

   Writing history as poetry exacts a price. The very emotion-tipped arrows that aim true for our hearts tend to obscure the more sober, factual evidence that is directed to our minds.

   Test yourself! Read through Ha'azinu and see to what extent you are able to define clearly what history is being told.

2. Here I will quote myself from chapter 7 of my recent book, *I Brought You unto Me*:

   [Rav Pinkus] begins by pointing out how vital it is that, whatever the undertaking in which we may be engaged, we never lose sight of what precisely is the purpose of that venture. It is always possible and forgivable to forget this or that detail that is important to the success of the project, but it is forbidden to forget what the project is all about. For example, we might agree that the essential nature of a business is to provide an income for the owner. So if I open a supermarket, I may make some silly mistakes in pricing my offerings. I may, for example, forget that Yom Tov is around the corner and that, for the next couple of weeks, there will be a tremendous surge in demand. That is forgivable. But if I forget that the entire purpose of the market is to help me make a living, and instead act as though the store is there to provide attractive displays of vegetables for my neighbors' esthetic edification, then I am not a grocer but a fool.

3. Maharal, throughout his work, deals with the meaning of numbers. His is an extremely sophisticated system, very much beyond our interests in this

book. If I understand him correctly, he explains the significance of "seventy" is as follows: Seventy is made up of the factors 7 and 10. Seven stands for physicality imbued with a spiritual core. (Think of the six days of Creation after Shabbos has made its entry into history.) Ten is the number that lifts disparate units into a new and higher reality. (Think of nine individuals milling around waiting to *daven Minchah*. When the tenth person arrives they have a "*minyan*." The individuals have been transformed into a *tzibur*.) "Seven" repeated "ten" times yields the highest level to which it ("seven") can aspire.

[I cannot say with absolute certainty that I have understood Maharal correctly. I believe that what I have written at least rises to a reasonable approximation. For our purposes in this essay, that suffices.]

4. R. S. R. Hirsch uses these insights to explain the avodah zarah that was rampant in those early years. To people who recognized that all that they were could be traced to the nurturing they had received from the country they called home, it must have seemed natural to pay obeisance to what they believed to be the locally based deities.

EIGHT

1. The fact that humanity is divided into nations must be recognized as Plan B. Here is the language of Midrash Tanchuma at the end of Noach.

אמר הקב"ה בעה"ז ע"י יצה"ר חלקו בריותי ונחלקו לשבעים לשון אבל לעוה"ב משוין כולן כתף אחד לקרוא בשמי ועובדין אותי שנא' כי אז אהפך אל עמים שפה ברורה לקרא כלם בשם ה' לעבדו שכם א' (צפניה ג) ויבטל שעבוד העכו"ם מישראל ...

[At the time of the Haflagah] the Ribono shel Olam said, "In this world, as a result of the *yetzer hara's* mischief, mankind split and was divided into seventy nations [with no communication between them]. But in the world that is yet to come they will all stand together shoulder to shoulder to invoke My name and to serve Me in one tongue . . . and their mastery over Israel will become a thing of the past."

The way the world would have looked had the Haflagah never taken place would have been very different from the one with which we are familiar. The concept of nationhood would have been completely unfamiliar to us. It is hard to think of a world without the UN, is it not?

2. I did a search on בעט and, to my intense surprise, found that ב ע ט used intransitively, as it is here, *simply does not recur anywhere in the whole of TaNaCh!* We have other terms for forsaking the Ribono shel Olam and turning to idol worship. Right in our neighborhood (in VaYeilech) we have זנה and פנה; in kri'as Shema we have ת ו ר.

3. Verse 14 in the earlier section also appears to switch to the second person, ודם ענבים תשתה חמר. However, see Ibn Ezra who toys with the idea that תשתה in this verse might be in the third person feminine.

If you have my book on Yosef HaTzadik (*The Riddle of the Bowing Moon*), you may want to look at chapter 11 (page 73) where I analyze Tehilim 81 (Thursday's שיר של יום), which has a very similar system of switches from second to third person. There, one switch is particularly striking because it occurs in a single pasuk. Verse 17 reads, ויאכילהו מחלב חיטה (third person) and ומצור דבש אשביעך (second person).

4. The rendering of נאץ as does the Gra (see the footnote), can, I believe, explain another irregularity in our verse. Ramban raises the issue why "daughters" are mentioned together with "sons." As everybody knows, throughout the Torah the masculine is always used to cover both genders. So why is "sons" (מכעס בניו) not sufficient? Ramban's answer centers around the fact that from various pesukim in TaNaCh it is evident that there were times in our history in which the women were somehow more drawn to idol worship than were the men. So in the present context they have the doubtful privilege of separate mention.

As I am reading the Gra, perhaps another answer is possible. When everything is objective—"Do such and such a mitzvah in such and such a way!"—women can comfortably be subsumed under men. However, in the area of personal relationships, when the Ribono shel Olam is repulsed by a disloyal people who flout their obligations, there is a real and substantive difference between the genders (כה תאמר לבית יעקב ותגד לבני ישראל). If, for example, it had been only the men who had served idols, but not the women (or, of course, the other way around), it is quite possible to conjecture that the Ribono shel Olam would not have uttered the dread אפאיהם. The two modes of relating are quite different from each other.

5. We ought, of course, to ask ourselves why the Torah should have chosen to tell such a huge story in so few verses. As a possible explanation I will quote a few lines from Rabbi Elie Munk's *The Voice of the Torah* on Ha'azinu. Since it touches upon sisrei Torah, I will simply quote the piece without any discussion.

From this verse (verse 1) to the end of the Song there are forty-two verses corresponding to the forty-two letters in the Great Name of HaShem (Kidushin 71a). God had, as it were, put His signature on this Song and each verse documents one of the mysteries of His name. Therefore, it is on account of the mysteries contained in each verse that Moses speaks here of rain and dew. The drops of moisture are so tiny compared with the vast surfaces of the field and forest that they cover. Similarly the Song is extremely short but contains the deepest secrets for the survival and existence of the world (*Tzror HaMor*).

6. If truth be told, for a careful reader who is guided by Chazal and is willing to go a little beneath the surface, there is a profound difference between the criticisms that these verses level against Klal Yisrael (R. Yehudah) and those that aim at the perfidy of the nations (R. Nechemiah).

The Sifrei tells us how each of them deals with the various phrases in this passage. My analysis will focus on the first phrase, כי גוי אובד עצות המה, *They are a people bereft of counsel*. For R. Yehudah, Sifrei offers, איבדו ישראל עצה טובה שנתנה להם, ואין עצה אלא תורה, שנאמר (משלי ח:יד) לי עצה ותושיה.... For R. Nechemiah, Sifrei suggests, איבדו האומות שבע מצוות שנתתי להם.

It seems obvious to me that, reprehensible as the lassitude expressed by both ourselves and the nations certainly is, there is still a vast difference between neglecting to seek out עצה ותושיה in the Torah, and failing to observe the שבע מצוות בני נח. We failed to seek the Torah's protection against our assimilationist tendencies and forthwith fell prey to the prevailing culture of idol worship. Nevertheless, at bottom, we remain human. We are damaged goods, profoundly damaged Jews. But, withal, we are still Jews. The nations, without their שבע מצוות בני נח, are back in the jungle. There really is no comparison.

Let me share a problem with you. A question has been nagging at me for quite a while. It is aimed at R. Nechemiah who believes that the passage under discussion is a description of the shortcomings of our enemies. *Why is this so important to us? Why, with only forthy-three verses available to the Ribono shel Olam (see endnote 6), waste four of them on what is seemingly* דברים של מה בכך? If we had been told none of this, would we not anyway have been shocked by the stupidity of the nations in claiming ידינו רמה ולא ה' פועל כל זאת?

I think that the theory we have worked out in this chapter can help. We suggested that in the very sameness of the language in which the criticism is couched lies the sharpness of the divergent fates of the two groupings: אלה לחיי עולם ואלה לחרפות לדראון עולם (Daniel 12:2).

As Chazal define the גוי אובד עצות for the two protagonists, it turns out that in the very sameness of the wording there lies an intimation of the divergence that is to follow.

NINE

1. The source for the assertion that Torah will not be forgotten by us is in Shabbos 138b. If we would only have the Gemara about which to worry, we could offer two reasonable explanations that could explain matters. The Gemara's language is as follows: רבי שמעון בן יוחי אומר: חס ושלום שתשכח תורה מישראל שנאמר כי לא תשכח מפי זרעו.... Without any untoward acrobatics we could interpret the Gemara as using a קל וחומר: The Ribono shel Olam has promised us that even a small shirah will not be forgotten, certainly the whole Torah will not be forgotten. Or, even though it is true that at this stage of VaYeilech Moshe Rabbeinu was being commanded to write Ha'azinu as a separate written work, eventually it was, of course, incorporated into the Torah. (See our analysis of the Ramban later in this essay.) Now we certainly do not have the original of what Moshe Rabbeinu wrote (separately) any more. So if we are going to remember Ha'azinu, it will be in its new incarnation, as a part of the Torah. The facts on the ground are now that if Ha'azinu is going to be remembered throughout our history, that can only happen if the entire Torah will also be remembered.

However, Rashi's language, הרי זו הבטחה..., implies that he is referring to the actual phrase, כי לא תשכח.... The implication is that a promise that the shirah will not be forgotten *is* in itself a promise that the Torah will not be forgotten.

2. ויתכן is an expression that Ramban uses frequently after he has already of-fered one reasonable explanation. That is precisely what has happened here, too. The passage that we are examining now is the second of two pos-sibilities. It is of extreme importance to pin down the point of disagreement between the two possibilities that Ramban is examining here.

An in-depth examination of this exciting Ramban would take many pages, and that is a luxury we cannot enjoy in the present context. I will simply lay out that which, after very careful study, I have concluded to be the issue. I do recommend that you do yourself a favor and study the entire Ramban carefully inside.

We are zeroing in on verses 24–26 in VaYeilech (that is, in chapter 31 of Devarim). Here are the two verses:

ויהי ככלות משה לכתב את דברי התורה הזאת על ספר עד תמם.

ויצו משה את הלוים נשאי ארון ברית יהוה לאמר.

לקח את ספר התורה הזה ושמתם אתו מצד ארון ברית יהוה אלהיכם והיה שם בך לעד.

These verses must be considered in the light of verse 9 where we read, ויכתב משה את התורה הזאת ויתנה אל הכהנים בני לוי .... So Moshe Rabbeinu had al-ready written the Torah and had already handed it to the בני לוי. So what are our verses 24–26 reporting that had not already been said earlier? Clearly verses 24–26 relate to verse 9 in the sense that what had begun in verse 9 but had not yet been finished was now brought to a successful conclusion. That is why the later pesukim stress ככלות משה, *When Moshe ended*, a term that had not been used earlier, and also עד תומם, *to its very end*.

It transpires that, originally, Moshe had written a Torah that was not yet complete and had entrusted it to the Levites on a temporary basis; he did not yet tell them what they were to do with it, as he does in the later passage.

What was it that Moshe Rabbeinu had to add to the Torah now that had not yet been a part of it earlier? It is on this question that the "ויתכן" (second) section disagrees with the first. The first section of the Ramban, the part that we have *not* quoted, keeps things very simple. In this inter-pretation Ramban agrees with the Rambam. Moshe Rabbeinu never wrote Ha'azinu on a separate piece of parchment. He took the sefer Torah back from the Levites to whom he had handed it earlier and inscribed Ha'azinu into it. The reason why he did not do this earlier is clear. He did not know that there was this extra piece that he would be told later. As soon as the Ribono shel Olam revealed it to him, he wrote it down in the Torah, thus completing it (ככלות) and bringing it to its very end (עד תומם).

The part of the Ramban with which we are going to deal now disagrees fundamentally. Ha'azinu had a life of its own. It had been written as a dis-crete composition, presumably on a piece of parchment, to serve a purpose that could be viewed as lying outside the Torah's concerns. Only later would Moshe Rabbeinu combine this self-justifying, self-sustaining composition together with the Torah, because the two shared a common purpose in that they are both intent upon providing testimony to the people. [For this last sentence, please see further along in this easy where I quote Ramban who says precisely this.]

3. In the first interpretation Ramban uses הוסיף לה על התורה, while here he uses שהיא מכלל התורה. A cursory glance at my search program shows that the Ramban attaches different meanings to these two terms. For הוסיף we can use Bereishis 1:4, "את האור" והוסיף בכאן. The question was why does it say וירא את האור כי טוב . . . ? Would the sentence not have been just as informative if those two words had not been used? Ramban has an explanation that does not concern us here. Be the answer what it may, it is perfectly obvious that now that the two words were added (הוסיף), they become a seamless part of the sentence.

For מכלל we can go to Bereishis 10:13. Here is Ramban's language there: כי כן מצינו לפתרוסים ארץ פתרוס, והיא מכלל ארץ מצרים. Ramban wishes to point out that countries tend to be called by the name of nations that lived there. Thus, there was no need to point out where the descendants of Cham's son Mitzrayim lived, since the country bore their name. All descendants of Mitzrayim (the man) lived in or around Mitzrayim (the land). Ramban points out that the same principle is at work with פתרוסים. Their land was called ארץ פתרוס although it was a part of Mitzrayim. Now clearly מכלל מצרים does not mean that when we say the word Mitzrayim we meant to include פתרוס. ארץ פתרוס is not called ארץ מצרים. It simply means that it was under Egyptian hegemony. It is not one continuum.

4. Tosafos to Sanhedrin 59a cites Rabbeinu Tam, who differentiates between אדם and האדם. Even עובדי כוכבים can be called האדם. Only Klal Yisrael is called אדם. I have been taught that this difference lies in the fact that a proper noun never takes the definite article. האדם is not the name attached to the particular man whose story is told in Bereishis. It can only mean "man" in general. That, of course, would include all other nations as well. However, אדם without the definite article refers to אדם הראשון and his descendants. Of these, only Klal Yisrael makes the grade: בהנחל עליון גוים בהפרידו בני אדם . . ., precisely as I explained that verse in chapter 7A.

5. At the beginning of this essay (second footnote on p. 83), I raised the apparent problem with the strange reading at Sanhedrin 21b. There the Gemara derives the obligation upon each of us to write a sefer Torah from verse 19 in VaYeilech, [. . . כתבו לכם את השירה הזאת], leaving out the word הזאת. We noted that this reading leaves "השירה" dangling since without הזאת we do not know which shirah is meant. We also noted that Rambam in Hilchos Sefer Torah does have the "הזאת."

After what we have learned, we may suggest the following. Rambam, who interprets the verse as meaning *Write a sefer Torah so that you may be able to write this shirah into it* was consistent in reading השירה הזאת. However, Rashi and Ramban, who read the pasuk as referring only to *Shiras Ha'azinu,* need to understand how the Gemara could derive the obligation to write a sefer Torah from this verse.

I think that what we have written within is sufficient to provide a reasonable and simple answer. Since it was incumbent upon Moshe Rabbeinu to write down Ha'azinu—a shirah that is itself a mini-Torah—it follows that there is also an obligation to write the Torah itself. However, that deduction cannot use the language of "השירה הזאת" since that refers specifically to Ha'azinu, not to the whole Torah. Therefore the Gemara omits הזאת. The *limud* is that since the שירה הזאת is to be written down, so, too, must that other shirah, the sefer Torah itself, be written. But, the sefer Torah that is to be written is not "השירה הזאת". That term refers only to Ha'azinu.

(N.B: The logic that I have used here is not the same as the קל וחומר that I suggested in endnote 1. A קל וחומר deals, by definition, with two discrete limbs [A and B]. A and B are in no way identical. They relate to each other only in the sense that B is somehow more powerful in its sphere of relevance than is A in its sphere. Logic therefore demands that if a certain stringency applies to the weak A, it should certainly apply to the stronger B. As I am presenting the facts in the current and previous essays, the Torah and *Shiras Ha'azinu* are equal to each other. They both have the character of a shirah because they both make clear that we are the segulah of the Ribono shel Olam with all that that status implies, and that the relationship in which we stand to the Ribono shel Olam guarantees that, in spite of all the rocky paths we will have to traverse along the way to אחרית הימים, the ultimate vindication of our history is guaranteed. If Ha'azinu must be written down, so must the Torah. This is not because logic demands it in the sense of a קל וחומר, but because they are identical to each other where it counts.)

TEN

1. My good friend R. Eliyahu Hakakian has directed me to the בן איש חי on parshas Devarim, who writes that in Baghdad it was indeed the custom to substitute Ha'azinu for אז ישיר on Tish'ah Be'Av, and that he permitted that usage to continue, although he personally did not follow this lead and said אז ישיר as on every other day. However, even he *did* say Ha'azinu on Tish'ah Be'Av, not as a substitute for אז ישיר, but after the עמידה. He writes that this was the custom followed by החכמים ויראים ואנשי מעשה.

HaRav Dovid Yosef (the son of HaRav Ovadiah Yosef) writes in his *Toras HaMo'adim,* וכן פשט המנהג בארץ ישראל, לומר שירת הים כמו בשאר ימות השנה. ואחר, סיום התפלה, קודם אמירת איכה וקינות, אומרים פרשת האזינו.

R. Eliyahu Hakakian tells me that there is a סידור called חמש תעניות, which is used among those who daven נוסח ספרד. In these *siddurim* the האזינו is printed before *Ma'ariv* in the section dealing with Tish'ah Be'Av. So, at least in the Sephardic community, Ha'azinu seems to be firmly entrenched, in one form or another, on Tish'ah Be'Av.

2. I believe that the affinity between Ha'azinu and Tish'ah Be'Av can help in what, for me, has always been a knotty problem when I tried to live within the spirit of this day of mourning. I did not know how to deal with that other part of Tish'ah Be'Av, the part that relieves us from saying Tachanun because Tish'ah Be'Av has the character of מועד. It immediately struck me

that the issue that has kept us so busy in the last few chapters, the fact that Ha'azinu, in spite of the grisly accounts of trespass and retribution, can nevertheless be defined by the Ribono shel Olam, and through Him by all of us, as a shirah is probably the key to understanding. If Ha'azinu can be a shirah, Tish'ah Be'Av can be a מועד. In both cases the absolute certainty that even when things are terrible beyond imagination, it does not mean that the Ribono shel Olam has deserted us, can act as a counterweight to the otherwise unrelieved pain.

I believe that the fructification moves in both directions. It is not only that Ha'azinu helps remove a problem from Tish'ah Be'Av; Tish'ah Be'Av can also help us to understand Ha'azinu in ways that, up to now, have escaped me.

It was language used in the Mishnah Berurah that alerted me to the possibility. In Orech Chaim 559:17 he explains the omission of Tachanun on Tish'ah Be'Av as we would have expected: Tish'ah Be'Av is called מועד. He then continues: *Nevertheless it is permitted to deliver a* HESPED *for a sage who has died, and also to sit on the ground even after midday, because the entire day is one of crying and* HESPED. *Relative to such matters we pay no attention to the fact that it has the character of a* מועד. Why not? This cannot possibly be an arbitrary differentiation. Somebody must have decided that for some reason there is a difference between omitting Tachanun on the one hand and making *hespedim* and sitting on the ground on the other. He must have had a logical reason for so doing.

The term that is used by the *poskim* to explain the omission of Tachanun on Tish'ah Be'Av is that Tish'ah Be'Av is איקרי מועד, *it is called* A TIME OF MEETING *with the Ribono shel Olam*. With the help of my search engine I tried to trace the source of this concept. I found this expression three times in *Shas*, but none of the references was in connection with Tish'ah Be'Av. Each time the expression occurs, it is dealing with the issue of whether or not *Rosh Chodesh* is called a מועד. The practical applications do not concern us here.

The Gemara's proof that Rosh Chodesh is called מועד is based on the pasuk in Eichah (1:15), . . . קרא עלי מועד. . . . What bearing does this pasuk that refers to Tish'ah Be'Av have on Rosh Chodesh? The Gemara's reasoning is as follows. Tradition teaches that the Meraglim left on the twenty-ninth of Sivan. Furthermore, we have the tradition that they returned on the eighth of Av with their message of despair, which makes the "night of crying" that followed their return come out on Tish'ah Be'Av. The Torah tells us that they were gone for forty days. All these factors can only come out correctly if we assume that *beis din* decreed that year that Tamuz should be "מלא," that is, that it should have a full thirty days. That way we have two days (29 and 30) in Sivan, thirty days of Tamuz, and eight days in Av—a total of forty days. The Gemara understands "קרא עלי מועד" to refer to beis din's decision to adjust Rosh Chodesh Tamuz (the "מועד" of the pasuk) of that year by pushing it off for one day (allotting thirty days to Sivan rather than the more normal twenty-nine), thus making all the traditions interlock satisfyingly.

So where does this leave us with Tish'ah Be'Av? Where in all this shuffling of text is Tish'ah Be'Av called מועד? I believe that we must assume the following. We are used to calling our Yamim Tovim by the name מועדים (מועדים לשמחה, חול המועד, and so on). Because of this we tend to translate the word as *a festival*. That, however, is not the correct translation. The root word י ע ד from which מועד is formed means *to set aside an appointed time*. A מועד is a day of significance for which prior arrangements are made. Since the hashgachah decreed that Rosh Chodesh (a מועד, *a day of significance* in its own right) be moved around just in order that the return of the Meraglim would be timed correctly to fall on the ninth of Av, and on no other date, it is clear that that date is itself of utmost significance. If Rosh Chodesh is a מועד, then Tish'ah Be'Av (for which this adjustment in Rosh Chodesh was necessary) must certainly be considered a מועד.

I believe that the reason why we do not say Tachanun on a מועד is not because it is a happy day. A day can be "appointed" for sorrow as much as it can be appointed for joy. I believe that the reason why we do not say Tachanun is that this prayer, by its very nature, is concerned with the individual. *I* am worried about *my* transgressions; *I* weep about *my* shortcomings and beg for forgiveness, and so on. When the Ribono shel Olam "appoints" a certain day for whatever reason He wishes to appoint it, I am required to desist from importuning Him with my personal needs. That Tish'ah Be'Av is such an "appointed" day suffices to remove Tachanun from the agenda. It does not interfere with its nature of being a day on which tears and *hespedim* are in order.

I believe that this is what the Mishnah Berurah had in mind.

I asserted earlier that the fructification born of the twinning of Ha'azinu with Tish'ah Be'Av moves in both directions. I had the following in mind. The absence of Tachanun on Tish'ah Be'Av is not because the day is happy, but because it is of great significance. We can understand the shirah nature of Ha'azinu in the same manner. We do not sing Ha'azinu because we are joyful, but because we are important. The direct hashgachah that is manifest in everything that Ha'azinu describes, the heavy suffering no less than the moments of love and caring, are something to sing about!

3. As I was thinking about this issue, I found that Ha'azinu seems to have had some claim to recognition even on regular days.

Here is Rambam in Hilchos Tefilah 7:13:יש מקומות שנהגו בהן לקרות בכל יום אחר שמברכין ישבתח שירת הים ואחר כך מברכין על שמע ויש מקומות שקורין שירת האזינו ויש יחידים שקורין שתי השירות הכל לפי המנהג. So even on ordinary days there were those who substituted Ha'azinu for אז ישיר, and there were individuals who would say both shiros every day.

ELEVEN

1. In the following footnote we discover that the formal term for induction is

צוה. That word does not appear in verses 7 and 8 where Moshe Rabbeinu is apparently introducing Yehoshua to his new role. On the strength of that apparent omission we might suppose that what Moshe had spoken did not have the character of a formal induction.

That, however, is very unlikely. We need only look back to parshas Pinchos where Moshe Rabbeinu was first informed that Yehoshua was to be his successor (BeMidbar 27:18 and 19). There the Ribono shel Olam tells Moshe Rabbeinu specifically that he is to introduce Yehoshua to Elazar HaKohen and to all the people (והעמדת אתו לפני אלעזר הכהן ולפני כל העדה) and then to induct him (וצויתה אתו לעיניהם). Later on, in verse 22, we are told ויעש משה כאשר צוה ה', that *Moshe did as God had commanded him*. Ramban in Pinchos to verse 12 writes expressly that ויעש משה does not mean that Moshe Rabbeinu did it at that time. It means that he did it on the day of his death, meaning the induction by Moshe Rabbeinu that is described in VaYeilech. Although Rashi does not address this issue expressly, Gur Aryeh (in Pinchos) writes that Rashi agrees with Ramban in this matter.

2. I have taken the verb ואצונו as describing a ceremonial induction, although צ ו ה usually means *to command*. In this I based myself on Ramban to BeMidbar 27:19, who adduces a number of proof texts that this same root can also mean an appointment to a post (מנוי). I have come across a number of commentators who surmise that this use of צ ו ה came about because a part of an induction ceremony would likely also include a charge (command) to take his new responsibilities seriously.

3. This explanation and the various conclusions that I will draw from it do not rise above the level of conjecture. I cannot, at least at this point, prove that all this is true. All I can say is that after careful examination, it seems to me to be yielded by the text. I have discussed my thoughts with friends and colleagues who agreed with me and felt my ideas to be reasonable. It is on this basis that I offer my thoughts in the rest of this essay.

4. The shirah defines who and what Klal Yisrael really is. Absent that knowledge, the leadership of a future leader would be hopelessly compromised.

Let us take these thoughts a little further.

The shirah, at least in the way Ramban sees it, has a unique standing as *Torah SheBiKsav*, written Torah, relative to Yehoshua. Let us concentrate really hard on this endnote. It will yield some very significant insights. We will start our analysis from verse 19 in VaYeilech where the Ribono shel Olam tells Moshe, ועתה כתבו לכם את השירה הזאת. The verb כתבו לכם is of course in the plural, so more than one person is to be involved. Ibn Ezra, in line with Chazal who learn from this pasuk that every Jew is obliged to write a sefer Torah (שירה = כל התורה כולה), interprets כתבו to be addressed to כל מבין לכתב, *whoever is capable of writing*. Ramban, however, goes his own way in both details. He maintains that the word שירה as used here refers to only Ha'azinu, and that the plural, כתבו, is addressed to both Moshe and Yehoshua, but not to anybody else.

Now, it would seem that Ramban is going to have a major problem with verse 22, which states clearly ויכתב משה . . . . , indicating explicitly that only Moshe Rabbeinu wrote. We will have to see how Ramban deals with this issue.

Here is what he says. על דרך הפשט למשה ויהושע שניהם יצוה שיכתבוה כי רצה לעשות יהושע נביאו בחיי משה. והנה משה כתבה ויהושע עומד עמו וקורא ורואה . . . . That seems very difficult to understand. Yehoshua, together with Moshe, was commanded to write. Moshe writes and Yehoshua "reads and watches," as Ramban quite clearly asserts. But, how can "reading and watching" be considered to be the equivalent of writing?

I believe that Ramban means the following.

We must first point out that, as far as Yehoshua is concerned, the shi-rah is unique. Nothing in the Torah equals it. We all know that we have a Torah SheBiKsav, a written Torah. However, as far as ordinary Jews were concerned, they learned this "written Torah" orally. Throughout the forty years in the wilderness, Moshe Rabbeinu learned the mitzvos from the Ribono shel Olam and then taught them orally to the people. The commit-ting of all this to writing was the next stage. By the time the Torah was writ-ten, the people's approach to the text would have been influenced by the oral presentation to which they had first been exposed. It was only Moshe Rabbeinu who heard the words directly from the Ribono shel Olam and then wrote them down, who saw in the written record precisely what he had learned directly from the Ribono shel Olam.

In this matter, the shirah was different from any other section in the Torah. Moshe Rabbeinu first wrote it down: ויכתב משה את השירה הזאת ביום ההוא וילמדה את בני ישראל (פסוק כ"ב). The writing down *preceded* the oral teach-ing. To all the other Jews this made very little practical difference. After Moshe Rabbeinu had written it down, he presumably taught it to the people orally. But Yehoshua was different. He was "reading and watching." For him there was absolutely no dilution occasioned by any oral transmis-sion. It is true that he presumably did not hear the Ribono shel Olam com-municating with Moshe, but, as Moshe Rabbeinu was writing it down, he read what was being written. He saw the pristine words of the Ribono shel Olam with no dilution.

What a Ramban!

5. I would like to anticipate an objection that you, dear Reader, may raise at this point. By now you have probably guessed that I plan to build my whole edifice on this Rashi, maintaining that Yehoshua's leadership must be viewed as a continuation of that of Moshe Rabbeinu. You would be right. However, you might feel that Rashi's personalized wording, ". . . he sees him-self . . ." and so on, weakens the basis of my contention. Rashi is not offering an objective judgment [Yehoshua *was* a continuation of Moshe Rabbeinu], but a subjective feeling [Moshe Rabbeinu *felt* as though he continued living in his student].

I contend that the thesis that I intend to offer is not weakened. Rashi, correctly, molds his remarks to the circumstances. Moshe Rabbeinu is speaking, and Rashi hears the inflection that he uses in that speech. The context is personal. However, *once these words were fixed in the Torah, they became objective Torah.* The truth that they contain moves from the arena of the subjective to that of the objective.

TWELVE

1. I am not sure how to understand this Ramban. Does he mean that the Ribono shel Olam will shield us from ever committing a sin that is sufficiently heinous to require that we be destroyed, or does he mean that even if we were to commit such a sin, the Ribono shel Olam would not destroy us? At this point I am not sure whether this would make a practical difference.

2. Perhaps *merely* is not the best word here. Ha'azinu is not "merely" a repetition, but was taught to all the people with the anticipation that it would become a part of the living folklore, sung, recited, and loved by all. Certainly, the wrapping of these basic truths in such a packaging cannot be dismissed as insignificant. Still, while all this is true, it does not sound like the whole truth. The pomp and circumstance with which the shirah is introduced seems to imply something considerably more.

THIRTEEN

1. As I write this, it is just a couple of days after Purim and it is not half an hour ago that I put down the phone from an argument with a friend as to what role teshuvah played in Shushan HaBirah. My friend argued that teshuvah lies at the very center of the story. When Haman's decree became public knowledge, the people were brought to their senses (see Megilah 14a, גדולה הסרת טבעת...) and repented of all the evils that they had done. God accepted that teshuvah and brought about the salvation. I vigorously disagreed, since there is not even the tiniest hint in the text of the Megilah that such a teshuvah took place. My reasoning was and is that it is impossible that the text should remain silent concerning a crucial factor in the story. I maintain that it is perfectly possible that Chazal had a tradition that the people indeed repented (as is implied in the Chazal at Megilah 14a that we cited above), but *it is impossible to say that this teshuvah played an active role in the story.* Had this teshuvah been required for the story to make sense, it is impossible that the writer would have made no mention of it.

[I do not believe that the fast that Esther ordained for the entire people prior to her going to the king can be read as a communal act of penitence. Esther was very clear about her motivation for ordaining the fast. It was to protect her (וצומו עלי) from the crazed monster with whom she had to deal. If teshuvah had been involved, then it would have been reflected in the text much as this was done in *sefer* Yonah at the crucial moment when the *anshei Ninveh* realized that the Ribono shel Olam was serious about punishing them.

It is true that Esther 9:31 mentions דברי הצומות וזעקתם indicating that fasting and praying *did* take place (presumably accompanied by teshuvah) before the Jews joined battle with their oppressors. It is that fast that we recall on Ta'anis Esther (see Mishnah Berurah 686:2). Nevertheless, in my opinion, it is boundlessly significant that this is not recorded as part of the story as it happened. We know of it only because Esther mentioned it in her letter. I believe that this confirms my thesis. The actual salvation was *not* based on the fact that they had done teshuvah.]

I have always maintained that the whole power of Megilas Esther lies in the fact that teshuvah is *not* mentioned and therefore, even if indeed it took place, *cannot* be described as an active requirement in the story. When the chips are truly down, the Ribono shel Olam does not wait for our teshuvah. His covenant with us is not a conditional one.

Now that I am learning Ha'azinu, I have become more certain than ever that my position is the correct one. I base this upon the Ramban that we have quoted a number of times (beginning in chapter 1), in which he sums up his reading of this shirah. This piece runs from verse 40 through verse 43 and ends with Ramban's assertion that the end of Ha'azinu looks forward to the Messianic future. Here are a couple of sentences plucked from that Ramban.

והנה אין בשירה הזאת תנאי בתשובה ועבודה, רק היא שטר עדות שנעשה הרעות ונוכל, ושהוא יתברך יעשה בנו בתוכחות חימה, אבל לא ישבית זכרנו, וישוב ויתנחם ויפרע מן האויבים בחרבו הקשה והגדולה והחזקה, ויכפר על חטאתינו למען שמו אם כן, השירה הזאת הבטחה מבוארת בגאולה העתידה על כרחן של מינין ...

Now this shirah makes its promises dependent upon neither teshuvah nor any other form of divine worship. It is, on the contrary, an un-encumbered written statement that we will be doing all kinds of evil deeds in which we will in no way be hindered. It foretells that God will punish us in His anger, but will *not* destroy us. That, on the contrary, He will move away from punishing us to punishing our enemies with His mighty sword. In addition He will help us to atone for our sins for the sake of His name. It is clear from all this that this shirah constitutes a clear guarantee of future redemption, the infidels notwithstanding.

Why does Ramban insist upon stressing that no condition of teshuvah encumber the ultimate redemption? It must be because the absoluteness of God's covenant with us is a given that lies at the very center of His relationship with us. It is not just another detail. It defined our *bris* with the Ribono shel Olam in its very being.

Now, Haman's threat to destroy us utterly (להשמיד להרג ולאבד) was very real. Rashi to Esther 4:1 brings sources that assert that Haman's plans had found heavenly confirmation. The danger was not only real, but it was absolute. The very existence of Klal Yisrael hung in the balance. When such a fate threatens, there can be no waiting for teshuvah. Ramban makes this eminently clear.

2. Please note that Tosafos in Shabbos 55a asserts that even if we agree that it is conceivable that we could sink so low that זכות אבות will have nothing more to offer us, that chasm will only neutralize "ברית" אבות זכות אבות, *covenants*

into which the Ribono shel Olam entered with our Avos, will remain unaffected. An unconditional *bris*, in as much as it is a legally binding contract, cannot be abrogated and can therefore outlive even the mass defections of such generations as cannot continue to be protected by זכות אבות. It must therefore be stated here that when we describe the chasm that has opened up between ourselves and the Avos in the absolute terms that we use in this paragraph, the description could be misleading. The terms that we use in all earnestness to underline the sheer horror of a situation that can be described as תמה זכות אבות are nevertheless only true within the voluntary area within which "זכות" operates. *Brisos* remain inviolate.

3. At this point we should spend a few minutes thinking about the Ramban to Devarim 9:4–5. Those two verses do not pull any punches; they make us face some very unpleasant truths about ourselves. When the Ribono shel Olam allows us to drive out the Canaanite nations from Eretz Yisrael and to take over the land, we are not to think that we are deserving of all this largesse. It is the dreadful evil of the Canaanite people that precipitates their expulsion, and it is God's oath to the avos that allows us to settle the land. Our righteousness has nothing at all to do with any of this, for the very simple reason that we are not at all righteous. From verse 6 onward there is a long litany of our failings that make that judgment very, very clear. We can make no claim at all to any righteousness that would make us worthy of entering Eretz Yisrael.

Ramban asks a question that really all of us should have been asking if we listened to kri'as HaTorah a week earlier when VaEsChanan was being read. There (Devarim 7:7–8) we read, *It is not because of your numbers that HaShem craves your closeness and chose you, because the opposite is true; you are the smallest among the nations. It was because God loved you....* Now, God does not crave closeness to, or love, wicked people. How are we to make peace between the two passages?

Ramban answers: כי שם ידבר עם ישראל בכללם, וכאן יוכיח הדור ההוא שהיו ממרים את ה' מיום היותם במדבר. Ramban is erecting some very powerful amber flashing lights. Whenever the Torah speaks of us either with fulsome praises or harsh judgments, we need to be very sure who is being described. Sometimes the object of that description may be Klal Yisrael as a whole; at others it may be a specific grouping within that Klal.

When Ha'azinu speaks of the fierce loyalty that Jews have displayed under the most dreadful conditions, we will of course be aware that there may well have been exceptions to that rule. Ha'azinu is speaking about Klal Yisrael in its totality.

FOURTEEN

1. Please look back to chapter 1 where we discuss the division of Ha'azinu into six parts beginning with the letters הזי"ו ל"ך. Here, we need only point out that the second section begins with the ז of זכר ימות עולם. This leaves the ה for the first six verses. Now that ה is simply the definite article, that is, it defines

the message, *luster is Yours*, but is not a part of it. This fits in well with our assertion that the first six verses are to be viewed as no more than an introduction to the shirah proper.

FIFTEEN

1. At Bereishis 6:9 it appears that Ramban uses these two terms interchangeably. However, in the present context it appears to me that we will not err if we assign a slightly different meaning to each one. We can conceive of a brick inserted into a wall in order to fill in a hole. We would want it to be perfect in the sense that it is has no imperfections in its structure, texture, and so on. Even if it fills this requirement, it may simply be too small. The stoppage would not be complete. God's actions, taken within the rubric מדת הדין, are not only perfect in the sense that there are no rough edges, they are also complete in the sense that they cover all the bases.

2. This sentence has probably annoyed many of you since we have all been brought up to translate משפט as "law." (How did your teacher translate ואלה המשפטים אשר תשים לפניהם?) Here is my defense. Please read this note carefully; I very much want all of us to be on the same page on these profoundly important issues.

   First we should tackle the matter of synonyms. I am on the road and do not have any good dictionaries handy. Nevertheless, I have a passable Thesaurus on my computer and it will do to illustrate what I mean. I picked the word *anger* at random and my program offered the following, among others: rage, outrage, fury, wrath, ire, temper, indignation, resentment, exasperation. I suppose any of us might have picked some of these words if we had been asked to mention a synonym for *anger*. Now it seems to me abundantly clear that not even a single one of these words covers precisely the same ground as does *anger*. I cannot imagine myself using any of them to replace the word *anger* if that would have been the term that came naturally to my mind. Synonyms are not *equal* to one another, but are simply close in meaning.

   More problematic for most of us would be the well-known Rashi from VaYikra 18:4:

   את משפטי תעשו אלו דברים האמורים בתורה במשפט שאלו לא נאמרו היו כדאי לאומרן.
   ואת חקותי תשמרו דברים שהם גזירת המלך שיצה"ר משיב עליהם למה לנו לשומרן ואו"ה
   משיבין עליהם כגון אכילת חזיר ולבישת שעטנז וטהרת מי חטאת . . .

   So why am I saying that משפט does not mean "law"? From Rashi it seems quite clear that both חק and משפט do indeed mean "law" but are to be differentiated from each other by the definitions that Rashi offers.

   Actually, it does not "seem so" from Rashi at all. Here is why. We need to ask ourselves why it is that משפט means what Rashi says it means. What is it about the root word ש פ ט that indicates a law that accords with our sense of the appropriate and the reasonable?

   The base meaning of ש פ ט is *to arrange things in a way that they will exist in a harmonious relationship to one another.* That is why, as an example of the

fascinating ways in which language is fruitful and multiplies, we began using "משפט" for the collection of words that we know as a "sentence." It hits
precisely the right tone because that is precisely what a sentence is. It ar-
ranges words by particular rules so that, acting in harmony, they are able to
convey a desired message. (You might want to ponder that in English, too,
we write "sentences" and the judges hand down "sentences," certainly a family member of the clusters formed under the rubric, "law.") So משפט does not
really mean *law*. It means a complex of usages (sometimes imposed, thus,
in effect, "law") that are designed to promote harmony within society. It
is true that, as a convenience, we use the "law" translation, always bearing
Rashi's distinction in mind. However, this is only a kind of shorthand. The
word does not really translate as "law."

3. If only for the sake of consistency, I should point out that the translation of
    שופטים as *judges* is again no more than a convenient, but not fully accurate,
    shorthand. The correct translation should, I suppose, be, *promoters of har-
    mony among the citizenry.*

    I venture to suggest that this is more than pedantic nitpicking.

    In a vastly interesting passage in his commentary to the *dor Haflagah*,
    R. Samson Rafael Hirsch speaks about the birth of languages. He argues
    that the words that different societies chose to express various ideas de-
    pended upon how those societies perceived these concepts. One of his ex-
    amples concerns the word for a judge. In German the term is *Richter.* The
    German for "direction" is *Richtung.* The judge is perceived as a kind of traffic
    cop whose job is done when he has, so to speak, gotten the two litigants out
    of each other's hair, setting each one upon a different direction where they
    will no longer clash. The administration of justice is essentially negative. It
    simply avoids conflict. The Hebrew שופט, particularly as we have translated
    it, is charged with the positive establishment of harmony. By defining rights
    and obligations, he establishes positive relationships.

    As long as we are dealing with exact translations, I suppose that we
    should assume that the משפטים that Moshe Rabbeinu was charged with
    placing before the Benei Yisrael (Shemos 21: 1) should be understood as
    harmony-producing ordinances.

    This note is already extraordinarily long. Nevertheless, I feel that the fol-
    lowing should at least be considered in passing. A little earlier in this note
    we pointed to the often interesting, even piquant, directions in which the
    habits, I assume the unplanned habits of language, take us. I doubt that it
    was a conscious decision to apply the word משפט to the grammatical unit
    that we know as a sentence. It was just a natural שידוך and so people gravi-
    tated toward it.

    It seems to me that another example of language opting for the true
    meaning of a word (taking משפט as "promoting harmony" rather than as
    simple "law") is the association of the exercise of law with the concept of
    יופי, *beauty.* Chazal refer to a highly qualified beis din as a "בית דין יפה," really
    a thing of beauty (Sanhedrin 32b), and refer to the unfettered power of the

courts (where that indeed exists) as "כח בית דין יפה" (Yevamos 90b and else-where). Now one ought not to make too much of this because, certainly in the course of time, the word "יפה" took on the meaning of "power" without any apparent reference to beauty, as in יפה כח הבן מכח האב (Shevu'os 48a and elsewhere). But that itself is just another example of linguistic development. [We do not think of a harmoniously arranged group of words when in grammar we speak of a sentence.] However, I *do* suggest that the seed from which the association between beauty and law ultimately grew was the association between the exercise of law with "משפט" as we have defined it here.

4. Rabbeinu Bechaya does not explain why divine משפט partakes of both qual-ities while human משפט (משפט צדק) is not to be softened by mercy. I suppose that the explanation will be that once we are going to permit considerations of mercy to intrude, objectivity will go with the wind and nothing will re-main of the majesty of law. Only the Ribono shel Olam can be completely objective in His judgment (משפטי ה' אמת) and still measure out smidgens of mercy (צדקו יחדיו) that are appropriate to the case but will not upset the balance.

5. Mercy is so much a part of the משפט process of the Ribono shel Olam that it is possible for the דין aspect to be entirely displaced with only חסד remain-ing—and it would still be considered משפט. This is how Rabbeinu Bechaya interprets Yirmiyahu 10:24 where the prophet prays that God chastise him אך במשפט. The word אך, which always has a limiting function, is interpreted to mean that God is asked that in chastising him the Ribono shel Olam not employ the full range of *mishpat's* reach. The דין part is to play no role at all. Only חסד is to be in evidence.

6. In effect this emendation requires a comma after משפט, divorcing it from the word that follows it, which thus becomes the first word in the following phrase that reads דתמים הוא ולא בפועלו חסרון. This emendation seems to me to miss the mark for two reasons. First, the introduction of the new comma requires a restructuring of the sentence. It implies that up to the time of his emendation people had not only misread the word—something that can happen easily enough—but had misinterpreted an entire sentence. That is serious business and, I believe, should be avoided at all costs. Second, the new phrase, דתמים הוא ולא בפועלו חסרן, adds nothing to what had already been said in the earlier phrase, כי הפועל הבא ממנו תמים ושלם. For these reasons I will assume that the earlier reading was the correct one, as I will explain within.

7. I would not be honest if I were not to admit to a small caveat that I think you ought to heed before accepting my enthusiastic endorsement of this meaning of משפט]וה[רחמים. It is this: I have made a universal search on my search program and in the entire database there was not a single usage of the concept "משפט]וה[רחמים" except only this one Ramban. It seems to me that if the relatively simple explanation I offered were correct, one could have expected a widespread use of the term וכ"ע.

8. Here is Ramban's language in BeMidbar 20:8: כי הכוונה לרבותינו בבארה של מרים

שהיה מעולם באר ניסי מקור מים חיים נובע בכל מקום שיהיה שם הרצון עליו . . . **ונבקע בחורב**
מן הצור ההוא שהיה שם, ובשאר המסעים **נובע מן הצור במקום שיחנו שם**. וכאשר מתה הצדקת
מרים . . . .פסק המעין ועתה חזר על ידי משה להיות לו מקור נפתח **מן הסלע ההוא בעצמו**. Clearly,
throughout the forty years in the wilderness, this mighty nation drank wa-
ter gushing forth miraculously from rocks. Always, from rocks.

9. The idea of barren rocks overcoming their natural limitations and becoming the source for life-edifying sweetness is not limited to the בארה של מרים.
In Ha'azinu itself only a few verses ahead (verse 13), we learn of the Ribono
shel Olam feeding us with honey [flowing] from the stones and oil from the
flinty rocks. Dovid HaMelech picked up the same thought in Tehilim 81:17.

This theme is sufficiently ubiquitous to indicate that it touches upon
ideas that are central to Jewish thinking.

SIXTEEN

1. In Nefesh HaGer, a sefer that analyzes the Targum, I saw that Targum
chose to introduce a reference to idol worship into this verse because the
word "שחת" was used by the Ribono shel Olam at Shemos 32:7 when He
apprised Moshe Rabbeinu of the fact that the Jews had slipped into idol
worship when they made the golden calf: "לך רד כי **שחת** עמך. . . ." He notes that
there, too, the Targum renders שחת with חבילו in the plural.

[As a matter of fact, almost all the Targumim that are available to me
have חביל in the singular there. However, I have been told by Targum ex-
perts that the most reliable recensions do indeed have חבילו.]

A word is in place concerning Targum's treatment of this verse. His
rendering appears to do violence to the syntax. It seems obvious that the
Targum knew that the words that are used and the pattern in which they
are organized cannot possibly yield his translation.

Please note that what I am about to suggest is my own thinking. I have
not seen it in any sefer. This sentence puts you on notice that you must be
circumspect in accepting my explanation. It advises caution.

The Targumim that are extant did not have their genesis in the written
word. In the time of Chazal it was customary to have a Metargem translate into Aramaic each verse as it was read in shul for the benefit of the un-
learned folk for whom Hebrew was a closed language. Clearly, people who
were uneducated to the extent that they could not follow simple Hebrew
would also have lacked the sophistication to grasp the more subtle expressions and concepts that make up the language and ideas that constitute the
Torah text. It was necessary for the Metargemim to bend their translations
to the extent of the people's grasp. Accuracy was often trumped by educa-
tional expediency.

An example that comes to mind is from Bereishis 41:44 where Pharaoh
tells Yosef that ובלעדיך לא ירים איש את ידו ואת רגלו בכל ארץ מצרים. Now it is perfectly obvious that "לא ירים איש את ידו ואת רגלו" is an idiomatic expression con-
veying the idea: to do anything of importance. Nevertheless Onkelos renders,
לא ירים גבר ית ידיה **למיחד זין** וית רגליה **למרכב על סוסיא**. He certainly did this so that

190

people for whom idiomatic phrases were difficult to grasp should not wonder how it would be possible for anybody to refrain from using an arm or leg without obtaining express permission from Yosef.

That given, it is possible that Targum agreed with Ramban's rendering of the verse (see below in the essay) in which "לו" is the object of "שחת," meaning that, כביכול, the Ribono shel Olam was damaged by our trespasses. Targum may have felt that this concept could prove harmful to his unsophisticated listeners, and therefore took the liberties with the text that he did.

2. This Ramban is difficult to translate. I decided against quoting his words and translating them in the essay itself because things are confusing enough as it is. I offer the text of the Ramban here for those of you who do not want to rely on the paraphrase that I offer within.

שחת לו לא בניו מומם המום יקרא השחתה, כמו שנאמר (ויקרא כב כה) כי משחתם בהם
מום בם, וכן וזובח משחת לה', כי מומם של ישראל שחת לצור עמו ונחלתו וקראם "לא בניו,"
כאשר יקראם בניו בעת רצון.

3. It would take us too far from the subject of this essay to examine whether or not R. Yehudah argues with R. Meir on this point. If Ramban thought that R. Yehudah does indeed argue and that his proposal is based on R. Yehudah's opinion, it still seems that he should have noted that.

SEVENTEEN

1. Change of person in Ha'azinu is by no means limited to this verse. As just one example, we can take verse 15: [שמנת עבית כשית] [וישמן ישורון ויבעט] [ויטש אלוה עשהו]. Brackets 1 and 3 are of course in the third person; bracket 2 switches, for no easily defined reason, into the second. If you just read through the shirah, you will find some other examples.

Ha'azinu is not the only place in כתבי הקדש where this happens. In order to forestall the facile explanation that this is simply poetic license, and is therefore limited to the poetic sefarim in TaNaCh, we can go to Mishpatim where we certainly do not expect anything other than very businesslike prose. Nevertheless, in a long passage in which, as expected, the third person is used, we have verse 17: [מכשפה לא תחיה] followed by pasuk 18 [כל שוכב עם בהמה מות יומת]. The first phrase is in the second person; the second is in the third. Interestingly enough, verse 19 continues along in the third person as has been the case in Mishpatim up to now, while verse 20 introduces a long section that uses the second.

Of course, the fact that we have demonstrated that the sudden changes from one person to another is a not infrequent usage throughout TaNaCh does not mean that it is an arbitrary idiosyncrasy. Each instance in which such a switch occurs must have an explanation. That said, it must still be stressed that whatever explanation we might find for a particular case must not be assumed to be a panacea to be arbitrarily applied wherever the issue may arise. There could be any number of explanations for any number of situations.

Here is one explanation that I believe worked for me in one particular case. In my book on Yosef HaTzadik, *The Riddle of the Bowing Moon*, I had occasion to think about Tehilim 81, the שיר של יום for Thursday. Starting from verse 8 till the end, we have the following system: Verses 8 through 11 are couched in the second person. Verses 12 through 16 use the third person. Verse 17, the final verse in the *mizmor*, starts in the third person, as do the verses immediately preceding it, but ends in the second. In chapter 11 of that book I demonstrate that the Ribono shel Olam speaks directly to us (נוכח) when we carried ourselves in accordance with the standards that He expected from us, but switches to the third person (נסתר) when we deviated from that path. (Many of you will recall that this is very close to the ideas we suggested in the Introduction to our present book, when we quoted the unforgettable interpretation that the late R. Gedalia Schorr offered for Ha'azinu's verse 39, כי אני אני הוא.)

Here is what I wrote concerning the final verse in mizmor 81: [ויאכילהו מחלב חטה] [ומצור דבש אשביעך].

Verse 17: As we have noted above, this verse is the most intriguing of all. Here, within one sentence, God promises us both the *fat of the wheat* and *honey drawn from a rock*, the one promise still couched in the third person, the other shifting back to the second.

However, when we really think about what the mizmor has been telling us, it is really not strange at all. The message is one of movement. We can fall in and fall out of favor. The change of person in mid-verse lends a particular poignancy to God's speech. He does not wish to end on a note of alienation. He began the verse in the third person because that is what the logic of style demanded; it is part of a section that is couched in that form. However, He cannot bring Himself to leave His children out in the cold. The mere recital of the pity and the sorrow of what their refusal to listen has brought about should be enough to turn them around. The final phrase is one of triumphant reconciliation. God knows, and tells us, that in the end all will be well.

As a sample of what the possibilities are, this will do nicely. It does not absolve us from attempting to find a good explanation for our verse 6.

Who composed the first six sentences of Ha'azinu? Who is speaking when the first person is used (האזינו שמים ואדברה... אמרי פי... לקחי... אמרתי... אקרא...)?

The Torah's own evidence points squarely to Moshe Rabbeinu. Even without the final pasuk in VaYeilech, the one that introduces Ha'azinu, וידבר משה באזני כל קהל ישראל את דברי השירה הזאת עד תומם, there is Moshe Rabbeinu's own statement in Devarim 31:28, ואעידה בם את השמים ואת הארץ. It was he who, in the first verses of the shirah, called upon heaven and earth to bear witness. Clearly it is Moshe Rabbeinu who is talking.

With this established, we are ready to return to the essay.

2. Defined in dictionaries as: To make a mistake, especially by doing something in a stupid or careless way; to fail to keep working to reach a goal.

3. In the early days of the Medinah in Eretz Yisrael, there was a political orga-

nization of observant Jews who, for one reason or another, were subjected to unrelieved criticism by the Haredi world. An *adam gadol* once spoke in their defense. He asked why it is that while the hangman is universally hated, the judge who condemns people to be executed escapes such enmity. Logic would seem to demand the opposite. The hangman is only doing his job and providing for his family. He bears no responsibility for the verdict that the judge issued. On the other hand, nobody forced the judge to do what he did. It would be understandable if people resented him.

But that is not how the world works. People hate the hangman because *all he ever does is hang people*. It is true that the judge condemns the person to death—but not always. On many occasions he decides that the prisoner at the bar is innocent.

If we expect to be listened to when we point out faults, we must also be prepared to find something positive to say. Nobody can be expected to be always in the wrong.

4. I base this assertion upon the Mishnah, Avos 6:6 (ברייתא דקנין תורה), where it is taught that *malchus* is "נקנה" by means of thirty "qualities" and *kehunah* is נקנה by means of twenty-four qualities. The numbers thirty and twenty-four refer, respectively, to the thirty rights exercised by a king over his subjects (as enumerated in I Shmuel 8) and the twenty-four מתנות כהונה to which the *Kohanim* are entitled. Now neither kings nor Kohanim "acquire" their positions by means of the rights that accrue to them by dint of these positions. Since the noun קנה is *the stalk* that serves as the conduit through which the nutrients stored up in the earth are transferred to the grain that is developing atop the stalk, R. Samson Rafael Hirsch thinks that the root word ק נ ה describes *experiencing* or *establishing a relationship*.

There is much that can be said on this subject, but this is not the place.

EIGHTEEN

1. I offer the following paragraph for useful background.

In chapter 4 we quoted a Midrash that teaches that there are ten (significant?) שירות. The list starts with one sung by Adam HaRishon (in Chazal's tradition, Mizmor 92, מזמור שיר ליום השבת), continuing with one sung by Avraham Avinu (in Chazal's tradition, Mizmor 89, משכיל לאיתן האזרחי), continuing on to the tenth one, which will be the שיר חדש that we will all sing when the ultimate גאולה will have occurred. The fifth one in the list is Ha'azinu, or, as the Midrash identifies it, שירת משה.

2. A friend pointed out the following passage ascribed to Maran, the Brisker Rov: ואני בחסדך יגל לבי בישועתך אשירה לה' כי גמל עלי. ובשם הגר"ח. דיש לעיין ממתי אפשר לומר שירה על הנס, האם רק אחר שקרה כבר הנס, או גם אם יהא לבו בטוח שיקרה נס, וכגון שנביא שיאמר לו כן, יכול כבר לומר שירה על הנס. וזהו דמבואר בפסוק הנ"ל "ואני בחסדך בטחתי" היינו דבטוח רק בחסדך אזי רק "יגל לבי בישועתך," יש לי שמחה ע"ז, אבל מתי "אשירה לה'," דאומר שירה הוא רק "כי גמל עלי," כשקורה ונהיה הנס כבר. It seems to me that this passage strongly confirms that we do, indeed, have a problem here.

3. Please understand that this is not the same question that I discussed in the

Introduction and which makes a cameo appearance in a number of the other essays. There it was simply a question of finding something to sing about in the almost unbroken gloom of Ha'azinu's description of our history. It was, as it were, a local problem. Songs are sung by people when they are happy. What is there to be happy about in the unrelieved litany of our constant failings? All we had to do was to answer that question and our problem was solved.

Our problem here is anything but local. Maharal teaches us the very definition of shirah. It is an expression of "fulfillment" as I have translated it, שלמות as Maharal words it in the original. שלמות, if I understand it correctly, cannot be quantified. Let us not forget that Devarim 31:21 teaches, והיה כי תמצאן אתו רעות רבות וצרות, וענתה השירה הזאת לפניו לעד.... That is not a description of שלמות. The very directions that the Torah gives us for how Ha'azinu is to be used seem to me to negate any possibility of Ha'azinu being a shirah in good standing as Maharal defines it.

I feel that I owe you, dear Reader, the following rather expansive meditation upon what I have written till now. My source is a Chumash commentary in five volumes, called ספר ממעמקים, written by my *mechutan*, R. Alexander Aryeh Mandelbaum. It purports to be a reworking of some of the teachings of HaRav Moshe Shapiro שליט"א. I am extremely grateful to Rav Mandelbaum for having made available some of these profound insights to those of us who have no training in this דרך הלמוד.

The issue that I am going to share with you concerns the etymology of the word "שיר." The same word, שיר, occurs (once) in the Mishnah (Shabbos 5:1) and occasionally in the Bavli (see Bava Metzia 25a and Kidushin 48a) and more frequently in the Yerushalmi with the meaning of *bracelet*, hence a *circle*. Apparently geometric figures have significance beyond their mathematical properties and harbor profound concepts within their formations. The circle can be regarded as a curved line on a plane surface emanating from a point, which, if it continues along that same curve, will ultimately return to its point of departure. An important property of this figure is that the further the curve moves away from its point of departure, the closer it is getting to return to that same point from the other side.

Understood thus, the circle (שיר) can be symbolic of the way the Ribono shel Olam runs the world, סוף מעשה במחשבה תחלה. History unfolds and moves toward destiny with many detours and obstacles that seem to defy God's purpose. Its path, however, is circular. In the end it will return to its point of departure in the sense that we will all realize that the seeming diversions were really beneficial and that they all contributed toward the Ribono shel Olam's purpose. It is "שיר," the circular path that history travels, that evokes "שיר," *the song of jubilation*. I assume that the return to the source that I have just described is the very "שלמות" of which Maharal speaks.

That given, can Ha'azinu really be described as a "שירה"? It is to be used when the curve has a long, long way to go before it arrives back at its destination. The bracelet is still very far from locking.

It is important to me to add the following Excursus to this endnote. When I first learned of the purported relationship between "שיר" the bracelet to "שיר" the song, something in me rebelled against the association. "שיר" the bracelet (really שֵׁיר rather than שִׁיר; see Targum to BeMidbar 31:50) is Aramaic and appears nowhere in TaNaCh and, as far as I can tell, only once in the Mishnah. Of course I am aware that there are Aramaisms in TaNaCh because some expressions found their way into Hebrew, but the evidence seems to point to a late importation. How, then, can it be said that the Hebrew שיר is elucidated by the Aramaic שיר?

While I was thinking about these issues, I took a look at Mishnah Shabbos 5:1 . . . וסוס בשיר, and saw that this is followed by the phrase, וכל בעלי השיר. This, of course, means that all other animals that generally wear a ring, as does the horse, may also go out on Shabbos. I was struck by the expression בעלי השיר. Perhaps my linguistic intuition is faulty, but it sounded like a strange expression in this context. I did a universal search on my search program and did indeed find a Chazal that seems to me to be germane to our issue.

After maintaining that the night is a time of דין, it notes that (even so?) there are מלאכים who sing שירה by night. It continues by telling us that these מלאכים who sing שירה by night are the שרים (princes?) over all **בעלי שיר** and that, moreover, anyone who can understand their שירים will enter all the gates of wisdom.

It seems to me that the reason why just the שירה that is said by night (דין) is so profound must be stated in the very terms that are engaging our attention now. These are שירים that are sung when things are very sad and threatening. The concept that even under those circumstances שירה can be appropriate is one for which unusually profound wisdom is required.

For me, this discovery removed my doubts about the relationship between the two meanings of "שיר." My intuition tells me that the unexpected usage of בעלי שיר in both contexts points inexorably to a common thought world.

4. The term "השירה הזאת" seems somehow to be a natural description of שירות that were sung on various occasions. The שירת הים is introduced with the words, 'אז ישיר משה ובני ישראל את **השירה הזאת** לה. The שירת הבאר (BeMidbar 21:17) also has אז ישיר ישראל את **השירה הזאת** . . . . So too does שירת דוד at II Shmuel 22:1 begin with **השירה הזאת** את דברי . . . . וידבר דוד לה' את דברי **השירה הזאת**. In all those cases the words of the respective שירות follow immediately upon those introductory phrases. At a simple level one could assume that "הזאת" in those examples fills the role of "the following" that I suspect we would have used in English. "So and so sang the following composition."

Since we are learning Torah, it is also possible that הזאת in these cases has a deeper meaning. Perhaps it fills the role of a flashing amber light, alerting us to the significance of each of the words that make up the שירה: "Do not think that a choice of different words, perhaps creating a different ambience, would have done as well. It is, after all, 'only' a shirah. That is not the case." These shiros are all Torah and, in Torah, nothing is happenstance. It was "this song" and none other that was appropriate to the particular circumstances.

So it is not the usage of "השירה הזאת" in connection with Ha'azinu that troubles us here. It is rather the constant, and therefore conspicuous, repetition that is catching our eye at this point.

NINETEEN

1. Obviously, when I say that these horrors were "willed" by the Ribono shel Olam, I do not mean that He takes pleasure in our suffering. I mean, rather, that given the history of our religious, moral, and social failings, these somehow cleansing experiences became a necessity. The significant issue is that these things did not, and do not, happen because the Ribono shel Olam has forsaken us. The Ribono shel Olam is always with us and we can therefore sing Ha'azinu in even the most fearful circumstances.

How this fits in with the rules generally governing a shirah needs clarification, and I will try to address this further along in the current essay. In this endnote I limit myself to an examination of the statement that I have just made within. I will attempt to present a matrix within which to make some sense of the Ribono shel Olam "willing" suffering.

Please reread endnote 3 from the previous chapter. It is there that we discussed the relationship between "שיר," song, and "שיר," bracelet or circle. In an excursus attached to that endnote I traced my initial hesitation to accept this association and my ultimate conviction that it ought indeed to be countenanced. Here, I would like to make the point that that association can, with equal conviction, be expressed differently from the explanation offered there.

This explanation occurred to me when I checked out the definition of circle. I found the following as a fairly standard offering: A closed plane curve, every point of which is equidistant from a fixed point within the curve. The fact that all points along the diameter are equidistant from the center caught my attention. The circle can be as large as the universe with the various points along the diameter many thousands of miles apart, both in distance and in experiences. On the circle are the content and the harassed, the suffering and the joyous, the sick and the healthy, and all, all, all without exception are equidistant from the Ribono shel Olam. His fatherly interest extends to all of them—equally. With this picture in mind, it becomes easier to understand that the משפט אשירה is not so much different from the חסד אשירה.

It seems to me that as long as we are thinking along these lines, it makes sense to co-opt Ta'anis 31a: אמר רבי אלעזר עתיד הקדוש ברוך הוא לעשות מחול לצדיקים והוא יושב ביניהם בגן עדן וכל אחד ואחד מראה באצבעו שנאמר ואמר ביום ההוא הנה אלהינו זה קוינו לו ויושיענו זה ה' קוינו לו נגילה ונשמחה בישועתו. The circle does seem to be a Jewish symbol!

2. Please glance back at the last section of the introductory chapter. We quoted the Rambam that when *leining* Ha'azinu we ignore the usual rule of not ending an aliyah on a sad note. We suggested that Sefas Emes and his school might have argued that this dispensation is based upon the fact that, from Ha'azinu's vantage point, the "bad" is also good.

When I wrote that, it had not occurred to me to what unbelievable degree this truth is true. I was thinking of kri'as HaTorah as we know it—the entire sidrah is read—and the sad parts are made less sad by the context within which they are told. As we have learned so many times, Ha'azinu begins early on when we were chosen as the segulah of the Ribono shel Olam, and ends with *Yemos HaMoshiach*. Within this context it is easy enough to realize that everything that happened along the way was part of the Ribono shel Olam's inscrutable hashgachah.

That was then. However, as I went further and further into this book, it struck me that that was only part—and that, the easier part—of the story. Earlier in the Introduction we had described how Ha'azinu had been sung as the shirah that accompanied the Musaf sacrifice on Shabbos. We learned that it was divided into six portions (הזי"ו ל"ך) and that each Shabbos one of those portions was sung. At the end of the six-week period they started again from the beginning and repeated the pattern.

Now when we consider how these six sections were apportioned (see Rashi to Rosh HaShanah 31a), it is clear that at least one of them consisted of *only* unrelieved horror. Look at the fourth section, the one beginning with וירא ה' וינאץ (verse 19), which runs till אמרתי אפאיהם (verse 26). Try to imagine that part of Ha'azinu, on its assigned Shabbos, as an independent שיר *without* the softening introduction and conclusion of the complete shirah. One wonders how the Levi'im assigned to the shir for that particular Shabbos must have felt. It turns out that even that "bad" is good.

TWENTY

1. Well, yes and no. The fact is that just today, when I was about to surrender the manuscript for the final editing that has to precede the typesetting, I became aware of a major problem that jeopardizes the answer that I have just so lukewarmly endorsed. There are many good reasons to sweep the whole thing under the carpet and leave things as they are. However, there is one excellent reason to own up and face the music. תורה היא וללמד אנו צריכים!

I began writing this endnote on Motzo'ei Shabbos parshas VaEira. During Shabbos it had occurred to me that it was about time to come to grips with the seemingly significant role that the חרטומים, *Pharaoh's court sorcerers* (in verse 11 these are called מכשפים, *people who practice* כשפים), played in the drama. So I learned the section dealing with כשפים in Rav Mandelbaum's ממעמקים על פרשיות התורה and became acquainted with an entire world that up till now had been closed to me.

An endnote in a book grappling with Ha'azinu is not the place to discuss כשפים in detail. Suffice it to say that, other than the Rambam (Avodah

Zarah 11:20), who believes that the world of the occult has no reality at all, the consensus seems to be that indeed the Ribono shel Olam created an entire system outside our physical world, in which the cognoscenti are able to fashion their own reality (see Gra to יורה דעה קע"ט ו', רמח"ל, in דרך ה' ג' ב, and קונטרוס הזכרונות ב' in ר' צדוק). The Ribono shel Olam has forbidden us to enter this world; it is His wish that we function within the context that He has provided for us. But if we decide to go against His wishes, the option is ours in much the same way that we have the בחירה to engage in forbidden unions and bring ממזרים into the world.

For some reason Rav Mandelbaum does not reference Ramban to Devarim 18:12, who in his own way says much the same thing as do the sources mentioned earlier. For our purposes some of the language that he uses is highly significant and I will quote just a small section from that long and extremely important piece.

> ואסר לך הנחשים והקסמים בעבור שעשה לך מעלה גדולה לתתך עליון על כל גויי הארץ שיקים בקרבך נביא ויתן דבריו בפיו, ואתה תשמע ממנו מה יפעל אל ולא תצטרך אתה בעתידות אל קוסם ומנחש, שיקבלו אותם מן הכוכבים או מן השפלים בשרי מעלה שאין כל דבריהם אמת ולא יודיעו בכל הצריך, אבל הנבואה תודיע חפץ השם ולא יפול דבר מכל דבריה, **והוא שיפרש (בפסוק כב) הוא הדבר אשר לא דברו ה' והנה אתה חלקו וסגולתו שומע עצתו מפיו**, והם חלק המזלות הולכים אחריהם . . .

Very clearly, Ramban maintains that reliance on כשוף stands in direct and absolute contradiction to our segulah status. If you glance back at the second footnote on page 153, you will remember that Rashi had included two transgressions—כשפים and deviant relationships—under the rubric תועבה. Ramban had argued—apparently on both—maintaining that Ha'azinu deals only with avodah zarah. In the body of this essay I thought that the factor that makes avodah zarah special is the fact that it stands in direct contradiction to our segulah status. But we have now learned that in Ramban's own view, כשפים stand in precisely that relationship to the segulah status. So why should he disagree with Rashi's assertion that, besides avodah zarah, Ha'azinu also criticizes כשפים? I regard this as an extremely serious issue.

I suggest the following solution.

Ramban does not in fact argue with Rashi in the matter of כשפים. Ha'azinu does indeed criticize כשפים as much as it criticizes avodah zarah. When Ramban maintains that Ha'azinu deals with only avodah zarah, he takes that term in its broadest sense. He means anything, including כשפים, that militates against our segulah status. His disagreement with Rashi is limited to the source from which we know this. Rashi derives it from the use of "תועבה." Ramban cannot agree with that. This is so because if we are going to take "תועבה" broadly, it would also include deviant relationships, and with that Ramban cannot agree. Accordingly he limits the implications of "תועבה" to aspects of avodah zarah. He requires no textual basis for including כשפים in Ha'azinu's criticisms. The inclusion, by the very nature of this transgression, is self-evident.

I believe that a careful reading of the Ramban and the Sifrei that I mentioned earlier will yield the contention set out in the previous paragraph. However, there is no need to expand this endnote beyond its already unreasonably long size. Interested readers will be able to do their own research.

2. Needless to say, this statement is meant metaphorically. But then again, it may not be so metaphorical after all. If you can take the time, perhaps you would look once more at endnote 1 in the Prologue. There we discuss the apparently strange form that the Ribono shel Olam's induction of Yehoshua took. He had summoned both Moshe Rabbeinu and Yehoshua to the Ohel Mo'ed so that He might induct Yehoshua into his new leadership position and then seems to ignore him completely. Instead he speaks to Moshe Rabbeinu—about Ha'azinu. We suggested a possible explanation in that endnote.

It occurs to me that, in the context of our current discussion, another explanation is possible.

As I was thinking about משיחה, it struck me than neither in Pinchos (27:15–23) nor in VaYeilech (31:7–8 and 23) where the story of Yehoshua's induction is told, is there any mention of anointment with oil. From the simple reading of the relevant passages, it appears that the induction was more a personal matter between Moshe Rabbeinu and Yehoshua (וסמכת את... ידך עליו... ונתת מהודך עליו) than the objective transferal of leadership implied in the impersonal act of משיחה. There may, of course, be a perfectly simple and logical explanation for all this, of which I am simply not aware.

There is another puzzling quirk in the induction story. In Pinchos, where Moshe Rabbeinu first broaches the matter of the succession, he is simply told that when the time comes (see Ramban) he is to take Yehoshua and follow the prescriptions that were now conveyed to him. There is never a hint that, in addition to Moshe Rabbeinu's actions, the Ribono shel Olam Himself would also take a hand in the induction process. In VaYeilech we learn that Moshe Rabbeinu did exactly what he had been told to do in Pinchos, and, if the story had stopped there, we would have supposed that that was the end of the matter. Then, just a few pesukim later, the Ribono shel Olam tells Moshe Rabbeinu to bring Yehoshua to the Ohel Mo'ed so that He, the Ribono shel Olam Himself, could appoint Yehoshua as leader. Why were these two inductions necessary?

Here is my suggestion. Rashi explains in Pinchos that Moshe Rabbeinu's request that the Ribono shel Olam address the matter of the succession had involved a personal consideration. He had hoped that his leadership would pass on to his own children. That was not to be, and the Ribono shel Olam informed him that he would be passing his greatness (ונתת מהודך עליו) on to Yehoshua by his own action (וסמכת ידך עליו). Within that context it is not difficult to discern that this transaction was indeed a personal matter between Moshe Rabbeinu and his beloved talmid. He was appointing Yehoshua to be *his* heir in place of his children. In VaYeilech we learn that

Moshe Rabbeinu did precisely as he had been told. He passed on his personal prerogatives to Yehoshua.

However, there had not yet been a formal *objective* appointment. This the Ribono shel Olam now undertook to do Himself.

Why was no משיחה involved in that formal induction? Well, perhaps there was. I have suggested that Ha'azinu, based on its "otherworldly" standing, has precisely the same character as the שמן המשחה. It was that idea that generated this rather long endnote. And so, at the very end of this book, we have finally offered a satisfying answer to the question that we first raised in the first endnote to the introductory Prologue. The Ribono shel Olam had asked Moshe Rabbeinu to bring Yehoshua to the Ohel Mo'ed so that the Ribono shel Olam could induct him (ואצונו). The Ribono shel Olam then ignores Yehoshua and instead tells Moshe Rabbeinu about Ha'azinu. What is happening?

Perhaps we have hit upon an answer. In that context, *Ha'azinu was in fact* the שמן המשחה!

3. Throughout the book we have had the occasion to quote the Ramban that it is only our obdurate clinging to avodah zarah that stands at the center of Ha'azinu's concerns. In endnote 2 to the Prologue we made some attempt to understand how the fatal attraction that Klal Yisrael seems always to have felt toward this seemingly ridiculous mode of worship could have come about. Now that we are standing at the end of the book, I think that it is appropriate to revisit this issue.

I feel it best to introduce the subject by quoting some lines from Letter 209 in the first volume of the *Igros Chazon Ish*.

כשאנו קוראין את הדברים בפרשה דברים, ואתחנן, עקב, נצבים, וילך, אנו רואים הרבה השתדלות להציל את העם מעזוב ח"ו את כל התורה בההחלף היסוד ללכת אחרי אלהים אחרים, דבר שלפי מצבנו אנו אחרי שונכיס יצרא, הדבור בזה אינו מן המדה כלל. **ואין לנו שום מושג** איך יתכן יצר של השתחויה לפסל, **ואין זה עליה מצדנו אלא ירידה , כי הלא תכלית האדם הוא היצר, ונטול יצר הוא נטול נשמה.**

האדם הגדול בעל יצר של עבודה זרה זה קצרה דעתנו להבינו כמו שהמשילו שאין להסביר לסומא בחינת הצבעים ...

It may well be that after reading this passage, there is really nothing more to say. We simply have no idea at all how this יצר הרע worked. If that is how you feel, you may not have any interest in following me to the end of this endnote.

For those of you who are interested in my thoughts on this matter, here they are.

Sanhedrin 64a tells the story of how, at the beginning of the Bayis Sheini, the Ribono shel Olam listened to our prayers and agreed to distance the יצר הרע for avodah zarah from us. (As a side remark, it is worth noting the intensity of those prayers. As the Gemara describes them, they were a scream from the heart, a petition born of absolute desperation. They made it clear that there simply was no alternative. If this יצר הרע was not taken off their shoulders, Klal Yisrael would buckle under its weight. And, *what is more,* the Ribono shel Olam agreed—not only by actually removing the יצר הרע but also by "sending down a note from heaven" inscribed with the word אמת! There seems to have been nothing simple about this entire process.)

So the prayers were answered and the יצר הרע for avodah zarah disappeared. When this happened, a fiery lion cub came bounding out of the *Kodesh HaKodoshim.* A prophet who was there at the time told the people that this cub was the personification of the יצר for avodah zarah. *Toras Chaim* to Sanhedrin asks the obvious question. Why should the יצר הרע for avodah zarah have been housed in the Kodesh HaKodoshim? He answers that, relative to the world, the Kodesh HaKodoshim parallels the human heart. Just as in a person, inclinations, even evil inclinations, are housed in the heart, so, too, the inclination to serve avodah zarah had its place in the Kodesh HaKodoshim.

Why is the Kodesh HaKodoshim the heart of the world? Because the אבן שתיה, a stone on the floor of the Kodesh HaKodoshim upon which the ark rested, was so called because ממנו הושתת העולם, *from it the world was founded.*

What does that mean? Here is what Rashi says: ציון נבראת תחילה, וסביביה נדבקו רגבים עד סוף העולם מכל צד, *Tzion (the Kodesh HaKodoshim) was created first* and, round about it, clods of earth were added until, from every side, they reached to the ends of the earth.

Can this mean anything at all to us?

I think that it can. I think that it means that the Ribono shel Olam created the world by first providing the place (ציון) where His שכינה, *His Presence,* would be ensconced. Drawing its energy from the שכינה that rested there, a physical world pushed further and further outward, ultimately forming itself into the universe. Since that outward thrust was energized by the שכינה, it follows that every particle in the universe is the *Shechinah's* will and power made manifest in a physical form.

It seems to me that, viewed thus, we can understand why people who may have loved the Ribono shel Olam very much were nevertheless drawn to seek Him out in some physical form. I am not sure whether the following metaphor is a good one, but it appears to me to be adequate. We can imagine a child who, for some reason, is far, far away from his father. A friend is expected to arrive from the place where the father lives and the child is looking forward to the regards that this friend will certainly bring. The father has a choice. He can either send oral regards—"Please make sure to remember to tell our little son how much we miss him . . ."—or he can send a tape into which he has recorded the same message. It takes little imagination to conclude that the child would much prefer the tape. He would prefer it even if someone were to explain to him that what he hears is not his father's actual voice but a series of electrical impulses that by some legerdemain sound exactly like it. He does not care. As far as he is concerned, his father put those sounds on the tape and that is good enough for him.

Can we not understand why perfectly sensible people were inexorably drawn to avodah zarah? "This tree is standing here because the Ribono shel Olam willed it to be here. As I bask in its shade, delight in its fruit, and stand in awe of its power and symmetry, I experience the Ribono shel Olam communicating with me. I will choose this over praying straight to the Ribono shel Olam, Whom I cannot see or hear or touch, and Who therefore remains completely abstract to me, is in fact far away from me."

Why is avodah zarah such a heinous sin? Why does the Ribono shel Olam refuse to cater to our smallness?

That, too, we can understand very well.

The fact, of course, is that our little metaphor of the child away from home is seriously deficient. It is false, it is misleading, it is positively dangerous. It postulates that because we cannot apprehend the Ribono shel Olam with our physical senses, He is indeed far away from us. That, however, is not the case. We will conclude this contemplation of the pernicious allures of avodah zarah with the following quote from the recently published sefer, *Bilevavi Mishkan Evneh,* and then we will be done.

דברים ברורים בזה אמרו חז"ל, "לית אתר פנוי מיניה" כלומר שהוא נמצא בכל מקום, וכמו שנאמר "אתה הוא עד שלא נברא העולם ואתה הוא משנברא העולם" שכשם שקודם בריאת העולם הקב"ה היה בכל מקום, כן ממש גם לאחר שנברא העולם, אע"פ שיש עולם ונבראים, הקב"ה נמצא בכל מקום ממש, ואין דבר שמונע מן הקב"ה להיות בכל מקום . . . ממש . . . כי קרוב אליך הדבר מאד . . . ולכך אדם יכול למצוא את הקב"ה בכל מקום, ולהיות קרוב אליו בכל מקום.

The Ribono shel Olam's battle against avodah zarah is fueled by His refusal to permit His children, His greatest hope, His great pride, to choose the easy, the undemanding, the infinitely less fulfilling. His manifesto in this struggle is, "You can be great and therefore you must be great! The crass and limited physical world, in which what cannot be picked up by the senses has no practical existence, is not your real reality. Only reach for Me, pure and unadulterated, and you will find Me in your reach. In fact, you will find that reaching was unnecessary because I was always there with you, closer than the closest closeness that you can imagine. Do not shortchange yourself; you have the best *protektzia* in the world."

That is the message that lies in the stern prohibitions against avodah zarah.

And that is ultimately the message of Ha'azinu.

IN MEMORY

OF

OUR BELOVED

HUSBAND, FATHER,

AND

TEACHER

Solomon Ralph Bijou

HE LIT A LIGHT IN OUR HEARTS

THAT

WILL GUIDE US AND OUR CHILDREN

THROUGHOUT OUR LIVES.

—FROM HIS WIFE,

CHILDREN, GRANDCHILDREN,

AND

GREAT-GRANDCHILDREN

IN LOVING MEMORY

OF

Esther & Isaac Mezrahi

PILLARS OF OUR COMMUNITY,

THEY ALWAYS KNEW WHAT HAD TO BE DONE

AND, PROFOUNDLY CREATIVE,

FOUND WAYS TO DO IT.

ABOVE ALL THEY WERE A TEAM.

ONE HEART

ANIMATED THEM BOTH,

ONE SOUL

BREATHED LIFE INTO THEIR DREAMS.

AFTER FATHER PASSED ON,

MOTHER KEPT THE FLAME BURNING

FOR EIGHTEEN MORE YEARS.

MAY THEIR MEMORY BE A BLESSING

FOR US, OUR CHILDREN, AND GRANDCHILDREN.

IN LOVING MEMORY

OF

Joseph S. Jemal

REMEMBERED BY HIS FAMILY AND FRIENDS

AS A MAN OF CHARITY AND SENSITIVITY

WHO LIVED A LIFE OF LOYALTY TO THE TORAH

DEDICATED

BY

HIS BROTHER AND SISTER IN LAW

ABRAHAM S. AND RACHELLE JEMAL

THERE ARE MANY PEOPLE WHO OWE

THEIR LIVES TO

THE LOVING CONCERN OF

Ezra & Zekia Shasho

OF BLESSED MEMORY.

WE GRATEFULLY RECALL THEIR GOODNESS AND

THE WONDERFUL EXAMPLE THAT THEY SET.

THEY, AS ALSO

THEIR BELOVED DAUGHTER

Frieda Kredy

AND THEIR BELOVED SON

Egal Shasho

OF BLESSED MEMORY,

WILL FOREVER LIVE ON IN OUR HEARTS.

—BY THEIR CHILDREN,

GRANDCHILDREN, AND FAMILY

Albert Hamway זצ״ל

UNDERSTOOD WHAT JEWISH LIVING

WAS ALL ABOUT.

IN FARAWAY JAPAN HE RAISED HIS CHILDREN

WITH A LOVE FOR THEIR TRADITION.

THEY EACH BUILT

WARM AND LOVING JEWISH HOMES,

PASSING ON TO THEIR CHILDREN AND

THEY TO THEIRS THE FLAME

WHICH THEIR FATHER HAD PASSED TO THEM.

HE IS REMEMBERED WITH LOVE BY

HIS WIFE, HIS CHILDREN,

GRANDCHILDREN,

AND GREAT-GRANDCHILDREN.

מציבים אנו בזה

מזכרת נצח

לאבינו מורנו היקר

ר׳ לטמן

בן ר׳ חיים דוב בער ז״ל

איש צנוע

שכל חייו רץ כצבי

לעשות רצון אבינו שבשמים

ולאמנו מורתנו היקרה

רות רבקה לאה

בת ר׳ אברהם ע״ה

יהא זכרם ברוך

IN LOVING MEMORY

OF MY BELOVED PARENTS,

AND

MORE, MY GOOD AND PRECIOUS

FRIENDS

Jack & Jeanette Feldman

THEY WERE GENEROUS, WARMHEARTED,

AND GENTLE.

YOU COULD NOT MEET THEM

WITHOUT BEING TOUCHED BY THEIR

GOODNESS.

WITH A SMILE ON HIS WISE FACE

AND NOVHARDOK MUSSAR IN HIS HEART

HaRav
Chaim Mordechai
Weinkrantz זצ"ל

UNDERSTOOD US ALL SO WELL, SO VERY WELL.

NO PROBLEM,

BUT HIS WISDOM FOUND A SOLUTION.

NO PAIN, BUT HIS EMPATHY

WAS A HEALING BALM.

CHILD OF A CULTURE VERY DIFFERENT

FROM OUR OWN, HE NEVERTHELESS FOUND

COMMONALITY IN HIS AND OUR

JEWISH HEARTS.

WE WILL NEVER FORGET THE BOOKS

WHICH HE SO DILIGENTLY TAUGHT US,

NOR THE LIFE LESSONS

FOR WHICH HE WAS A LIVING TEXT.

—THE MONDAY SHIUR